"Jack Saul invites us to join him in his e
and destruction—a dark continent of
healing capacity of communities. Look .... as diverse as Kosovo, lower
Manhattan on September 11, and the Liberian refugees on Staten Island, he describes
how a group of systems thinkers, armed with an extraordinary trust in the power of social
connections, joins in partnership with communities in search of justice, reconciliation,
and resilience. Written with attention to the small details of survival, an understanding
of the power of cultures in history, and the healing capacity of art and theater, Saul
shows us the effort and endurance necessary to reconstruct life and restore sanity in
societies that have experienced chaos. It is a powerful testimony."

—**Salvador Minuchin, MD, founder of the Minuchin Family Center and**
author of *Families and Family Therapy*

"Jack Saul's book is terrific and truly compelling for professionals who work with
traumatized people. With first-hand stories, he artfully describes a range of out-of-office
interventions to help families, neighborhoods, and communities in the aftermath of
disaster. Dr. Saul is never better than when he writes about using the arts to understand
the complexities of human trauma and resilience. Yes, even improvisation!"

—**Pauline Boss, professor emeritus at the University of Minnesota, and author of**
Ambiguous Loss **and** *Loss, Trauma, and Resilience*

"With compassion and insight, Jack Saul shares his own journey through the aftermath
of September 11 as witness, participant, and healer, chronicling the power of collective
narrative to transform traumatic experience into communal recovery."

—**Alice Greenwald, director of the National September 11 Memorial and Museum**

"In *Collective Trauma, Collective Healing* Jack Saul takes us through a masterful journey
of his healing work addressing the ongoing tragedy of social and political traumas around
the world. His work is creative, rich, sensitive, and deeply felt. His writing gives rare
glimpses into how science and wisdom must be coalesced to treat the wounds of torture,
loss, and devastation. Psychological science, art, and anthropology are so thoughtfully
integrated in his work and writing to provide both a history of his intervention work
and a guidebook for those brave enough to treat the collective wounds that both nature
and humans too often cause. With this volume, Dr. Saul contributes meaningfully to
repairing our world."

—**Stevan E. Hobfoll, PhD, the Judd and Marjorie Weinberg**
Presidential Professor and chair of the department of behavioral sciences at
Rush University Medical Center

"Jack Saul's clear and compelling narrative, based on his immersion in several
catastrophes, offers practical knowledge on community resilience strategies for
responding to collective trauma that will be highly informative for practitioners across
many disciplines."

—**Stevan Weine, MD, professor of psychiatry at the University of Illinois at**
Chicago and author of *Testimony After Catastrophe*

"In *Collective Trauma, Collective Healing*, Dr. Saul provides a detailed documentation
of what it takes to recognize, develop, and sustain a community environment that
promotes healing from mass disaster. Throughout the multiple examples in the book,
including personal challenges to his own community in the wake of September 11, the
author emphasizes the importance of going beyond individual approaches to mount

a public health response after any disaster. Dr. Saul has a deep respect for systems and how they work, while never denying the inevitable tensions that occur and the competing agendas that can easily sabotage recovery efforts. As man-made and natural disasters increase in frequency and intensity, few of us are prepared by our professional training to know what to do when faced with the kind of social challenge that Dr. Saul describes. This book, with all the lessons learned, becomes a must-read book for public and private managers."

—**Sandra L. Bloom, MD, co-director of the Center for Nonviolence and Social Justice at the Drexel University School of Public Health**

"Jack Saul is a dedicated healer whose deep understanding of systems therapy has taken him to the aid of injured communities around the globe. Yet it was September 11 that literally brought these lessons home, making him an insider to catastrophe. This blend of outsider knowledge and insider wisdom makes this *the* book on collective recovery. It will transform our practice."

—**Mindy Thompson Fullilove, MD, professor of clinical psychiatry and socio-medical sciences, New York State Psychiatric Institute at Columbia University**

"Most books simply espouse principles or ideal goals, telling us what to aim for, but not how to get there, and almost never do they walk us through the messy process of working in the wake of conflict. Saul's book not only breaks critically important fresh ground in setting out the critical role that collective resilience plays in allowing individuals and communities to transform themselves after traumatic events: he also takes us with him on the journeys he travelled to make the discoveries he can now share. The various stories in his book convey the critical message that we cannot know the answer before we begin, at the same time as providing us with a toolkit of indispensible principles and resources for action."

—**Danielle Celermajer, PhD, associate professor and director of the Torture Prevention Project at the University of Sydney**

"Jack Saul's compelling book is a major achievement in the literature on trauma and recovery, nudging the discourse from the individual to the community. This must-read for mental health professionals and creative arts therapists blends psychotherapy and expressive therapy, reflection and action, featuring communities of dialogue front and center, capable of re-building destroyed edifices of the city and the soul."

—**Robert Landy, PhD, professor and director of the drama therapy program at New York University**

"Jack Saul brings to this book years of outstanding contribution and experience addressing the psychological needs of those exposed to many different types of disaster. As governments at all levels seek better ways to make communities resilient, this book offers much needed practical guidance for policy and practice. It is a unique contribution to an emerging field that is understanding that early intervention is always better, but that it's never too late to offer help in culturally appropriate ways."

—**Michael Ungar, PhD, professor of social work at Dalhousie University and co-director of the Resilience Research Centre**

Collective Trauma, Collective Healing

Collective Trauma, Collective Healing is a guide for mental health professionals working in response to large-scale political violence or natural disaster. It provides a framework that practitioners can use to develop their own community-based, collective approach to treating trauma and providing clinical services that are both culturally and contextually appropriate. Clinicians will come away from the book with a solid understanding of new roles that health and mental health professionals play in disasters—roles that encourage them to recognize and enhance the resilience and coping skills in families, organizations, and the community at large.

The book draws on experience of working with survivors, their families, and communities in the Holocaust, post-war Kosovo, the Liberian civil wars, and post-9/11 Lower Manhattan. It tracks the development of community programs and projects based on a family and community resilience approach, including those that enhance the collective capacities for narration and public conversation.

Jack Saul, PhD, is assistant professor of clinical population and family health at Columbia University's Mailman School of Public Health and director of the International Trauma Studies Program. As a psychologist he has created a number of programs for populations in New York City that have endured war, torture, and political violence including the Bellevue/NYU Program for Survivors of Torture, REFUGE (Refugee Resource Center), Theater Arts Against Political Violence, the Post-9/11 Downtown Community Resource Center, and African Refuge. He consults with organizations on staff welfare in response to trauma-related work and has a private practice in Manhattan.

ROUTLEDGE PSYCHOSOCIAL STRESS SERIES
Charles R. Figley, Ph.D., Series Editor

Editorial Board

Collective Trauma, Collective Healing

Promoting Community Resilience in the
Aftermath of Disaster

Jack Saul

Routledge
Taylor & Francis Group

NEW YORK AND LONDON

First published 2014
by Routledge
711 Third Avenue, New York, NY 10017

Simultaneously published in the UK
by Routledge
27 Church Road, Hove, East Sussex BN3 2FA

Routledge is an imprint of the Taylor & Francis Group, an informa business

© 2014 Taylor & Francis

Library of Congress Cataloging in Publication Data
Saul, Jack.
Collective trauma, collective healing : promoting community resilience in the aftermath of disaster / Jack Saul. – 1 Edition.
pages cm. – (Routledge psychosocial stress series)
Includes bibliographical references and index.
ISBN 978-0-415-88416-7 (hardback : alk. paper) – ISBN 978-0-415-88417-4 (pbk. : alk. paper) – ISBN 978-0-203-84218-8 (ebook) 1. Psychic trauma. 2. Post-traumatic stress disorder. 3. Social psychology. 4. Community organization. 5. Emergency management–Citizen participation. I. Title.
BF175.5.P75S28 2013
362.2'2–dc23

2013003427

ISBN: 978-0-415-88416-7 (hbk)
ISBN: 978-0-415-88417-4 (pbk)
ISBN: 978-0-203-84218-8 (ebk)

Cover image painting: "The Shield" by Rocio Rodriguez

Cover design by Zohar Nir-Amitin: www.zoharworks.com

Typeset in Adobe Caslon
by Wearset Ltd, Boldon, Tyne and Wear

Contents

Tables

Series Editor's Foreword

As series editor of the Psychosocial Stress Series I would like to welcome *Collective Trauma, Collective Healing: Promoting Community Resilience in the Aftermath of Disaster* to the book series. The purpose of the book series is to provide busy professionals with useful and timely information to guide their work with those seeking help in facing and overcoming significant adversity. Like the first book in this series, *Stress Disorders Among Vietnam Veterans: Theory, Research, and Treatment* (Brunner-Routledge, 1978), *Collective Trauma, Collective Healing* is an extraordinary contribution to the field of psychological trauma that focuses on ways of enhancing community resilience following disaster.

The author, Dr. Jack M. Saul, is a well-known trauma psychologist who is the founding and current director of the International Trauma Studies Program, affiliated with Columbia University's Mailman School of Public Health. Professor Saul's work in New York and around the world is well known by both researchers and practitioners.

The idea for this book emerged from discussions with Dr. Saul several years ago. We talked over coffee at the Mille-Feuille Bakery Café, a popular spot squeezed between upscale condos and trendy Manhattan boutiques close to New York University's main campus. It was nearly ten years before this that Jack and I had first met, along with several dozen of his colleagues, days after the 2001 terrorist attack that changed his city, and the United States, forever. He makes reference to this meeting early in his book.

Over coffee, he talked of his many humanitarian efforts of the last 20 years, why he established the International Trauma Studies Program, and a new paradigm for promoting resilience in communities—one that would not simply focus on crisis intervention and PTSD-prevention in the wake of disasters. He discussed how 9/11 energized his trauma program and his colleagues to move toward this new paradigm of pragmatism. They began to focus on the fundamental principles of working with collective trauma that can lead to collective healing. His writings, lectures, and training emphasized the importance of culture, meaning, and hope.

In this book, Dr. Saul lays out guidelines and practices for psychosocial responses to various types of catastrophes. At the same time, he establishes a framework that practitioners can use to develop their own community-based, collective approach to treating collective trauma and providing and timing clinical services that meet precise cultural expectations and requirements.

This book emerged over the last three years through reviewing more than 300 hours of video and other data gathered from more than a decade of work around the world and throughout the United States. It is also a distillation of a two-year disaster-response workshop series and discussion group with mental health professionals. Moreover, to grasp the significance of collective trauma interventions, Dr. Saul interviewed many dozens of community members who participated in community-based recovery work and leading professionals worldwide who are currently engaged in family and community resilience approaches to massive trauma, which included good and bad examples of effective trauma resilience efforts.

The book is a beautiful collection of the wisdom of human collective behavior, the philosophy of helping, and a blueprint for approaching, fitting in with and assisting the traumatized community of survivors. Like the first book in this series, *Collective Trauma, Collective Healing* will quickly become a classic and highly referenced text because it challenges the current approaches to trauma response and, in doing so, significantly improves our chances of forging significant and sustainable healing.

Charles R. Figley, PhD
Series Editor
New Orleans, January 2013

Preface

This book is the story of my professional and personal journey over the last 15 years working with survivors of political violence, their families and communities. I started working as a psychologist in clinics in New York City and moved to the streets, schools, churches, theater studios, and community centers to work as a collaborator with refugees who were rebuilding their lives. It was not only a geographical move, but also a conceptual shift in which I grew to appreciate the role of social context and the collective capacities in families and communities to recovery from massive psychosocial trauma and loss. My personal story is inseparable from the story I tell here, for just weeks after returning from Kosovo, the September 11 terrorist attacks on the World Trade Center took place in my neighborhood, having a tremendous impact on me personally as well as on my family, my community, and my country. I found myself in the role of an insider practitioner after having collaborated with many who had played that role in contexts where they themselves had endured major catastrophe. I realized I had learned a great deal from these and other colleagues about how I could help promote a process of collective recovery in New York City. After working with my own community, I applied that experience to a community resilience project with the underserved Liberian refugee community across the Hudson River in Staten Island.

Today, we often hear the term resilience in the context of disaster—which usually refers to an individual's capacity to rebound or bounce back following adversity. Researchers and practitioners have increasingly come to see that the resilience of an individual does not exist in a vacuum—it is a function of one's social and cultural context. It is commonly referred to today as community resilience—we are looking at the collective capacities in families, communities, organizations, and society at large that are more than the sum of individual capacities. We have come to recognize today that community resilience is a crucial factor in recovering from adversity, and in preventing long-term mental health and social difficulties (Norris, Friedman, Watson, Byrne, Diaz, & Kaniasty, 2002; Padgett, 2002).

This book is for mental health professionals working in the aftermath of disaster as well as emergency management professionals. It will be especially useful for insider practitioners from affected communities as well as community members who have decided to take an active role in promoting a process of collective recovery in their own neighborhoods, communities, or cities.

I received a great deal of guidance and support from the community research writing group at Columbia University's Mailman School of Public Health, which urged me to spend a lot of time first documenting in detail the narrative unfolding of my experience working on these projects. Then, with a team of research assistants, we reviewed and analyzed more than 300 hours of videotapes of interviews, community meetings, and implemented projects, in order to better understand how the process of collective recovery unfolded. During the process, it forced me to relive without avoidance some of the most difficult experiences I lived through with my family in the months following 9/11. As a result, it has also more firmly anchored my understanding of collective recovery in my experience carrying out these projects.

Acknowledgments

In writing this book I drew upon many connections with teachers, colleagues, and friends from many disciplines. Hillel Klein and Elie Wiesel set the stage in graduate school for my professional work on collective trauma. Salvador Minuchin, Randy Gerson, Jorge Colapinto, Carlos Sluzki, Peter Fraenkel, Pauline Boss, Froma Walsh, you have been important teachers and colleagues in the field of systemic family therapy. A special thanks to Judith Landau, who provided the framework and mentorship for many of the projects described in this book. Soeren Buss Jenson, my co-founder of the International Trauma Studies Program (ITSP), I value your ongoing support. Steven Reisner, Nancy Baron, Deborah Munczek, Madelyn Miller, Saralee Kahn, Donna Gaffney, Marsha Shelov, Nancy Wallace, Saliha Bava, and Sonali Sharma have been my trusted fellows at the International Trauma Studies Program. To the actors and directors of Theater Arts Against Political Violence: Abigail Gampel, Lucy McLellan, Carlos Caldart, Meagan Auster-Rosen, John Burt, Garretson Sherman, Arianne Zaytzeff, and Robert Gourp—thank you. The ITSP has been blessed by the contributions of noted colleagues and friends, among them Melinda Meyer, Bessel van der Kolk, Sandra Bloom, Stevan Hobfoll, Fran Norris, Yael Danieli, Alastair Ager, Winnifred Simon, and Robert Jay Lifton. My colleagues from the Kosovar Family Professional Education Collaborative: Ferid Agani, Stevan Weine, Shukria Statovci, Shqipe Ukshine, Afrim Blyta, Jusef Ulaj, Mimosa Shahini, Ellen Pulleyblank-Coffey, Corkie Becker, John Sargeant, Mellisa Elliot, John Rolland, Jim Griffith, Kaethe Weingarten, and Jane Ariel—our work together may soon continue. From the Chilean immigrant community in New York City, Ernesto and Maryanne Castillo, Victor and Nieves Torres, and Emelio Banda, you have been a great inspiration. To those who were instrumental in promoting the post-9/11 community resilience work in New York City—Claude Chemtob, Jack Rosenthal, Carol Prendergast, Linda Mills, Esther Cohen, Liz Margolies, Hally Breindel, Fred Wistow, and the many staff and participants of the Downtown Community

Resource Center. To Jacob Massaquoi, Gene Prisco, Serena Chaudhry, Ernie Duff, Juma and Gerald Brumskine, Ilene Reilly, Janice Cooper, Bob Jacobs, Reverend Phillip Selwranye, Rufus Arkoi, Esther Sharpe, Cheryl Nadeau, Annemarie Dowling-Castronovo, Nilafor Naqvi, and Brandon Brockmyer, our work with the Liberian community in Staten Island is now approaching the end of its first decade. And special thanks to Liberian TRC Commissioners Massa Washington and Jerome Verdier, for their contributions. To my colleagues in the field of journalism and trauma—Frank Ochberg, Bruce Shapiro, David Handshuh, and Adam Lisberg. I want to also acknowledge Brandon Hamber and fellow members of the INCORE project on Trauma, Peace-building, and Development—you have been a tremendous source of inspiration to me during the writing of this book.

I am truly grateful for the contributions of the research team at the International Trauma Studies Program—Nat Pinkerton, Ali Rodriguez, Rachel Lev, Amanda Goodman, Perry Nagin, Cyril Benounna, Lauren Cubelis, Laura Merryman, Julia Richter, Vanessa Smith-Levine, and Nira Shah—this was truly a collective endeavor. And to those who have contributed as editorial advisors: Jennifer Dworkin and Victoria Horowitz; and to the book's editors in its final stage, Jennifer Wholey and Griffin Shea. A special thanks to Rocio Rodriguez, my artistic mentor, for offering her painting for the book's cover and to Zohar Nir-Amitin for the cover design. A special acknowledgment to Mindy Fullilove and the Columbia University writing group—Lourdes Hernandes, Ann Burack Weiss, and Helena Hanson—who provided the shape and encouragement for this project. And thank you to Charles Figley for the invitation to write this book and to Anna Moore, my editor at Routledge. My deepest appreciation goes to my family, who not only supported me but also contributed to the book—my sons, Noam and Adam, and my wife Esther Perel.

Introduction

Collective Trauma, Resilience, and Recovery

In recent years, it seems we have faced increasingly frequent natural disasters, conflicts, and other major catastrophes. As I am completing this book in New York City at the end of 2012, we are just recovering from super-storm Sandy, which left thousands of people along the northeast coast with their homes, businesses, and property ruined from the floods of a surging ocean. The civil war in Syria rages on with more than 40,000 deaths and hundreds of thousands displaced in and from a country that has seen such destruction that recovery will take decades. Weeks ago the conflict erupted again between Gaza and Israel, exacerbating tensions that now make peace seem farther off than ever. And just before the winter holidays, one of the worst school shootings in U.S. history took place in Newtown, Connecticut.

Disasters, whether their causes are natural or man-made, strain the ability of local systems to respond to needs. They bring an array of stressors to populations—from direct threat to life, physical injury, exposure to the dead and dying, bereavement, loss, societal and community disruption, and ongoing hardship (Norris, Friedman, Watson, Byrne, Diaz, & Kaniasty, 2002). The mental health consequences of disaster are many and include depression, anxiety, posttraumatic stress disorder (PTSD), physical health problems, chronic problems in living, interpersonal relationships, and financial stress, as well as the loss of resources such as actual and perceived social support. In their study of 142 disasters, Norris et al. (2002) found the disasters that had the greatest impact were those in which two or more of the following were present: extreme and widespread damage to property, serious and ongoing financial problems, a deliberate human cause, and impact associated with previous traumatic events such as injury, loss of, or threat to life. An inevitable consequence of natural and human-caused disaster is what we refer to as "collective trauma," the shared injuries to a population's social, cultural, and physical ecologies.

1

This book describes how communities strive to recover from collective trauma and the ways that practitioners both outside the events and within them may assist in that process by promoting resilience and well-being. Over the last 15 years, I have worked as a family systems-oriented psychologist with populations that have endured genocide, torture, ethnic cleansing, terrorism, civil war, and forced migration. The situations vary in terms of the severity, duration, and impact of violence and destruction as well as the communities' social and material capacities to recover. This book tracks this work in a number of different community contexts in which my role shifted from that of an outside to inside practitioner: my work with immigrants and refugees in New York and with war survivors in Kosovo, strengthening resilience in my own neighborhood in Manhattan following the September 11 terrorist attacks, and then again collaborating with the Liberian refugee community in Staten Island, New York.

For some time now, I have been interested in collective contexts and capacities for recovery, particularly the importance of public spaces and communal activities. In this light, I have focused on collective narration as an important process in recovery, and thus many of the projects that I have developed utilize narrative, testimony, the arts, and theatrical performance as collaborative social interventions. Like many people working in this field, I have a family history of relatives having survived persecution, political violence, and migration. My grandfather survived the anti-Semitic pogroms in Kishinev in present-day Moldova at the beginning of the twentieth century (see Saul, 2003). My wife's parents were the sole survivors of both their large extended families and their towns in Poland during the Holocaust of World War II. My interest in the human capacities for recovery following major adversity is certainly derived from my family experience.

The major thesis of this book is that recognizing and strengthening the adaptive capacities or "resilience" in families and communities promotes collective recovery after mass trauma. These capacities for recovery may be enhanced through the structure and support provided by outside practitioners, may be initiated from within communities themselves, or may be driven by various insider/outsider collaborations. Adaptation following massive traumatic events requires both flexibly responding to changing circumstances over time and at the same time developing a positive vision of recovery. Thus, collective recovery is a creative and emergent process; its content and form are constructed over time through cycles of collective action, reflection, and narration.

Collective Trauma

Collective trauma refers to the impact of adversity on relationships in families, communities and societies at large. This includes natural and human-caused disasters as well as the cumulative effects of poverty, oppression, illness, and displacement.

American sociologist Kai Erikson, in a report on the Buffalo Creek disaster of 1972, a terrible flood that wrecked a hollow in Appalachia, made the distinction between "individual trauma" and "collective trauma." To quote him:

> By individual trauma I mean a blow to the psyche that breaks through one's defenses so suddenly and with such brutal force that one cannot react to it effectively. This is what clinicians normally mean when they use the term, and the Buffalo Creek survivors experienced precisely that. They suffered deep shock as a result of their exposure to death and devastation, and, as so often happens in catastrophes of this magnitude, they withdrew into themselves, feeling numbed, afraid, vulnerable, and very alone.

Erikson 1976, pp. 153–154

Erikson continues:

> By collective trauma, on the other hand, I mean a blow to the basic tissues of social life that damages the bonds attaching people together and impairs the prevailing sense of communality. The collective trauma works its way slowly and even insidiously into the awareness of those who suffer from it, so it does not have the quality of suddenness normally associated with "trauma." But it is a form of shock all the same, a gradual realization that the community no longer exists as an effective source of support and that an important part of the self has disappeared.... "I" continue to exist, though damaged and maybe even permanently changed. "You" continue to exist, though distant and hard to relate to. But "we" no longer exist as a connected pair or as linked cells in a larger communal body.

Erikson 1976, p. 154

Erikson pointed out that people might experience either individual or collective trauma in the absence of the other. But it is common that after a catastrophe people experience both, and the two are very much interrelated. As he observed in his studies, people who suffer from individual trauma usually have difficulty recovering if the community to which they belong remains shattered. Similarly, individual therapy is usually most successful when done in concert with a nurturing and supportive environment.

What is often a component of collective trauma, according to Erikson, is the way that those who are responsible for an accident, as in the case of the Buffalo Creek disaster, deny responsibility, and retreat from the victims without any expression of regret or apology. This betrayal of social trust leaves one feeling devalued and humiliated, with a sense that previously established communal trust and decency is no longer present. Restoring social trust thus becomes one of the greatest challenges for survivors of collective trauma and often takes the form of demands for acknowledgment, accountability, and justice.

For traumatized people, betrayal of social trust is often associated with feelings that one's most basic views about life have changed. Traumatized individuals may no longer share the same sentiments and beliefs that usually make life's risks and dangers feel manageable for others.

Trauma, loss, and displacement, according to Mindy Fullilove (2013), disrupt social networks and shared sentiments and may cause a collapse of morale. As identified in her research on the long-term health and mental health effects of neighborhood destruction and displacement due to urban renewal, collective trauma may lead to increases in structural and individual violence, the inability to react to patterns of threat and opportunity, and cycles of social fragmentation (Fullilove, 2004). Catastrophic events often open up or exacerbate previously existing fault lines of racism and other forms of discrimination, social and economic inequalities, and prior historical traumas.

From a family systems perspective, the term "relational trauma" is used to refer to the impact of adverse events on significant relationships in families and communities. These events, ranging from domestic violence and child abuse to disaster and mass violence, reduce the sense of trustworthiness, safety, openness, and emotional quality in relationships. Such events have negative impacts on interactions between persons and their social context as well as on their internal experience—affecting their thoughts, feeling, memories, and sense of personal agency. The traumatic impact on relationships may occur even in an absence of individual symptoms (Scheinberg & Fraenkel, 2001; Hardy & Fraenkel, 2002). Thus, focusing exclusively on individual symptoms and psychopathology following disasters may miss some of the more troubling relational impacts and serious risks of effective coping.

The relational perspective draws attention to the ruptures of relationships that can occur at multiple levels due to injury, loss of a loved one, friend or associate, the loss of employment, the violation of basic assumptions about the world as a safe, predictable, and reasonable place, and the loss of a place itself, i.e. one's city or town as a secure base. The sense of betrayal by trusted others, by nature, by government, and by helping systems is also a frequent source of relational distress.

In the field of traumatology, Charles Figley (Figley & McCubbin, 1983; McCubbin & Figley, 1983) has addressed the impact of catastrophic events, war, and disaster on relational systems. Families may experience severe distress in response to one or more members' traumatic experience or the entire family may be directly affected by mass trauma. Both may lead to serious disruptions of family functioning such as difficulty parenting, or diminished capacity for effective communication. It follows that, to effectively address the impact of major trauma, family and community resources will need to be mobilized for effective recovery.

Catastrophic events often involve multiple losses of life, property, livelihood, and even dreams for the future (Walsh, 2007). Hence an important feature of collective trauma is what we call traumatic loss. This may refer to deaths that are untimely, sudden, and/or violent and are experienced as the most traumatic of losses (Norris et al., 2002). During and following catastrophes, due to the disappearance of people and the uncertainty about whether they are dead or alive, families often experience "ambiguous losses." In such an experience of loss, the person is physically absent but emotionally present. Conflicts over accepting the death of the missing person versus continuing to believe that he or she might be alive may cause families immobilizing stress and further traumatization (Boss, 1999). The absence of a body or remains may prevent the carrying out of expected mourning rituals, thus leaving families in a state of limbo, unable to adequately grieve their losses. Massive trauma and loss may also lead to the intergenerational transmission of particular coping styles and emotional sensitivities (Klein, 1982; Danieli, 1985, 1998).

Massive trauma often involves a serious loss of resources. According to conservation of resource theory (Hobfoll, 1998), people strive to obtain, retain, and protect that which they value. Stress occurs when people lose their resources, when they are threatened with resource loss or are unable to develop or enhance resources despite significant effort. Following major traumatic events, those with fewer resources are more deeply impacted and may fall into rapid and turbulent loss cycles in which the loss of one or more resources triggers further losses. Such downward loss spirals, which are extremely difficult to reverse, may lead to anxiety, depression, and loneliness, as well as reduced social involvement, diminished interest in life, feelings of social detachment, and a sense of alienation. In order for communities to recover, these vicious loss cycles have to be interrupted and resource gain cycles reintroduced.

Somasundaram (2007) described the multiple impacts of collective trauma that were the consequence of civil war in Sri Lanka. As a result of the destruction of family relationships, networks, processes, and structure, whole communities suffered a sense of pervasive despair, passivity, and silence, as well as a lack of motivation and a loss of values and ethical mores. Somasundaram noted that in collectivistic cultures (in which the individual's sense of self is submerged in wider social contexts), collective events and their consequences may have more significance than in Western individualistic societies. In Tamil society, a person's identity is defined by the village, which through its traditions and institutions provides the foundations and framework for daily life. Recovery then must address the impact on the collective. To be most effective, he recommended that relief, rehabilitation, and development programs address the problems of collective trauma through integrated multi-level approaches.

Even in Western societies, the disruptions to families and communities by terrorism and natural disaster warrant an approach that addresses the larger social impacts at multiple levels (Saul & Bava, 2008). However in the United States following September 11 and Hurricane Katrina, individually oriented ideologies and institutional practices often posed tremendous obstacles to addressing the collective consequences of massive trauma.

As collective trauma refers to disruptions of relationships at all levels of human systems, recovery then involves collective processes of readjustment and adaptation and the mobilization of capacities for resilience in families and communities.

Family and Community Resilience

Usually defined as a person's ability to overcome stress and adversity, the term "resilience" was first applied to an individual child or adult. There is a large body of work on resilience in children ranging, for example, from children of war and communal violence (Garbarino, 1992; Garbarino & Kostelny, 1996), to studies of children living in large cities (Bell, 2001), to children facing major depression and suicidality (Anthony & Benedek, 1975) and to children and adults in the aftermath of terrorism (Bonanno, 2005). This exclusive focus on resilience as an individual trait has been seen as problematic in that it does not take into account the person's social and cultural context. More recently, there has been a focus on resilience in families, communities, and society at large. The pertinent characteristics of families who cope well with stress have been developed by numerous authors (Antonovsky, 1979; Boss, 1999; Boss, 2006; Figley, 1985; Figley & McCubbin, 1983; Walsh, 1998). In the mental health field, a resilience approach shifts the perspective from a focus on pathology to one that emphasizes helping individuals, families and communities access their strengths and capacities for healing and recovery.

Kirmeyer, Sehdev, Whitley, Dandeneau, & Isaac (2009) make the important distinction between two interpretations of community resilience. On the one hand, it may look at how the individual's resilience is fostered by social networks and cultural resources embedded in communities. On the other, it may consider the collective capacities or ways that communities themselves exhibit resilience in their response to stress and challenges (Norris, Stevens, Pfefferbaum, Wyche, & Pfefferbaum, 2008; Landau & Saul, 2004; Walsh 2007; Ungar, 2008, 2011; Pfefferbaum, Reissman, Pfefferbaum, Klomp, & Gurwitch, 2007; Kirmeyer et al., 2009). This may involve adjustments and adaptations of subsystems within the community, i.e. individuals, groups, and organizations, or it may involve the interactions of the entire community with its environment, including other social, economic, and political entities (Kirmeryer et al., 2009).

While much of the focus on community resilience has been on strengthening the adaptive capacities of communities to prepare for and respond to disasters (Norris et al., 2008), other approaches also mobilize families and communities to address the impact of war and forced migration (Rolland & Weine, 2000; Weine et al., 2006) as well as such mental health problems as substance abuse (Landau & Garrett, 2003) and serious mental illness (Agani, 2005; Weine et al., 2005).

Froma Walsh, who has been instrumental in developing the concept of family resilience, defined resilience as "the capacity to rebound from adversity, strengthened and more resourceful. It is an active process of endurance, self-righting, and growth in response to crisis and challenge ... the ability to withstand and rebound from disruptive life challenges" (Walsh, 2007). She has called for a multisystemic, resiliency-oriented approach to recovery from mass trauma and loss. She stressed the contextual factors in practice, by situating the traumatizing event in a communal context while attending to the relational networks and practice focused on "strengthening family and community resources for optimal recovery."

Walsh identified belief systems, organizational patterns, and communication/problem solving as the key family and social processes to facilitate resilience (Walsh, 2003, 2007). These processes include:

- *belief systems*: making meaning of traumatic loss experience; a positive outlook, transcendence, and spirituality;
- *organizational patterns*: flexibility, kin and community connectedness, and economic and institutional resources; and
- *communication/problem solving*: which includes clear, open emotional expression and collaborative problem solving.

Walsh approached resilience as a systemic process from micro (family) to macro (communal). She cited the studies of strong families by Stinnett and DeFrain (1985) who found that "75 percent of families in crisis experienced positive occurrences in the midst of hurt and despair, and believed that something good came out of the ordeal" (Walsh, 1998, p. 7).

Landau and I defined community resilience as: "A community's capacity, hope and faith to withstand major trauma and loss, overcome adversity, and to prevail, usually with increased resources, competence and connectedness" (Landau & Saul, 2004). We saw this as an inherent competence present in us all. For the human spirit to prevail and be perpetuated across generations, we need to be able to access and utilize our biological, psychological, social, and spiritual resources to cope with the impact and immediate consequences of trauma, and to be able to promote long-term recovery and healing (Landau, 1982).

According to Landau, traumatic events cause a disconnection and discontinuity of people's "transitional pathway"—the pathway that creates continuity among past, present, and future, bridging their entire ecosystemic context smoothly through time. As a result of this discontinuity, people may lose access to their inherent competence, their resilience, the strengths and resources that their families and tribe had accessed and utilized across time (Landau-Stanton, 1990; Seaburn, Landau-Stanton, & Horwitz, 1995). When people are able to access past resilience by being in touch with their history, they can reconnect their transitional pathways, knowing where they came from and where they are now. With this knowledge, they can make informed choices about what to keep from their past to draw on for the future, and what they choose to leave behind. Making these choices allows them to plan not only where to go, but also how to get there (Landau & Saul, 2004).

Landau highlighted the importance of knowing one's past family history as a protective factor for families (Landau, 2007). She cites that adolescents who knew of and shared family stories, even those involving themes of vulnerability, had more protective tendencies and lower sexual risk taking than those who did not. Discussing themes of resilience was associated with greater self-esteem.

In humanitarian crises, multisystemic approaches, with the active participation of local residents, facilitate both family and community resilience (Landau & Saul, 2004). Community-based coordinated efforts, involving local and national agencies and international assistance where needed, are essential to meet challenges. Major disasters that disrupt family systems, work organizations, and community structures and services are most debilitating because they may lead to community fragmentation, conflict, and destabilization. Unresponsiveness by larger systems compounds the traumatic impact.

Both Walsh and Landau not only emphasized the capacity to rebound and withstand adversity in their definitions of family and community resilience, but also included the notion of increased capacity, connection, and growth, incorporating ideas from the clinical research on "posttraumatic growth" or the positive psychological changes resulting from struggling with adversity (Tedeschi & Calhoun, 2004).

A number of perspectives on community resilience have been put forth in recent years. Some perspectives focus on the accessibility of resources to a community and the extent to which the community utilizes these resources to face challenges. Others focus on social capital—defined as the extent to which a community invests its resources (physical, symbolic, financial, human, or natural) in social relations.

Norris et al. (2008) provided a conceptual framework on community resiliency for disaster preparedness based on an extensive review of the literature. They developed a conceptual framework that draws out economic development, social capital, information and communication, and community competence as four primary sets of "adaptive capacities" that foster community resilience. They emphasized that resilience rests on both the resources themselves and the dynamic attributes of those resources (robustness, redundancy, rapidity). Like Landau and Walsh, they stress that the transformational characteristics of "community resilience" distinguish it from other ways of characterizing community strengths, such as social competence or social capital. Their framework included this set of network adaptive capacities:

Economic development refers to the basic physical and material resources of a resilient community such as land, accessible housing, health services, schools, and employment opportunities, as well as economic growth and the equitable distribution of income and assets within populations. Community resilience is a function not only of the volume of resources but also of their diversity.

Social capital is defined as the aggregate of the actual or potential resources that are linked to the possession of a durable network of relationships (Bourdieu, 1986). Putnam (1993) as cited by Kirmeyer et al. (2009) emphasizes the role of relationships, networks, trust, and norms and defines social capital as consisting of five principal characteristics:

> (1) Community networks: number and density of voluntary, state and personal networks; (2) Civic engagement: participation and use of civic networks; (3) Local civic identity: sense of belonging, of solidarity and of equality with other members of the community; (4) Reciprocity and norms of cooperation: a sense of obligation to help others, along with a confidence that such assistance will be returned; and (5) Trust in the community.

p. 75

An important component of social capital is "social support," which refers to social interactions that provide individuals with actual assistance and embed them into a web of social relationships perceived to be loving, caring, and readily available in times of need (Barrera 1986). Research on social support (Kaniasty & Norris 2004) has distinguished the necessity of both "received support" (actual receipt of help) and "perceived support" (the belief that help would be available if needed). Norris et al. (2008) highlighted citizen participation as a fundamental element for community resilience. Pfefferbaum et al. (2007) hypothesize two aspects of citizen participation: one describes member involvement and engagement and opportunities for such that are sensitive to the diversity, ability, and interests of members; and the other describes structures, roles, and responsibilities, referring to leadership, teamwork, clear organizational structures, well-defined roles, and management of relationships with other communities.

Information and communication are primary resources for enabling adaptive performance and depend on common meanings and understandings that allow community members opportunities to express their needs, views, and attitudes. The presence of communal narratives is an important community capacity that gives the experience shared meaning and purpose. Landau and Saul (2004) conclude that community recovery depends partly on collectively telling the story of the community's experience and response. Media may also be an important contributor to collective narration, shaping how a community understands its situation as well as providing important information for accessing resources and conveying useful information on solutions to difficult challenges (solution journalism).

Community competence is the extent to which a community has the capacity to engage in collective action and decision-making. Norris et al. (2008) referred to Cottrell's (1976, p. 197) description of a competent community as one in which

> the various component parts of the community: (1) are able to collaborate effectively in identifying the problems and needs of the community; (2) can achieve a working consensus on goals and priorities; (3) can agree on ways and means to implement the agreed upon goals; and (4) can collaborate effectively in the required actions.

Importantly, these arise out of a commitment to the community as a relationship worthy of substantial effort, participation, and discussion.

The capacity to engage in collective action is complex and unpredictable and, according to Norris et al. (2007), may depend on the extent of collective efficacy, mutual trust, and shared willingness to work for the common good of a neighborhood. Collective action may also be closely linked to processes of empowerment versus disempowerment, and adversarial versus collaborative community politics.

Based on this framework Norris and her colleagues concluded that community resilience to disaster depends on: (1) the development of economic resources, the reduction of risk and resource inequities, and attention to areas of greatest social vulnerability; (2) the meaningful engagement of local people in every step of the mitigation process; (3) relying on pre-existing organizational networks and relationships for rapid mobilization and ongoing support; (4) boosting and protecting natural support to ensure that communities and families retain the capacity to exchange emotional and instrumental support (Landau and Saul 2004); and (5) planning ahead, but at the same time planning for not having a plan. Responding to a disaster means that communities must be flexible and rely on trusted sources of information and communication in the face of tremendous complexity and uncertainty. Thus, promoting community resilience, whether in the context of disaster preparedness, emergency response, short or long-term recovery, is an emergent process requiring flexibility and creative improvisation.

Promoting Community Resilience and Recovery

Michael Ungar (2008) presented five principles of resilience as applied to practice. They are as follows: resilience is nurtured by an ecological, multileveled approach to intervention; resiliency shifts our focus to the strengths of individuals and communities; resiliency research shows that multi-finality, or many routes to many good ends, is characteristic of populations of children who succeed; resiliency studies show that focus on social justice is foundational to successful development; and resiliency research focuses on cultural and contextual heterogeneity related to children's thriving (Ungar, 2008). He defined resilience thus:

> First, resilience is the capacity of individuals to navigate their way to resources that sustain well-being;
> Second, resilience is the capacity of individuals' physical and social ecologies to provide these resources; and
> Third, resilience is the capacity of individuals and their families and communities to negotiate culturally meaningful ways for resources to be shared.

pp. 22–23

His definition emphasizes the individual, family, and community while contextualizing the constructive nature (meaningfulness) of how the resources are utilized. His research is focused on pathways to resiliency, particularly for children and youth. His multilevel ecological intervention moves from a micro to macro perspective of accessibility and resource availability.

Kirmeyer et al. (2009) see community resilience in response to disasters as encompassing three different capacities:

Resistance: the community may resist change, counteracting the impact of challenges by adjustments and adaptations, withstanding disruption before undergoing significant lasting change.

Recovery: a community may change for a period in response to challenges but return to its previous state when the challenges have been resolved. A resilient community thus would return to its pre-disaster state more quickly than a less resilient community.

Creativity: a community may be transformed by adversity, developing new ways of functioning and new directions, by creating new institutions and practices that carry its values forward.

Thus Kirmeyer et al. (2009) assert:

> As these terms make clear, resilience is a dynamic property of systems. A system may express resilience, insuring its own continuity, in ways that maintain its components but it may also transform or eliminate components. Thus, a community may express resilience that maintains its continuity and growth as an entity in ways that are distinct.

p. 72

In the field of international psychosocial response, there have been attempts to place psychological programs in response to massive trauma and loss into a larger social context. Ager (1997) has pointed to tensions that have existed between approaches that are conceptualized as unique, indigenous, and community based and those that are conceptualized as generalizable, technical, and targeted. Most trauma programs are defined by the latter characteristics. He has proposed a four-phase framework that puts psychological interventions within a larger context: (1) an initial phase, in which planned interventions avoid disrupting intact protective factors such as community structures, meanings, and networks; (2) the second phase, in which social resources that are considered too weak must be actively re-established—family reunification, community development, vocational training, etc.; (3) the third phase, in which particularly vulnerable groups may need compensatory support; and (4) only when the other phases have been implemented is there a place for a fourth phase, in which there is targeted therapeutic support. What is crucial for the effectiveness and sustainability of such a program is that the voices of those for whom services are intended contribute to the design, implementation, and evaluation of such assistance (Ager, 1997).

A multilevel approach that integrates the fostering of collective resilience with targeted clinical approaches has been articulated in a set of guidelines to train local professionals and practitioners in mental health and psychosocial response by the Task Force on International Training of the International Society for Traumatic Stress Studies (Weine, Danieli, Silove, van Omerren,

Fairbank, & Saul, 2002). In 2007, the Inter-Agency Standing Committee of the United Nations published the *IASC Guidelines on Mental Health and Psychosocial Support in Emergency Settings* (IASC, 2007) with input from more than 200 NGOs (non-governmental organizations). These new guidelines focused on implementing steps in complex humanitarian emergencies that take into consideration the particular social, political, and cultural context of the recipient populations. The guidelines also propose a multilevel approach and have the following core principles: promoting human rights and equity, maximizing the participation of local populations in humanitarian response, doing no harm, building on available resources and capacities, integrating support systems, and developing a multilayered set of complementary supports that meet the needs of diverse groups. An important contribution to standards for mass casualty intervention has been developed by Hobfoll, Watson, Bell, et al. (2007) which proposes five essential elements of intervention based on empirical studies. These are promoting: (1) a sense of safety, (2) calming, (3) a sense of self and community efficacy, (4) connectedness, and (5) hope. The importance of strengthening the social milieu as a crucial factor in promoting recovery from trauma has been emphasized by Bloom and Farragher (2013).

The project on Trauma, Peace-building, and Development sponsored by the International Conflict Research Institute (INCORE) has generated a number of practice recommendations for psychosocial support and social transformation initiatives (Hamber & Gallagher, forthcoming). These include:

1. A comprehensive, coordinated approach that interconnects psychosocial support and peace-building, particularly in post-conflict environments;
2. An adaptive approach to the context, including the political environment, engagement with the state, and the political implications of psychosocial work;
3. Avoiding a narrow focus on the individual trauma and deficits, and focusing on strengths, assets, resilience, and collective processes. Building on existing natural supports and cultural practices while avoiding romanticized, fossilized views of culture;
4. Taking into account the value of dialogue, issues of gender, masculinity and women's empowerment; the value of education and the importance of including and learning from the voices/perspectives of children and youth; the importance of tailoring support to the distinctive needs of different subgroups (e.g. youth, girls, young men, etc.);
5. Historical and intergenerational awareness;

6. Multilayered psychosocial support, engaging with different subgroups, and working into diverse spaces, such as schools, religious sites, community centers etc.;

7. Working on livelihoods and attention to the economic context;

8. Recognizing large-scale crises as opportunities for constructive social changes, practitioners should think about how their work promotes such change;

9. Attending carefully to ethics issues beyond confidentiality and informed consent.

Ager, Strang and Abebe (2005) present a framework for building community support in war-affected populations that includes three domains; *human capacity*, *social ecology*, and *culture and values*. War may deplete resources in each of these domains. The facilitation of resource development in communities consists of processes engagement, negotiation, and transformation.

An established methodology for fostering community resilience is the LINC Community Resilience Model developed by Judith Landau (Landau-Stanton, 1986; 1990; Landau & Saul, 2004; Landau, 2007), which has been applied to an number of major disasters including Lower Manhattan Communities following the 9/11 terrorist attacks, and the impact of political and economic instability and the "disappearances" of dissidents in Buenos Aires, Argentina. This LINC model provides a basic framework for promoting community resilience illustrated in this book (see Chapters 6 and 9) through case studies with different communities. The LINC model includes strategies for assessing communities, mapping resources and resilience, joining with the community, and working with natural change agents to develop effective and sustainable prevention and intervention programs.

The Purpose of this Book

Collective Trauma, Collective Healing tracks my progression as a psychologist. I first address collective trauma in different global situations, then delineate my role as an inside and outside practitioner addressing the impact of 9/11 in my neighborhood and city, and then my work collaborating with a community of war survivors living in New York City. This book examines the issues of collective recovery in a number of different situations—from moderate to massive trauma, from the immediate aftermath of violence to second- and third-generation effects, from a local to a national and transnational project, and in the context of intact and well-resourced communities to those that are extremely fragmented and poorly resourced.

Since the content of the book is based on implemented projects rather than research studies, I wrote it as a narrative drawn from reviewing more than 300 hours of video of community forums, presentations, narrative projects, and interviews with key participants. The book was written with the intent to reveal concepts and themes in promoting community resilience and recovery as they emerged in the process of carrying out the work. This includes a host of mistakes as well as successes, wrong turns, and changes of direction. I try to convey this kind of community-oriented work as complex and dynamic, requiring a great deal of flexibility, improvisation, reflection, and adherence to some basic principles. This book is for practitioners and community members affected by catastrophe. Since much of what was implemented in these projects was inspired by what others had done in similar circumstances, it is my hope that it will be an inspiration for future creative projects that promote collective recovery.

Organization of This Book

Part One, "Collective Trauma and Recovery: Global Perspectives" lays out foundations for promoting resilience and recovery in international contexts. It includes the following chapters:

Chapter 1, "Families and Generations" presents a view of survival from mass trauma that focuses on adaptive capacities rather than primarily on symptoms and psychopathology. It presents a wide-angle view of recovery taking place in families and communities over life spans and generations.

Chapter 2, "Treating Refugees: From Clinic to Community" presents a social ecological perspective on working with refugees in New York City and follows a shift to address collective capacities for recovery, including a theater of witness project with members of the Chilean refugee community.

Chapter 3, "Promoting Family and Community Resilience in Post-War Kosovo" documents both an approach to enhancing the mental health community's professional capacities through collaboration as well as the resilience of Kosovar families and communities.

Part Two, "From Global to Local: Urban Terrorism in Lower Manhattan" applies approaches from working in international contexts to my own neighborhood and community in New York City following September 11. It presents the stages in a community resilience approach to the disaster in five chapters.

Chapter 4, "9/11: The First Three Weeks" is about the initial response to the terrorist attacks in Lower Manhattan by the school community and by local mental health professionals. I locate my own position in the community as well as my own personal initial reactions and those of my family.

Chapter 5, "School and Community: Forging Collaboration" describes how parents, teachers, and school staff came together to address the needs of children and adults in the school community. A series of community forums are presented, which were sites for exchange of information, problem solving, and needs assessment. Integral to this phase of response were efforts to prevent and address community fragmentation.

Chapter 6, "Promoting Collective Recovery" tracks efforts over the next year and a half after 9/11 to sustain attention to issues of community recovery, and not just individual therapeutic responses. These efforts took place in a number of places—with city agencies, with the media, between community organizations across the metropolitan region, in the development of a community resource center in Lower Manhattan, and in providing ongoing training for mental health professionals that integrated clinical and community perspectives on disaster response.

Chapter 7, "Community Initiated Recovery Activities" describes four projects initiated by community members with support from the Downtown Community Resource Center in Lower Manhattan. These projects simultaneously strengthened bonds in interest/occupational groups while forming new connections and collaborations with groups and organizations outside the community, some even extending their global reach.

Chapter 8, "Collective Narration and Performance" presents two projects run by the Downtown Community Resource Center that encouraged the expression of a diverse range of voices and experiences about 9/11, community membership and identity, and the process of collective narration and reflection. The chapter shows the development of a narrative video and a theater project that incorporated stories of community members for public performance and conversation.

Part Three, "War and Migration—Little Liberia, Staten Island, NY" describes the process of fostering community resilience within a neighborhood in New York City populated by more than 6,000 Liberians, most of whom migrated during the recent civil wars in their country.

Chapter 9, "Little Liberia: Promoting Community Resilience" tracks the organic development of a neighborhood drop-in center run by Liberian residents in a community fragmented by the impact of war and migration, tribal affiliation, class difference, and local political conflict. It examines a number of ways in which the collective and creative capacities of the community were enhanced despite a paucity of material resources, ongoing neighborhood crime and communal violence, corruption, mistrust, and intense community polarization.

Chapter 10, "Seeking Truth and Justice" describes the interplay between local and global processes beginning with the participation of the Staten Island Liberian community with the national project of the Liberian Truth and Reconciliation Commission (TRC). Initially inspiring hope for the future of their country and a process of local communal reconciliation, the TRC's loss of support by the Liberian government reverberates in Staten Island. Following a community-initiated theater project and academic forum to discuss the TRC and implications for the future of Liberia, an opposition political movement is established.

The Summary ties together a number of approaches and principles for working with communities to promote collective recovery.

COLLECTIVE TRAUMA AND RECOVERY

GLOBAL PERSPECTIVES

Families and Generations

The Second Generation

In the fall of 1981, I drove to New York City with a friend, Yaakov Naor, to attend the inaugural Children of Holocaust Survivors conference, where more than 600 children of Holocaust survivors gathered for the first time. I had met Yaakov, an Israeli psycho-dramatist, at Danvers State Hospital, just north of Boston, where I worked during graduate school as a psychology intern. Yaakov's parents, like thousands of others, had immigrated to Israel from Europe after World War II. Growing up as a Jewish American, I had studied the Holocaust and, while in graduate school at Boston University, I immersed myself in Holocaust studies under renowned professor Elie Wiesel. But Yaakov's recollection of his experiences growing up with survivor parents finally brought home the reality of this genocide for me.

Before the conference, many Holocaust survivors' children already realized that they somehow were affected by their parents' experiences from the war. Even though they might have endured nightmares about the camps and running from Nazis, they were not yet sure that the commonality of their experiences warranted its own description "children of survivors."

The conference was also attended by professionals who had been working therapeutically with survivors and their families. Following a keynote presentation by Helen Epstein, author of the book *Children of the Holocaust*, the conference took an awkward turn when professionals began presenting research on the pathology of survivors and what was commonly referred to as "survivor syndrome." The survivors' children, who had come together to celebrate their movement as a peer support organization, were upset to hear such stark clinical presentations, particularly addressed at their parents. They soon fought to have their own voices heard amidst the generational gap. The conference managed to end on a positive note: Dr. Henry Krystal, a psychiatrist and survivor himself, called attention to the warm connection and harmony between the generations underlying their difficulties and misunderstandings (Peskin, 1981).

Until the early 1980s, much of the clinical research and writing on Holocaust survivors was focused on pathology, e.g. "survivor syndrome": a description of symptoms and difficulties as they were presented in the clinic. This perspective began to change, highlighted particularly in the work of two clinicians—Yael Danieli, a New York psychologist who researched adaptation styles in survivor families (Danieli, 1982), and Hillel Klein, an Israeli psychiatrist and psychoanalyst whose clinical and research interests led him to examine the adaptive or resilient processes in survivors, their families and communities (Klein, 1982).

Dr. Klein, himself a survivor, had worked for over 35 years as a clinician and researcher with survivors and had done extensive work on survivors' reintegration in kibbutzim and in families within the context of psychotherapy. Eva Fogelman, an active leader in the children of survivors' movement, introduced me to Dr. Klein. Later I assisted him with his writing on "survival and revival," which was posthumously published in English (Klein, 2012).

Much of the early approach to understanding the Holocaust's impact on survivors focused on psychopathology. This was in part due to the task of clinically documenting the massive trauma and loss they had experienced in order to make claims for restitution from Germany. Government-financed support proved to be extremely important for survivors for economic and therapeutic reasons, but also as acknowledgment of Germany's culpability.

A former student of Donald Winnicott at the Tavistock Clinic in London, Dr. Klein was interested in how survivors maintained emotional connections to lost loved ones, enabling them to mourn. In contrast to the prevailing view of survivor guilt as a psychological problem, he saw survivor guilt as a way of maintaining an emotional connection to those who had died, facilitating the process of mourning and engaging in the difficult task of finding meaning in one's survival. He often saw many survivors express this by transforming feelings of guilt to a sense of responsibility to the dead, such as "How can I live my life in a way that honors the memory of those who did not survive?"

In the early 1980s, Dr. Klein encouraged other mental health professionals to look at the "adaptive mechanisms" that enabled survivors to endure horrifying experiences and then go on to rebuild their lives and create new families. For Dr. Klein, this capacity was crucial to the recovery process. He wrote,

In studying the different ways in which survivors coped with disaster, with "normal" life, and with re-establishing family ties, I have been repeatedly impressed with the diversity rather than the uniformity of these ego-adaptive and coping mechanisms within the life histories of survivors.

Klein, 2012, p. 28

The survivor's process of healing or revival includes retaining a sense of self-cohesion and continuity, he said, "connecting the nuclei of his previous identity and world of past representations and values with the duties and responsibilities of his present world" (p. 28).

For many Holocaust survivors, marriage represented a re-emergence from the *Weltuntergang*—the end of the world. It was a life-affirming act, not just of love, but as a way to counter the massive disruptions in their lives, and to attempt to remedy the dehumanization and loneliness they had experienced during the war (Danieli, 1985). A new family was a symbol of rebirth, providing a sense of continuity with the past and hope for the future (Perel & Saul, 1989). The family context was then crucial for the process of recovery and re-adaptation—a place for intimacy after having lived for years without privacy or protective boundaries.

Survivors often feared that they had been emotionally scarred by what they had experienced in the camps and that somehow this would damage their children. Yet many quickly married and started a family—having a child meant that they were still human. A child was a tangible reaffirmation of life and symbolized the replacement of lost loved ones.

Dr. Klein believed that survivors struggled to work through the themes of loss, separation, dependency, guilt, and hopelessness within the family context. Survivor families often had intense emotional interdependence, which expressed itself in difficulties with separation. Parents tended to place strong demands on children for achievement, to both adhere to external values as well as internally generated standards. While Dr. Klein rejected the notion of psychopathology transmission from one generation to another, he believed families could transmit common motifs and emotional sensitivities between generations.

Most survivors immigrated to the United States, Israel, Canada, and Australia after the war and experienced a profound sense of dislocation, which contributed to closed boundaries between families and the outside world. These immigrants faced the usual litany of problems: the decline of parental authority, lower social status, and a clash of values with the new society. Children often became liaisons between the family and the new environment.

Families' sense of isolation was further intensified by a "conspiracy of silence," the collusion between survivors and society to avoid talking about the Holocaust. This silence often prevented these families from accessing important social and material resources that would have been helpful to their adjustment and cultural transition.

Many survivors' children came to feel that they were imbued with a special mission in life—to make up for the parents' disrupted lives and those of lost family members. This created a particular bond between survivors and their children, and kept the parents overly involved in their children's lives.

When children of survivors read *Children of the Holocaust* (Epstein, 1979), they often felt that the book accurately captured what had gone on in their own homes. Frequently, these children questioned how any of their own suffering had any legitimacy compared to what their parents had gone through. In the same circumstances as their parents, they wondered, would they have been able to survive? Many felt that they carried a heavy burden and placed impossible demands upon themselves about how to live their own lives. They often felt that they had to make up for all those whose lives had been cut short. Some felt compelled to accomplish something meaningful, while others felt that whatever they accomplished, it would never be significant enough.

Whether their parents spoke or were silent about their Holocaust past, children often felt that their parents' past had somehow penetrated them as if by "osmosis." Adult children of survivors spoke about not being able to remember actual moments when their parents told them about their past, yet somehow they could recall images, phrases, and incomplete memories related to what their parents had experienced during the war.

Parents' sharing their Holocaust experience with their children can be a unifying experience and an important part of the process of mourning for the survivor. This disclosure could help the family emerge from an atmosphere of secrecy, demystifying and clarifying important components of the family's history and its losses—such as explaining to young children why they had no grandparents, uncles, or aunts. It might provide new opportunities for intimacy among family members and may lead to mutually empathic exchanges between the generations (E. Fogelman, personal communication, 1988). However, most families in these circumstances must negotiate between silence and communication. It may be too overwhelming for some survivors to speak about their past, and parents may choose to spare their children from some experiences they endured. The practice of "speaking about speaking" is equally important for families whose members have experienced other traumatic events. Mutually acknowledging that some experiences may be shared in time and some may never be shared at all can preserve family connections despite the fact that secrets do exist.

Due to the experience of massive loss, the dominant motifs for many Holocaust survivor families are the restoration of lost family and moving beyond the destruction (Klein, 1982). Despite the tendency for parental over-involvement and over-protectiveness that this might trigger, survivor families have found ways to maintain cohesion and loyalty to the past while facilitating the maturation of their children. But a traumatic past can easily overburden families who are dealing with the stresses of normal developmental challenges, and these families do not always attribute their coping strategies, resilient or not, to the family's Holocaust past.

For many families, the structure and support provided by community and culture were crucial to their successful adaptation. Most Jewish survivors of the Holocaust did not go to therapy, and often viewed it as an admission of being harmed by their experience. Instead, they engaged in an array of supportive community activities—informal peer networks, rituals of remembrance, gatherings of survivors from the same European town, creating testimony archives, planting thousands of trees as symbols of rebirth and life, and situating their personal suffering within the context of the history of the Jewish people. Dr. Klein saw Jewish culture, religion, and identity as key factors in survivors' adaptation during the war and in rebuilding their lives afterwards.

A Return to Poland

We sat in the town square of Zarki, preparing for lunch. Only recently were tourists appearing in small Polish towns, and the locals kept their distance, inquisitively eyeing our small group. A young girl about 12 years old curiously watched these foreigners for some time. Sala asked her in Polish to join us for some cake, and in their conversation she discovered that the girl attended the same school that Sala had attended some 50 years before, when she was 12. Sala began to sing a Polish song and the girl joined her; together they sang a number of songs that were still taught at the school. The girl was curious about Sala and offered to take us to the local community center a few blocks away. When we arrived, Sala recognized the building as the synagogue she had attended each week with her family before the war.

In the early 1990s, with the Soviet Union dissolved and the Eastern Bloc finally open, many Jews who had emigrated before and during World War II returned to visit the countries of their youth, often accompanied by their children. My wife Esther's parents, Sala and Icek, had spoken for years about possibly visiting Poland together, and now they felt ready, though the family knew that it would be an emotionally difficult trip. They wanted their son, Leon, and Esther to know about their lives before the war.

Both Sala, 66, and Icek, 72, were extraordinarily hearty people, both physically and mentally. They grew up in the country in the Upper Silesia region of Poland. Each would have said that maintaining a sense of dignity despite all odds, remaining hopeful to reunite with surviving family members, and sheer luck, had enabled them to survive the Holocaust.

Sala grew up in an educated and aristocratic Hasidic family in the small town of Zarki. She was the youngest of seven children. When the war broke out, 18-year-old Sala fled the ghetto of Zawiercie and spent a year living in hiding in the woods, stealing strawberries, potatoes, and eggs from the local farmers. When this life proved too difficult to sustain, she surrendered herself to a men's labor camp, hoping they might need someone like her to work in the kitchens. She preferred the predictability of the camp to the dangerous uncertainty of life in the woods. She spent the next five years living in nine different labor camps. She had a great deal of pride in how she was able to fend for herself and maintain her self-respect through attention to her hygiene and her ethical behavior toward others. After liberation in 1945, she eventually realized that of the 80 or 90 members of her extended family, she was the sole survivor. She was one of only a few Jewish survivors from her entire town.

Icek was from a religious family in the small village of Koziegłowy. A hard worker in his family's construction material factory, he made deliveries by horse and carriage from age eight. His physical stamina later served him well in the Nazi labor camps near Russia. He too was the sole survivor of a large extended family, eight siblings, and the only Jewish survivor from his village. After liberation, Icek met Sala on the road, recognizing each other from the vicinity where they had lived. Like many Holocaust survivors at the time, they felt elated to be free and quickly wanted to build a new life. Knowing each other's respective families was sufficient to establish they were suitable as partners. They eventually arrived in Belgium, where they connected with other Jewish war survivors. They lived in and ran a clothing store in Leuven, not far from Brussels.

Like many survivors at the time, after laying the foundations for a new life Sala went eventually for "treatments" paid for by the German government.

For several years she spent the month of July at a spa, taking baths, receiving hydrotherapy (water treatments for pain and stress relief), being massaged, and walking barefoot on the wet grass at dawn. Spa treatments had been used for centuries to cure nervous disorders and soothe the body. While at the spa, the survivors also attended ballroom dances and classical music concerts. Despite this, Sala was plagued by memories from the camps during the rest of the year; she regularly suffered nightmares and often engaged in fits of screaming.

Sala and Icek often met with other survivors in Belgium, and a few years after the war they moved again, to Antwerp. There they felt safe and supported in a thriving Jewish community, primarily made up of other Polish survivors. Some survivors found themselves only able to speak about their past in ways that were debilitating. Sala and Icek somehow found the strength to speak openly about their camp experiences and life before the war with friends, business associates, and customers at their clothing store. They were storytellers, speaking about their triumphs in the camps. Both had come close to death numerous times, either through disease, the harsh conditions, or at the hands of the guards. Icek had been caught sending love letters to a woman who was a prisoner in the adjacent camp, and he was almost transferred from the kitchen to the work factory where he probably would not have survived. But he had also run a black market for food at the camp, which enabled many inmates to receive the extra nutrition they needed to survive. A German guard, himself benefiting from the food distribution, prevented Icek's transfer.

Eventually, some years after the war, Sala and Icek began to contact survivors from the neighboring towns where they had grown up before the war. Together they created memorials for the towns' inhabitants whose deaths had never been formally acknowledged.

It was not until 1991, two years after martial law was lifted, that they decided to visit Poland with their children. When Icek walked down the main street of his village many people recognized and greeted him. They were glad to see him and wanted to know about his life during the war and afterward in Belgium. Icek spent hours speaking with villagers. He wanted to find out what had happened to one of his brothers, who had been in hiding. He met a man who had been nine years old when the Nazis took over Poland. This man's father had sent him to warn Icek's family when Nazi soldiers approached the town. Icek learned that his brother had given everything to be hidden by one of the peasants in the village, who eventually turned him in anyway.

Sala and Icek had not anticipated the intensity of feelings they would face when they visited the Auschwitz and Birkenau death camps, confronted with the reality of their friends' and family's murder. Nevertheless, the visit to Poland was an important experience of transmission for the family. Esther learned how her father had started life as an illiterate poor migrant and eventually became a successful businessman in Belgium. Due to the war and the Holocaust, his previous life had been destroyed, but it was replaced with the opportunity for a life he would never have anticipated. Icek appreciated this new life, even though he had lost everything and everyone from his old one. Icek was much less angry than his wife, and distinguished between Germans and Poles who had been good people and those who had been cruel. It was important for him to see the humanity in each person. Sala idealized her past and her relationship with her parents. They had very different styles of mourning their lost families. Icek and Sala were able to convey to their children that Poland had been a place of life for them, not just a place of tragedy and death. The act of visiting the villages, schools, and parks, walking down the streets where the parents had grown up, and speaking with the townspeople physically connected Esther and Leon to their parents' youth, which had been eclipsed by the dark years of the Holocaust. The physicality of place evoked positive memories of the past for the parents and brought to life stories of their families.

Beginning 45 years after the war, families of survivors began to visit their former hometowns with increasing frequency. Survivors felt more comfortable after they had rebuilt their lives and established themselves, and were thus better able to reflect on their past and pass on their history to their children. These visits were part of many collective healing rituals that were created by survivors and their families. These rituals re-established the family's transitional pathway, its continuity with the past, and its inherent strengths and resources. The process of recovery from a collective trauma such as the Holocaust is a lifelong process and even extends into future generations. As in other cases of extreme trauma, it may take decades for families and communities to come to terms with the impact of their losses.

In 1991 my wife Esther Perel, who is a marriage and family therapist, and I were invited to Oslo to present about the long-term effects of massive trauma on families of Holocaust survivors. We made a presentation to staff working with Bosnian and Iraqi refugees and torture survivors at the Oslo Center for Refugees. Esther spoke about the community of Holocaust survivors in which she grew up in Belgium. There were two groups of people there, she said: those who didn't die and those who came back to life. The people who "didn't die" were often very fearful. They didn't take any risks to go out into the world. The world to them was a dangerous place. They generally could not experience much joy without guilt and, consequently, neither could their children. They were surviving, but they did not truly live. The other group, who had "come back to life," comprised the kind of people who understood the "erotic"—that sense of aliveness that is an antidote to death. It was that life force that had enabled them to transcend their condition in the camps. And having survived, they wanted to make the best of life and live it to the fullest.

Following the conference, I became interested in the kinds of mental health services New York City offered to our present population of refugees and torture survivors. I began to inquire about how such services could be developed.

Refugees in New York City

From Clinic to Community

I was walking down the streets of Santiago.
I was arrested. He was arrested?
I was arrested. He was arrested?
Pablo Gomez. Pablo Gomez?
They don't believe what you say. What did she tell them?
They don't believe what you say. What did she tell them?
I was arrested. One year blindfolded.
What did I tell them? I told them they knew everything already.
They don't believe what you say.
They cannot eliminate what you stand for.
O my back. Seven times under torture.
That was the easy part.
Electroshock? They did that to everyone.
You get very thirsty.
Torture.
It's like a carousel.
Chile...

From "Victor's Body" (Theater Arts Against Political Violence)

Torture Survivors in New York City

In 1995, Dr. Allen Keller and I established a clinic at Bellevue Hospital for torture survivors, aided by my colleagues at the Oslo Center for Refugees where I had recently given a presentation. We were also given support and guidance by other centers including the International Rehabilitation Council for Torture Victims (IRCT) in Copenhagen, where the movement to treat survivors of torture had originated, the Center for Victims of Torture in Minneapolis St. Paul, and the STARRTS Program in Sydney. Through contact with these centers, we created a framework for providing clinical services for survivors in New York.

The research of an Australian psychiatrist, Dr. Derrick Silove, was instrumental for our work. His model emphasized five core adaptive systems: (1) the re-establishment of safety and security; (2) the restoration of interpersonal bonds; (3) the creation of systems of justice; (4) the development of a social framework that allows survivors to develop new roles and identities; and (5) the revival of institutions that confer meaning, whether political, social, religious, or spiritual (Silove, 2004).

Manu, a West African asylum seeker, was one of the first referrals to our newly founded program for survivors of torture and their families. When he first arrived in New York City, Manu was approached by members of a local church who had noticed him wandering aimlessly in Times Square. The church members invited him in for a meal, found a place for him to stay with a family in Brooklyn, and referred him to our newly formed clinic at Bellevue.

Barely three weeks before, Manu had been a graduate student in political science. Just shy of graduation he was arrested for participating in a student pro-democracy movement on campus. Police confronted him in his dorm room one evening, blindfolded him, and carried him away to an undisclosed location where he was tortured by strappado. For the next week, he was hung from chains attached to his hands, which were tied behind his back. Fortunately, he was released and warned that, next time, things would be much worse.

The situation in his country had become increasingly dangerous. Two of his friends had recently disappeared and were presumed dead. Manu quickly sold his belongings and arranged to buy an airline ticket to New York City. He left the country within the week without telling his mother and fiancée. When he came for an intake at Bellevue Hospital, he needed medical attention for the chain burns on his wrists and hands and his dislocated shoulders.

Manu greatly desired to speak with his family to assure them that he was all right, but it was too risky to contact them at the time. He was also very interested in documenting his torture to submit to the United Nations Special Rapporteur on Torture. He started to write a series of letters to his family documenting the events that led to his exile, but he did not send them. The letters were in the emotional vernacular of his native language and dialect, with shared memories and references from his past family life. He also began writing letters to fictional characters in order to force himself to be as factual as possible about the events that had taken place; he hoped this could become the basis for a written testimonial. He found this process painful, but also helpful in placing the traumatic events in the past and experiencing his freedom in the present. Eventually he found a way of writing letters that could actually reach his family; he addressed the letters from fictional characters and wrote in a code, which did not reveal his identity to authorities. He then was able to reconnect to his family and speak with them by telephone.

Over the next few months, Manu made a good adjustment to life in New York City, though it was not easy earning a living without a work permit. Within a year, he had received political asylum and resumed his graduate studies. In appreciation of the staff at Bellevue Hospital, he offered to give an in-service training entitled "What American Psychologists Need to Know About Working with African Clients." About 15 psychology interns and other staff attended Manu's presentation. He began by saying that when he first met with the doctor and me, just days after his arrival in New York City, he was still in a state of culture shock, confused and disoriented. On his second or third visit to meet with me, he said he became terrified when he saw that I came in wearing a black shirt. For him, meeting someone wearing black signified bad fortune, such as the death of a relative. For weeks, he avoided coming into the clinic, until a fellow African told him, "Don't worry, in New York City everyone wears black."

Manu emphasized to the staff at our clinic that he and his fellow African immigrants have a very different hierarchy of needs than Americans, and therefore a very different set of needs than professionals often presume. One thing he found most frustrating about being in the United States, despite the generosity that Americans had shown him, was this assumption that people knew what he needed without taking the time to listen to what he was feeling. He appreciated the fact that our team mostly didn't make assumptions about his needs, but when we did we were open to hearing his perspective.

By the time many asylees or refugees reach a host country like the United States, they may have endured multiple traumas, often living through years of violence inflicted upon their family and community. Following imprisonment, it is not uncommon for them to live in hiding, or under chronic threat of arrest. They often become marginalized in their society, stripped of their previous occupation, status, and property. Refugees who are also parents may find it extremely difficult to provide for their family and continue child rearing. Furthermore, physical and/or sexual abuse they received in detention often leads to problems in their marital relationship.

The process of fleeing their country is also dangerous. When refugees finally arrive in a host country, they must then deal with problems of residency status, racial prejudice, and numerous other types of obstacles—socioeconomic, educational, occupational, and linguistic. And still, the stresses from the past are ongoing: concern about family and friends back home, ambivalence and grief about fleeing their country, and additional physical and psychological sequelae of torture and related traumas.

Many political asylees become socially isolated. They often do not join their ethnic community in their new country because of factionalism within the community or an ongoing fear of reprisals from agents of repressive regimes. The asylee or refugee is in a state of continuous stress due to unresolved political and family calamities in the home country compounded by difficulties they have in adapting to their new and often alienating environments.

While trying to establish new lives in exile, they are still confronted with the impact of the multiple losses—of their relational web, home, possessions, work, culture, lifestyle, language, and political agency. They may consider forced migration as a kind of continued punishment and persecution; for some, exile is considered worse than torture. Many refugees are continually plagued by traumatic stress reactions—the uncontrolled intrusion of haunting memories and nightmares, the constriction of their lives in order to avoid experiences, people, or cues that may trigger traumatic memories, and disorders of concentration, sleep, and arousal. Some will suffer from severe depression, anxiety, mental impairment, substance abuse, and sexual dysfunction.

In providing clinical services for asylum seekers like Manu, who had recently arrived in New York and were socially isolated, we quickly learned of their profound needs for social support. The clinic team, with other patients at the clinic, came together for group meetings, which acted as a kind of "transitional family" for these men and women who were in the process of finding or establishing a support network of their own. The ability to interact with supportive staff members and fellow clients was an important step in their recovery.

Tibetans in the Café

A number of Tibetans needing health services and assistance applying for political asylum soon started showing up at the clinic at Bellevue Hospital. We happened to have a Tibetan psychiatric resident, Dr. Sophia Banu, on staff who offered to help out. Dr. Banu and I decided that one way to provide services for this population was to offer a support group for incoming refugees. We created a flyer in Tibetan advertising the group, and within the first week 15 young men and women met us at the clinic. Since space was scarce at Bellevue, we found ourselves having to meet in the coffee shop.

Some of the recently arrived Tibetans were seeking asylum, and already meeting with evaluators in the clinic who would prepare a medical or psychological evaluation to support their asylum claims. We continued to meet each week until the group grew too large for the café; we eventually found a conference room. The Tibetans discussed issues they had adjusting to life in the United States, including problems finding fair work and financial support. After a number of weeks, however, we found ourselves in a conundrum. In order to justify working with the Tibetans in the hospital, they all needed to be registered as patients with a clinical diagnosis and receive psychotherapy. However, they were not all seeking help for mental health reasons. One day, two of the leaders of the support group came in and asked whether we could help the group form its own non-profit community support organization. For many members, their priority was not just to receive support from the group; they also wanted to help other recently arrived refugees and asylum seekers navigate the bureaucracies of New York City. These refugees valued helping others as an adaptive way of dealing with the trauma and loss they had experienced as a result of torture and migration, and separation from their families. I found myself caught between the requirement of the hospital to give each person a diagnosis and the need I felt to shift my role from clinician to mediator.

One challenge of setting up a mental health clinic for torture survivors at Bellevue was that psychotherapy—speaking about one's experiences as a means to healing—was an alien concept for many refugees. The clinic served emigrants from such diverse countries as Mauritania, Sierra Leone, Iran, Iraq, Jordan, Palestine, Afghanistan, Tibet, China, and the Philippines. Most came to us with ideas about what they needed, both psychologically and socially.

Without a doubt, individual counseling and therapy can be extremely helpful to many torture survivors. We've now developed a set of effective clinical practices that range from psychodynamic and cognitive behavioral therapy to eye movement desensitization and reprocessing (EMDR), and art and group therapy. We realized that the predominant client coming into the clinic was an asylum seeker referred for an evaluation to support their asylum claim, or for medical services. Most were not seeking mental health services directly. Unfortunately, at Bellevue Hospital there were constraints on delivering social services, such as help with housing and financial support, which were often the most important services needed. Research shows that what best promotes the positive mental health of refugees is attending to a variety of social needs including employment, housing, raising a family, and political stability (Porter & Haslam, 2005).

We began to realize that other approaches to working with survivors of torture and refugee trauma were needed, especially if we wanted to reach the greater part of this population, which was not seeking asylum, but already living in the many ethnic communities throughout the city. Miller and Rasco (2004) proposed an ecological, community-based model when working with refugees. They cautioned that professionals should not assume that refugees with elevated levels of traumatic stress will necessarily have impaired psychosocial functioning. Despite high levels of stress, refugees may function very well in many areas of their lives. Furthermore, the impact of displacement is often the most challenging for refugees, rather than the previous exposure to violence and war. Thus, Miller and Rasco recommended that refugee mental health programs prioritize enhancing the capacity of refugee communities to cope effectively with these numerous displacement-related stressors as well as help them manage symptoms of trauma and traumatic loss.

In our situation, the refugees also appeared to need services held in community settings rather than in hospitals and clinics. These services needed to be based on a collaborative relationship with community members that took into consideration their hierarchy of needs and cultural beliefs about illness and health. Miller and Rasco highlighted that interventions need to: address problems in the ecological settings in which refugees live and work; reflect the concerns and priorities of the community; and, when possible, prioritize prevention over treatment. They also emphasized that interventions should incorporate local values and beliefs regarding well-being and distress, be integrated whenever possible into existing activities and services, and build the capacity of the community to address mental health issues (Miller & Rasco, 2004).

The International Trauma Studies Program

In the context of a growing need for a comprehensive community-based psychosocial approach to assist refugee survivors of torture, I began to look at the need to create opportunities for advanced training at New York University. We also needed a system to more intensely train staff and interns to work with these severely traumatized survivors of human rights violations. It was then that I met Dr. Soeren Buus Jensen, a psychiatrist from Denmark who had spent three years (1994 to 1996) working with the World Health Organization in the former Yugoslavia. As the WHO program manager and later as the head of the humanitarian aid program, he implemented a trauma-training program for Bosnian, Croatian, Serbian, and Macedonian mental health practitioners providing services during the war, involving many who had suffered through the same traumatic experiences as their patients. The "regional model" provided a year-long training program in 13 different areas for 30 to 32 professionals each, mainly psychiatrists and psychologists.

Dr. Jensen developed a network of international trauma-training advisors for an NGO he created in Denmark called the International University Center for Mental Health and Human Rights. Meeting with experts from around the world to learn about trauma-training programs, to his surprise, he found very few training programs in Europe and the United States. Dr. Jensen and I decided to develop an intensive trauma-training program at New York University similar to the one he had developed during the Yugoslavian war.

Prior to his work in the former Yugoslavia, Dr. Jensen and Dr. Inger Agger had done research with survivors of state terrorism in Chile. In the course of that work they became interested in the uses of testimony to promote the healing process from political violence. As recalled in their book, *Trauma and Healing Under State Terrorism* (Agger & Jensen, 1996), psychologists in Chile found that survivors giving testimonies to create documentary evidence for later war crimes trials were found to have improved mental health compared to those who had not given testimony and were still waiting to do so. Based on this work, Dr. Agger and Dr. Jensen developed a method of testimony therapy with refugee survivors of torture living in Denmark (Agger & Jensen, 1990).

Dr. Jensen brought to the curriculum a human rights framework from South America, referred to with the acronym DITE—documentation, investigation, therapy, and evaluation. The mental health and human rights perspective advocated a position of therapeutic non-neutrality in working with victims of human rights violations; it was important to establish an alliance with victims to condemn the inhumane practices that they suffered.

The training program, named the International Trauma Studies Program (ITSP), began in the fall of 1998 at New York University with more than 40 students participating. We held two separate course tracks, with one more intensive track for clinicians. Another, requiring fewer hours, was oriented toward building community-based practices and was open to practitioners other than mental health professionals—lawyers, community activists, youth workers, etc. The program revolved around workshops run by visiting faculty who were at the forefront of the trauma field, and leaders at the International Society for Traumatic Stress Studies (ISTSS), the most prominent organization promoting research and clinical practice in work with trauma survivors. The training was divided into didactic work on trauma theory and intervention, case studies, and self-care. Students worked in small groups to discuss cases, to engage in role-play and other experiential learning methods, and to discuss the impact that the work had on them personally. In the tradition of the Yugoslavian training program, students were required to carry out a project in order to complete the program. These projects ranged from workshops, to small clinical studies, to the development of citywide advocacy activities for trauma survivors. Three students teamed up the first year to create a program honoring survivors of torture on the U.N. day commemorating survivors.

The ITSP pursued its commitment to community-oriented work with survivors of torture and refugee trauma by establishing a not-for-profit organization called Refuge. It formed an alliance with three other organizations assisting torture survivors in the New York area—Solace/Safe Horizon, Doctors of the World USA, and the Cross Cultural Counseling Center of the International Institute of New Jersey (IINJ)—and was titled the Metro Area Support for Survivors of Torture Consortium (MASST). The MASST Consortium, under the leadership of the Solace/Safe Horizon director Ernest Duff, received a Torture Victims Relief Act (TVRA) grant from the U.S. Office of Refugee Resettlement, and over the six years of TVRA funding support, the MASST Consortium developed a range of services for over 2,000 survivors of torture and their family members. Services included information and practical assistance, support for families and youth, social services, referrals for legal and medical assistance, programs for educational and vocational development, individual, family, and group counseling, community development and capacity building, community arts and cultural programming, and medical and mental health evaluations for political asylum.

Refuge's role was to provide technical assistance to Solace and IINJ to develop family-oriented clinical services, train clinicians and community workers, and develop a network of mental health professionals in the New York area that would provide pro bono therapeutic services to survivors of torture and their families. In 2000, Refuge became a member of the National Consortium of Torture Treatment Programs with the other members of the MASST Consortium.

From the Clinic to the Stage

One project Refuge developed was Theater Arts Against Political Violence. Dr. Steven Reisner—a psychoanalyst and former actor and theater director—and I headed the project, along with another theater director, Robert Gourp. I was the producer. In our work with torture survivors, it became increasingly apparent that many of them desired to speak publicly about the injustices they had endured in their country of origin. They hoped not only to bring attention to injustices that were still present, but also to encourage intervention.

We began to see value in creating a public forum where survivors could speak about their experiences, and felt that it was necessary to create an open exchange with survivors. In the mental health profession, a lot of emphasis is on working with individuals or families in the privacy of a therapy office. However, this type of clinical work addresses primarily individual trauma reactions, while many survivors yearned to address shared trauma and the social and political contexts which informed them. The theater program was our alternative to one-on-one therapy. With this approach, the survivors and artists could collectively create art where all were free to contribute their ideas and experiences.

Theater Arts Against Political Violence originated at Bellevue Hospital in another project in partnership with the former U.S. Department of Immigration and Naturalization Services. We were tasked with training asylum officers to sensitively interview applicants for political asylum who were severely traumatized. To accomplish this, we hired a theater group and trained the actors to play traumatized refugees—a unique challenge for the actors. We cast actors to play composites of torture survivors from countries in the Middle East, Africa, Latin America, and Asia, blending cultural styles of coping and distress into each character. The asylum officers role-played interviews with the actors, and we occasionally froze the action to highlight what was happening at different points during each interview.

After these training sessions, the theater group expressed interest in creating a play about the issue of human rights violations, and the collective responsibility we all share to deal with them. The theater group began to explore themes related to political violence and the life of a refugee; we invited refugees who had been political prisoners to meet with the theater group and talk about their experiences. Eventually both groups would collaborate to create scenes based on the survivors' stories and creative input.

We found that the refugees felt honored to have the opportunity to speak with artists about their lives. For many, it was the first time any Americans had asked about their experience. We brought Tibetans, Guatemalans, Africans, and, eventually, a group of Chileans to meet with the theater group.

The three Chilean men and one woman had been living in New York City for over 15 years and had rarely spoken to others about their pasts. When we met for the first workshop, a refugee named Ernesto Castillo thanked us and introduced the rest of the Chileans.

> We are very honored to be here and want to thank you for inviting us to share with you our stories. The three of us are ex-political prisoners. Emelio was a student leader when he was arrested. Victor was a trade union leader. He spent three years in prison before he was expelled from the country. I was a trade union leader too. I was in prison for two years. We went through interrogation centers, to concentration camps, to prisons. Thanks to international pressure ... we were able to survive. We are survivors.

The three men told each other's stories of imprisonment and torture; their bond and the trust among them allowed them to tell their collective story. Emelio continued:

> I was only five days under torture ... I never had the opportunity to see my experience on stage. I have been to plays and they try to communicate such pain to you, but I think that the pain was like a carousel, like you are on a horse moving, smiling, having a fun time ... but instead of the good sensations, you feel pain, and all your body feels pain.

The Chilean survivors continued to meet with the theater group to speak about their experiences during the era of Augusto Pinochet, and of their oppression, imprisonment, and torture. The actors engaged them in dialogue, but it was not the same kind of dialogue therapists or journalists might have used. The actors were interested in how they physically and emotionally embodied their stories—the sensations, gestures, images, and movements they used to convey their experiences. The actors took what they saw and heard, combined with the conversations on video, and then worked improvisationally on the material.

The artists brought a scene to the group entitled "Victor's Body" (see opening text in this chapter), which portrayed a shattered narrative of arrest, imprisonment, and torture. Five actors each portrayed a different part of Victor's "body," and they echoed phrases the three men had used in the interview to describe their experiences of torture.

As each scene was previewed, the Chileans critiqued the portrayal and made recommendations: "You portrayed the pain very effectively, but what we didn't see were the moments of humanity, warmth, and humor that were so important to us," Ernesto said. In a particularly poignant interview, Nieves Torres told the group about a humorous experience she had with her torturer, which allowed them both a momentary acknowledgment of their humanity. Overall, the theater work opened up new stories and conversational spaces among survivors, actors, and mental health professionals in ways that had not been anticipated.

The Theater Arts Against Political Violence group premiered the performance at Tibet House in New York City during an event to honor torture survivors. Prior to the theater work, the Chileans had not told their children about their time as political prisoners, to protect them from the atrocities they had lived through. By the time of the performance, four months after we began our work with them, they had opened up to their children and to other members of the Chilean and broader Latin American communities in New York City. We had not anticipated that the work would have such a ripple effect through their families and communities.

Two months later, one of the Chilean couples took the unedited video of the theater work and the performance video on their first visit to Chile in 15 years. They met with other activists and theater groups in Chile to share their work. The theater work opened up communication within families and communities, and in the larger transnational community. Theater had become a language to share their experience that could easily cross geographic and cultural boundaries. In 2009, 11 years after the theater work, we organized a reunion to speak to a class in performance studies about the work we had done and to reflect on its meaning. The survivors spoke about how the work had positive effects on their marriages and family life, and enabled them to feel less distressed about their experiences during imprisonment.

In 2000, Theater Arts Against Political Violence was invited to collaborate with the International Organization for Migration on a project that integrated theater approaches in the training of psychosocial counselors in Kosovo. The project culminated in the production of a theater piece performed at the National Theater in Pristina, Kosovo (Reisner, 2003).

Promoting Family and Community
Resilience in Post-War Kosovo

Resilience in the Kosovar Family

We took off our shoes and were led into a family's home in the small town of Slovia, 30 kilometers outside of Pristina, the capital of Kosovo. The living room floor was covered with oriental carpets. We sat on the floor as the women of the family brought out tea, poured it into small glasses, and offered us slices of cake. During the past year, our colleagues from the Department of Neurology and Psychiatry at the University of Pristina had been visiting families in this agrarian village of 2,000 people to provide mental health support. I was with a group of U.S. mental health professionals being given our first introduction to Albanian Kosovar families and how they were coping with their recent war experiences. We visited the home of an extended family: children, women, and one elderly man lived together in the six-room house. The previous year, the family had witnessed the execution of five men and teenage boys by Serbian paramilitary forces.

Albanian and Serbian Kosovars had lived together in the village of Slovia for decades. But one evening in May 1999, Serbian military forces had a group of Serbian Slovians identify the male Albanian leaders in their village. The following day, Serbian forces entered the village, took the Albanian men from their homes and shot them, often in front of their families. One group of villagers briefly managed to escape, but they were later caught and slaughtered. The violence lasted an entire day. Bodies were buried in mass graves just outside the village.

Days later, Serbian forces returned to the village and attempted to remove the evidence of their atrocities; they dug up most of the corpses and trucked them out of the area. On a hill above the village, half of the graves of the 58 massacred people were now empty and likely to remain that way. Hardly one Albanian family was spared the massacre; some families lost as many as five loved ones that day. The grief they sorely felt would soon be compounded by their inability to hold proper Muslim funerals.

We conversed with this family through English and Albanian translators. According to tradition, we spoke first with the elder man, then with his sister and sister-in-law, then with each of the young widows, then the children. We were deeply struck by their warmth and hospitality despite their profound grief. One of the elder women told me that she was unable to find the body of her son who had been killed in a massacre. Because her family could not locate the son's remains, his funeral had to be postponed. With no grave to visit and no way to care for her son's body, the woman was in a great deal of pain. She told us that she turned to prayer in order to cope. When she prayed, she said that she asked God to grow flowers around her son's grave in paradise. She imagined herself taking care of the flowers. She said that her prayers were like water that enabled the flowers to stay alive and grow. In her imagination, she had created a place where she could symbolically overcome her frustrated desire to visit and tend to her son's gravesite.

After the war Albanian Kosovar mental health professionals initiated mobile teams. These teams went to hundreds of villages to work with families who had suffered the most severe trauma and loss during the massacres. Reports estimate that more than 10,000 Albanian Kosovars had been killed. One psychologist, Shqipe Ukshine, had undertaken previous family therapy training with the Hungarian family therapist Ivan Boszormenyi-Nagy. She had organized a mobile crisis team that traveled from village to village to meet with families on a regular basis.

Ms. Ukshine described the case of one Albanian family in which the surviving patriarch was an 83-year-old man named Avni. His wife, brother, and two sons had been murdered and their bodies were burned during the war. The first time Ukshine met with him, Avni told her that he no longer felt needed in what was left of his family. Ukshine reminded him of the Albanian saying: "A house without an aging old man is like a house without a basement," that is, missing an integral piece of itself.

"I don't know," he said. "I'm not sure if there is anyone else who thinks like you." He gave her a strange look, as if he couldn't tell if she were speaking from the heart. Then, he smiled.

"My life experience is very, very long," Avni said. "I have too much experience."

"I would like to hear about your experience," Ukshine said, "but do your grandchildren know about it?"

It turned out they did not. They were young, and they had not learned about the wars in school yet. Ukshine asked him to share the story of his life experience with his grandchildren in attendance, and he accepted.

Ukshine and Avni began to visit his grandchildren's family every week for three months, and on major holidays, such as Ramazan Bayrami, the end of Ramadan. During these visits, he spoke about his family's history and realized that the children were carefully listening to what he had to say. He told them about the important people in the family and explained why the family had moved to the village. He spoke about his sons who were murdered during the war and the particular family values they embodied. He emphasized the need to cultivate these values in the new generation and encouraged the children to let God punish those who were responsible for the atrocities instead of taking revenge themselves.

Through his weekly discussions, Avni was able to help restore the relationships within his family. These family meetings also helped Avni and his sisters to temper the pain of their enormous losses. He resumed praying and other religious practices that he had ceased after the war. Whenever he took his cows to graze, a grandchild accompanied him, eagerly listening to his stories. One of his surviving sons took over as the family authority, and respectfully consulted his elder Avni before making any important decisions. Ukshine's work with the family illustrated an approach that capitalized the entire family's resilience, in a way that benefited each member. Offering services only to individuals who exhibited problems would have missed this crucial resilience that benefited everyone (Saul, Ukshini, Blyta, & Statovci, 2003).

The Kosovo Family Professional Education Collaborative

In the aftermath of the war in Kosovo in 1999, Albanian Kosovar society faced having to build a mental health system while still contending with the widespread experiences of loss, violence, and geographical displacement. The Serbian authorities had permitted very few formal services in the previous decade, therefore most mental health and social services for Albanian Kosovars were provided by a parallel system of professionals and paraprofessionals who worked underground, usually without pay. During the war, most Albanian Kosovar mental health professionals had fled the country with the rest of the population. Many had lived in refugee camps, faced serious danger, and lost family members and friends. Despite this, the few mental health practitioners had continued their education when they returned to Kosovo, and went on to provide services at the University Hospital in Pristina. This small group of psychiatrists, psychologists, and nurses took on the responsibility of building a mental health system and providing services to a large number of families in need.

Unsurprisingly, the war in Kosovo had a devastating effect on the population's mental health. According to a study in the *Journal of the American Medical Association* in 2000, 62% of the population reported near-death experiences, 49% had been tortured or abused, 42% were separated from family, 26% witnessed the death of a family member, and 4% reported sexual abuse (Agani, Cardozo, Vergara, & Gotway, 2000). According to the Center for Disease Control's Kosovo mental health survey in 2000, 25% of Kosovo's two million inhabitants had signs and symptoms of PTSD. In 1999, the World Health Organization reported: "The people are severally traumatized and a mental health system is almost non-existent. There is little hope for the future of mental health" (Agani, 2005).

According to psychiatrist Ferid Agani, many families in Kosovo were left without a common network of support, due to the large-scale physical destruction, displacement, and poverty. The existing mental health services were centralized, hospital-based, and employed a biological model of services. There were no services for the chronically mentally ill, no intensive care psychiatric services, no child and adolescent services, no forensic services, and no drug and alcohol services. For a population of two million Kosovars, there were 19 adult psychiatrists (one per 110,000 inhabitants), one child psychiatrist, two clinical psychologists, 57 nurses, and no social workers with a psychiatric background. At the time 51.6% of the population of Kosovo was under the age of 20. As had been the experience in Bosnia, in the immediate aftermath of the war, there was an influx of NGOs that imported "copy/paste" programs bypassing local professionals and systems of care. There was wide-scale corruption of public health workers and very little interest in sustainable public mental health services (Agani, 2005).

The Kosovo Ministry of Health set up a task force for mental health, supported by the WHO and the participation of local mental health-oriented NGOs. Their policy document made clear the strategic decision to develop a community-based, family-oriented mental health system rather than focus on psychiatric asylums.

Because family is the fundamental social unit in Kosovar culture, the Ministry decided that working with Kosovar families would be a more culturally appropriate solution to the country's mental health difficulties. In a low-income country such as Kosovo, it was necessary to bolster the indigenous strengths and competencies in the society and culture. They also chose to focus on developing evidence-based practice and they prioritized the needs of the large and previously neglected chronically mentally ill population (Baron, Jensen, & de Jong, 2002; Dixon, McFarlane, Lefley, Lucksted, Cohen, Falloon, et al., 2001). Changing the behaviors of health and mental health professionals in Kosovo, as well as the behaviors of policymakers and civil society, was strategically important. Raising funds to develop psychiatric capacities and to develop human capacity and expertise also became a priority (Agani, 2005).

The war in Kosovo began in early 1998 and ended in the spring of 1999. When I first visited in the spring of 2000, the country was still in shock. A few months earlier, Dr. Stevan Weine, a psychiatrist from the University of Illinois in Chicago, called me to say he was putting together a project with members of the American Family Therapy Academy to create a family-oriented mental health project in Kosovo. We had worked together on an International Trauma Training Task Force for ISTSS in 1999. More recently, Dr. Weine had been working with a committee on mental health reform in the countries of former Yugoslavia and had initiated contact with leaders in the mental health field in Kosovo.

We collaborated with a team of 19 psychiatrists and psychiatric residents at the Department of Psychiatry and Neurology at the University of Pristina Medical Hospital. The team also included one clinical psychologist, one psychiatric nurse, and one social work professor. Our team from the United States comprised at first of six psychiatrists and psychologists and a nurse who were all family therapists and members of the American Family Therapy Academy, a sponsoring partner of the project.

The leader of our collaborative team in Kosovo was Dr. Ferid Agani, who was soon to become the assistant commissioner of mental health. His uncle Femhi Agani was a well-known Kosovar philosopher and human rights activist who had established the founding faculty at University of Pristina. Dr. Agani embodied the Albanian cultural value of "Besse": he had a profound sense of hospitality that he demonstrated time and time again through his strong leadership and care for his team and our visiting group of professionals.

The project was called the Kosovar Family Professional Education Collaborative (KFPEC). The collaborative was based upon a family strength and resilience approach, which assumed that the family unit has a powerful, and often positive, role in shaping responses to adversity (Bell, 2001; Rolland & Weine, 2000; Walsh, 1998). In the first phase of the project, 36 Kosovar mental health professionals were trained in clinical approaches centered on needs of families and on building of family resilience to psychological stress and trauma. This first stage included the formation of two working teams. One team assessed training needs and planned training sessions and ongoing long-distance supervision. The other, a writing group, documented the development of the collaboration and training process (Rolland & Weine, 2000; Agani 2005). In the project's second year, focus shifted to developing family-oriented mental health services.

The professional relationships on the teams were built upon mutual respect and shared participation and expertise. The collaborative had identified the family-centered "practical knowledge" of Kosovar mental health professionals as more relevant to their work than the individually centered "scientific knowledge" of modern psychiatric practice (Scott, 1998). There were a number of initial goals of KFPEC: to supplement this local "practical knowledge" with "scientific knowledge" concerning families and interventions, to enhance the Kosovar professionals' ability to draw upon untapped strengths and resources of Kosovar families to address their mental health needs, and to teach the skills to engage the family as the basic unit for mental health services (Agani, 2005).

The focus on the dynamics and strengths of the Kosovar family provided an important foundation for the "collaboration" between the American and Kosovar team. Though Kosovar and U.S. professionals were equal partners in all phases of the project, from design to implementation to evaluation of the training activities, we found that the idea of collaboration was defined and redefined as the project developed. On a number of occasions, the team reflected on the meaning of collaboration, a concept itself shaped by cultural and situational factors. The team particularly took into consideration the position of the Kosovar mental health professionals, who were involved in multiple negotiations and partnerships with European and American professionals. At first, the idea of shared expertise may have been an alien concept for professionals educated within a Soviet system, with its emphasis on an authoritarian approach to education. But the project was able to simultaneously teach mental health approaches that enhanced capacities for resilience in Kosovar families and communities and build the collective capacities of our collaborative relationship.

We came up with a plan. Each training program had panel presentations given by a paired team of one American and one Kosovar professional.

Identifying topics most relevant to the issues faced by Kosovar mental health professionals with their patients occupied us for the coming year. Our U.S. team would visit every two months, but maintain ongoing contact through email and telephone. For the first training session, our Kosovar colleagues took us to different villages to meet and learn about Kosovar families. This was followed by conferences at the University Hospital in Pristina that were open to the public.

Hosting Solution-Focused Conversations to Foster Resilience

At the Kosovar Family Professional Education Collaborative's first training conference, my co-presenting partner Dr. Shukria Statovci—a psychiatric resident—and I spoke about a solution-focused approach to promoting resilience in individuals and families. The solution-focused approach in psychotherapy places an emphasis on the individual's or family's strengths rather than on their problems or on explanations of pathology. It is a pragmatic and common-sense approach that has been utilized as a therapeutic intervention by de Shazer (1985), Berg and Miller (1992), O'Hanlon and Bertolino (1998), Furman and Aloha (1992), and others. Traditional psychotherapy approaches aim to decrease dysfunctional patterns in order to create room for functional behavior. This approach, however, attends to the functional aspects of clients' lives in order to foster and expand helpful actions. By focusing on strengths and solutions, problems and symptoms are not denied, but are rather explored in the context of respectful conversations that enhance the person's dignity and sense of agency. These conversations reinforce people's sense of self-efficacy or competence by highlighting the good in their lives and helping them to recognize how they have contributed to those positive processes. This approach encourages taking advantage of the unique resources and opportunities in persons and families, and in their environments.

The solution-focused approach offers valuable ways to help people re-narrate or ascribe meaning to traumatic experiences. This approach assumes that there are many narrative possibilities to reconstruct the past, and that these possibilities are shaped by the types of conversations in which we participate. By framing questions in the context of a conversation about strengths that have enabled a person to survive an ordeal, he or she will more likely feel a greater sense of control and feel less victimized as he or she describes these past experiences. This conversational context can inspire greater optimism and confidence while exploring solutions.

The way one relates to memories of past events is crucial to the process of healing from trauma. Conversations that situate painful experiences within a vision of the future that includes solutions add an important dimension to processing or narrating traumatic experiences. Strengthening the resilience of people and their families, this approach helps build a foundation for a new life, establish connections with new sources of social support, reconnect with important people in life, and helps people regain a sense of agency in relation to past injury. When people can weave new sources of continuity and connectedness into their life stories, they are better able to overcome the disturbing discontinuities they endured as a result of violence, tragic loss, or displacement from home, country, or culture.

Dr. Ben Furman, a Finnish psychiatrist and self-proclaimed "incurable optimist," proposed that collaboration, creativity, and hope are the most important ingredients in a solution-focused approach. To explore solutions most successfully, people need to work together in an open, non-secretive exchange which respects the resources and areas of expertise of all those involved. Rather than take on the role of an expert, the therapist must instead act as the moderator and/or facilitator; the therapist can then make sure that everyone in the solution-seeking conversation has a voice and shares responsibility to construct and carry out the steps toward the solution. It is very important in this collaboration that the therapist creates an empowering context for change.

The creative use of imagination is an important resource to deal with traumatic events, though it is often initially constrained by trauma. In his book, *Playing and Reality*, Donald Winnicott (1971) proposed that people give meaning to their lives through imaginative acts. We know that playful creativity in children is often a powerful tool to help them regain mastery over difficult experiences. Representing stories either literally or symbolically reduces the destructive power of negative experiences. In the process of externalizing painful memories, children may change their relationship to the experiences from passive to active, and at the same time make it easier to speak about these experiences with others.

Restoring hope is also key to helping people who have recently experienced traumatic events. For people who have endured tragic loss or dehumanizing ordeals, their previous notions of the future may have been annulled by events of the past. Trauma survivors who carry a sense of shame or guilt often feel undeserving of a promising future. Exploring sources of hope was very important in working with survivors of the recent massacres and displacement in Kosovo, and, as described by our Kosovar colleagues, often a crucial step in promoting the process of healing from trauma and massive loss.

Dr. Statovci had engaged her clients in solution-focused conversations after the war, at a time when it was most important to reawaken their sense of hope. In her presentation she spoke about conversations she had with clients. In her experience, she said families usually intuitively know how to cope with adversity. When she was unsure how she could help most, she often realized that she could seek the answers from the families themselves. The first step in conducting solution-focused conversations with families is finding their sources of strength to help them reconnect. She found that one of the most important sources of strength for Kosovar families is caring for children. Children were always at the forefront when families envisioned the future.

Dr. Statovci spoke first about her own experience during the war. During the NATO bombing, she had the misfortune to be in Blasé—a "no man's land" between Macedonia and Kosovo. Together with her family, she experienced some of the most severe conditions of the war. About 50,000 people in Blasé were gathered in very inhuman conditions and not permitted to leave for more than a week. Many women and children endured extreme shortages of food and water and often did not know the whereabouts of their relatives.

After three days, Dr. Statovci, her mother, and two brothers found a bus to take them away, but they did not know where it would go. They waited for the bus in a very dangerous location with Macedonian police raining down violence upon them. Suddenly, Dr. Statovci's mother said, "I would like to go back to the place where we were before." Dr. Statovci was surprised by her wish to return to the nightmare of the camps.

She asked her mother, "Why do you want to go back to those conditions where you could easily die from disease?"

"Over here, if the police start to beat you then I don't need my life anymore. Because of you, I am here. In the other situation, I would be in my home and killed by the Serbs. I prefer to go back together to these nylon tent camps and die all together by diseases than to stay here and see you killed by the Macedonian police," her mother answered.

At the time, she did not have a chance to fully consider what her mother had said. Later, when they did return to Kosovo and she was working with families, she continually saw that children were parents' source of strength, and then she understood her mother's response.

She finally realized why a single mother of one remaining child could choose to live and cope with all the problems she faced. Even though God had taken her husband, she believed that God had given her a gift by sparing her child. Through the child, an image of the future could be forged and linked to the past.

In one example, a child witnessed his uncle's murder in a massacre. The child had been very close to his uncle and had severe PTSD symptoms after his loss. He was admitted to the hospital. Gradually his condition improved, and one day he came to Dr. Statovci and said, "My memories start to pale, but what I cannot cope with is that I was in a very close relationship with my uncle, and I don't know how to go forward without him."

"When you and your uncle were together, did you have any sort of conversation about the future?" she asked him.

"My uncle's wish was that I would be educated. He very much wished that I would become someone whom he would be proud of," the boy said.

"Would you like to accomplish his wish to continue with your education or what do you want to do?" asked Dr. Statovci.

"I never thought about it before, but I think that this is a good idea," he answered. In this way, he was able to make a connection between the future and the past.

Dr. Statovci concluded: "Everyone makes plans for the future and life can bring obstacles in realizing these plans. But we may use these plans or visions of the future to cope with the crisis situations in our current lives" (Saul, Ukshini, Blyta, & Statovci, 2003).

As part of the training program, Dr. Statovci and I conducted a session with a family that was being seen at the hospital. A group of psychiatric residents joined us in the room with the family. The older daughter in the family had been hospitalized for suicidal behavior. But there was more to this story than the daughter's pathology. The family had been under tremendous stress, and this stress had led to intense conflict with their older daughter. The goal of our family session was to explore the meaning of the daughter's behavior in the context of her family relationships. It became quickly apparent that the parents had found it challenging to establish clear and consistent limits with the young woman and that communication between them had broken down, leading to conflict and exacerbating their daughter's behavior. The parents' authority was further undermined by a foreign NGO, which was making arrangements to fly the daughter to another country in Europe for treatment.

The psychiatrists on the team each had a chance to ask the family members questions about their relationships, which stemmed from their own understanding of the dynamics in Kosovar families. As a result, the psychiatrists were better able to understand the young woman's problems and were better positioned to help the young woman and her family as a whole.

After the family meeting, the team's excitement was palpable as they discussed what they had observed in the session. Using the language of family relationships liberated them from a psychiatric discourse that focused exclusively on individual psychopathology. It was apparent that our colleagues in Kosovo could comfortably navigate between the different mental health discourses that circulated at the hospital.

A Mental Health System Based On Family and Community Resilience

In the fall of 2000, I invited Dr. Agani to present at the International Trauma Studies Program (ITSP) at New York University to give an overview of the state of mental health services in Kosovo and discuss the strategic plan that had been developed. The presentation was also an opportunity to meet potential funders for the project's next phase. Afterwards, Dr. Agani was approached by Marcia Presky, a representative of the Joint Distribution Committee in New York, which already had a presence in Kosovo after the war. Ms. Presky requested that we submit a proposal, so, later that fall, I returned with members of the American team to continue our work with the KFPEC training program and to plan the project's next phase.

We returned to Kosovo during Bayram, a Muslim holiday observed by fasting from sunrise to sunset. Once again we conducted joint training sessions, public presentations, and site visits, but we also met to develop a proposal for a family and community-based resilience project with the chronically mentally ill. An image that remains with me from this second training visit was that of the group of male and female psychiatric nurses standing in black leather jackets against the hotel cafeteria wall, fasting and waiting patiently as the American team sat down for lunch.

On this trip I met Dr. Judith Landau, a psychiatrist on our team. Dr. Landau, a leader in the field of family therapy, had done groundbreaking work in the family treatment of substance abuse and had developed the model of "transitional family therapy." This was the first team visit for Dr. Landau, a professor at the University of Rochester in New York. Born and raised in South Africa, she had experienced some of the tragic events of apartheid, as the daughter of a doctor who was deeply committed to social justice and worked as a community-oriented psychiatrist with disadvantaged populations. Her early experiences nourished what would later become her LINC

Community Resilience Model. The model was based on identifying effective change agents in a community, i.e. leaders or "links" who could mobilize a broad range of constituencies to address what the community members themselves perceived as their most pressing problems.

Dr. Landau masterfully demonstrated this approach one afternoon during our joint training workshops. A Kosovar clinician had invited a middle-aged man, who was feeling quite depressed, to join us. He had lost many relatives during the recent war. The man sat across from Dr. Landau, and, with the help of an interpreter, he recalled his history, which included tragedies experienced before the recent war. During the interview, Dr. Landau asked him to give a detailed family history and his family genogram was drawn on the large pad of paper. During their conversation, the man was able to describe the resources that had enabled him to survive and become a leader in his extended family and take initiative to promote the family's well-being. Dr. Landau demonstrated how to encourage the man to take on the role of a community "link" with his extended family, giving him a renewed sense of purpose. At the end of the session, the man rose to give a hug to all of the team members who had witnessed his struggle from hopeless to hopeful.

During another workshop, Dr. Landau and I and our Kosovar colleagues explored how to work with families facing a difficult cultural dilemma. In the Kosovar patrilineal family, women widowed during the war were often asked by their husbands' families to leave their children and return to their family of origin. This cultural practice compounded the traumatic loss with the additional trauma of separation between a mother and her children. Should families adhere to this tradition or seek a new solution to preserve the integrity of the entire family? This situation was highly stressful and had the potential to evoke intense conflict and fragmentation. One approach was to work with family members who were ambivalent about this cultural norm of expulsion. These members might be able to engage the rest of the family in a conversation about whether this practice was in the best interest of the children, the mother, and the family as a whole. We created a role-play in which about 15 Kosovar mental health professionals acted out the roles of family members facing this dilemma.

As the role-play began, we heard gunshots from just below the windows of the Grand Hotel where our workshop was taking place. Dr. Landau, who had trained in civil defense, rounded up the entire group and sat us behind chairs piled up for our protection. It was unclear at that point whether a terrorist incident had taken place, and if they might be in the hotel looking for hostages. For an hour, we waited to hear what had transpired. Finally Dr. Agani arrived, deeply relieved to find that no one on our team had been hurt. A vendetta shooting had taken place at the front entrance of the hotel. We later found out that men from one family had taken revenge on a member of another family because of an insult at the public market the previous day. At that time, Kosovo had only a marginal police presence, and some families were taking the law into their own hands.

The shooting evoked a range of responses among the U.S. and Kosovar mental health staff. For some, it triggered frightening memories of the war. For the U.S. staff, it brought home the dangers still present in the country. The event provided an opportunity for the group to discuss important role group support as a protective factor against stress.

During the KFPEC's second meeting, team members worked on a proposal to develop a family-based community mental health program to help chronically mentally ill patients live successfully with their families.

"We all mutually agreed that one priority problem was how the severely mentally ill were being treated and how families didn't have adequate support to help their own," said Dr. Weine (personal communication, January 12, 2012). Our Kosovar colleagues felt that this vulnerable population could benefit greatly from multi-family psychoeducational groups. These groups focused on keeping the severely mentally ill person in the community under family care and supervision. Using this methodology, the project was called Services Based Training (SBT). Two teams of psychiatric nurses were trained to run multiple family groups at two newly formed community mental health clinics in Gjakova and Ferizaj. The teams made home visits to families, ran multiple family psychoeducational groups, and had ongoing supervision and monthly training sessions. The groups strengthened the capacities of families to care for members with severe mental disorders by helping them to understand the nature of these disorders and to develop skills to provide home care. They also helped the families develop a support system by meeting with other families facing similar challenges. The multiple-family groups learned about psychiatric symptoms and the clinical course of chronic mental disorders, medication use and side-effects, the role of psychosocial factors in precipitating or preventing relapse, responses to common problems, and resilience building approaches to severe mental illness (Weine et al., 2005).

In its first year, the SBT program helped many families overcome isolation and shame and despair, and also successfully increased medication compliance and decreased hospitalizations. Families reported that the program positively affected their family life, including a decrease in blaming family members, improved coping strategies, decreased fear in family members, increased socialization and quality of life, and enhanced hope (Weine et al., 2005). The program also had a positive impact on mental health professionals in Kosovo. They became better observers of family life and saw effective ways to help families develop successful strategies to cope with severe mental illness (Pulleyblank-Coffey, Griffith, & Ulaj, 2006).

After the initial success of the SBT teams in Gjakova and Ferizaj, the project was scaled up. By 2004, SBT teams were running groups for approximately 250 families and patients at each of seven community mental health centers. According to Dr. Agani, (2005) KPFEC's work had a profound impact on the development of Kosovo's mental health system, providing what he referred to as the "software" for the nation's mental health services. The project not only created awareness for collaborative work between professionals and with families, it also enhanced professional morale and grounded the newly developed mental health approach in its cultural milieu. Such community-based clinical work with families, Agani stated, stood in sharp contrast with the treatment approaches in which Yugoslavian and Kosovar psychiatrists had been trained. The family-based work also had a positive impact on the relationship between mental health professionals and families, enhancing their mutual respect, confidence, and self-esteem.

The four-year program was modestly funded by a $150,000 grant from the Joint Distribution Committee (JDC), plus in-kind contributions of professional time from its faculty of volunteer clinicians and educators. In 2005, I returned with fellow KFPEC colleagues from the United States to Kosovo for the completion of the SBT program. At a conference to mark the occasion, each community mental health center around the country presented on different components of the program. Multidisciplinary mobile teams composed of nurses, social workers, and psychosocial counselors were visiting clients at their homes. Nurses, trained and supervised by Kosovar KFPEC clinicians, were implementing multiple family psychoeducational groups and doing more than 70% of the work in the community mental health clinics. In a ceremony at the conference, Kosovo's Health Ministry formally recognized the work of the KFPEC team and then took responsibility for the continuation of the program.

PART

FROM GLOBAL TO LOCAL

URBAN TERRORISM IN LOWER MANHATTAN

4

9/11

The First Three Weeks

September 11, 2001: The First Day

On the morning of September 11, 2001, I dropped off my sons, eight-year-old Adam and five-year-old Noam, at the New York Public School 234 schoolyard at 8:30 a.m. As I headed home, I heard the first explosion. When I looked up, all I could see was sparkling silver confetti drifting down from the blue sky. When I finally glimpsed the building, I fixated on the gaping hole in its side. My mind flashed back to the memory of the post office tower in the center of Pristina, pierced by a misguided NATO cruise missile. I immediately called my wife Esther, who was getting into a taxi to go to her office in Midtown, where she works as a marital and family therapist. I told her to look up at the World Trade Center. "Oh my God," she said. Having lived in Jerusalem, she learned long ago that when there is a bombing on the left, you go to the right. She got into the cab and went to work.

I went home and turned on the television, trying to understand what was happening. I watched the events unfold with my houseguest, Alberto Spectorovsky, a Uruguayan political science professor. Because we were both familiar with political violence, we immediately suspected that the crash was a terrorist act. As we watched the second plane crash into the South Tower, our suspicions seemed confirmed, although the television announcer was still struggling with his theory that air traffic controllers had made grievous errors. I initially thought my kids were safer in school than on the streets, but when the South Tower collapsed into itself, I bolted toward PS 234. Alberto and I ran against the current of dazed, grey-dusted crowds of people rushing north, away from the World Trade Center.

As I ran, I tried to comprehend the scale of the destruction. Early news reports estimated that tens of thousands of people might have lost their lives. Even as I struggled to understand what had happened, the events took on a surreal quality. Like many New Yorkers, I was used to seeing action films shot

57

in the city streets where the police cars were fake, the disaster mocked-up, with large audiences stopped to watch the drama unfold. In a strange twist, this massive destruction sometimes felt like a real event based on fictional accounts.

The reality was overwhelming. By the time we arrived at PS 234, the North Tower was on fire and people were falling or jumping from the top floors. Fire trucks and sirens blasted at street level. People stared up at the tower in shock and in tears. It's a cliché, but the scene before me seemed to take place in slow motion. I was having a dissociative response, it occurred to me, and this sliver of clarity and comprehension allowed me to remain calm, think quickly, and act decisively.

Alberto waited outside the school as I went in to get the kids. I passed the Parent Association chairman, George Olsen, and his son, who were monitoring the entrance. When I got to the gym, Adam and Noam ran up to hug me. They asked me to explain what was happening outside. I said that I would tell them on the way home, but that we had to leave immediately. As we left, I told them not to look back at the tower, hoping to shield them from the sight of people jumping. Alberto was nowhere to be found. Hoping he had gone back to the apartment, my sons and I ran toward home, trying to take west-to-east streets to avoid a storm of debris from another collapsing building. We went to the roof of our apartment building and saw smoke rising from the site where the World Trade Center had been. The towers had been such an important part of our landscape, like a mountain range that could never disappear, and, inexplicably, they were gone. When we got back home and were seemingly safe, I took video of Adam and his friend dancing on the roof of our building—for now, at least, we were physically safe from harm—the image of their nervous excitement was a kind of natural response to the situation. We later learned that Alberto had gotten lost in the crowd outside of my children's school, and that when he tried to return to my apartment from uptown, he was denied entry at the checkpoint that had been set up around my neighborhood.

I checked my email in the afternoon, as I always do. My inbox was filled with messages from friends and colleagues from around the world offering their concern and assistance. That was when I realized I had just survived a disaster. Almost simultaneously, I thought: What should we do next? I was both a recipient of this trauma and an experienced helper in traumatic situations. And I was also a husband and father who wanted to get out of downtown.

At her office, Esther soon realized that this attack on the WTC was different from the one eight years earlier. On that day, her patients had been delayed on the subway; this time, they didn't show up. She went back to our house and our Muslim Senegalese babysitter, Fatou, arrived, quite shaken. Fatou had taken the PATH train into the city from New Jersey and her train had stopped underneath the World Trade Center as the planes crashed into the towers. The passengers waited for more than half an hour until they were led upstairs. When she emerged from the subway station, Fatou found herself in the midst of destruction and was led to shelter in the basement of a nearby restaurant. She was anxious to get home to her family, but the trains to New Jersey were no longer running. Esther spent the afternoon searching for a way to get Fatou home and eventually convinced someone with a boat to take Fatou across the Hudson River.

Like others in our neighborhood, our family packed up and stayed with friends that evening. We went to the Upper West Side of Manhattan, and found relief from the stench of burning that would remain in the air for months to come. With our friends, we recounted and grappled with the events of that day. Noam spoke about his second day of kindergarten. That morning he went into his classroom and within minutes he heard what he described as a "big bang." He thought he heard furniture dropping onto the floor. When he looked through his classroom window, he saw a huge fireball in the North Tower, which was three blocks south of his school. He and the other children were sent to the basement gymnasium where they waited for their parents.

The First Week: Starting to Mobilize

I began to experience firsthand what international colleagues had told me about post-disaster situations elsewhere. Ubiquitous journalists chased after the story. International relief organizations arrived on the scene and began to interview local professionals to inform their own funding applications. Missionaries and outreach workers flooded in, as did trauma and grief counselors and therapists of all kinds. Downtown Manhattan had become a spiritual and therapeutic supermarket.

It didn't take long for us at the International Trauma Studies Program to wonder what competition we would face as local mental health providers. My international colleagues and I surmised that hundreds of organizations would seek funding, as they had in Bosnia and most recently in Kosovo.

Unfortunately, the vast majority of these funds went to external agencies that lacked a toehold in the communities and to mental health practitioners who favored individual treatment over preventive social support. When working with mental health professionals in Kosovo to develop a successful response to the war, I learned that it's crucial to have a first line of mental health care that focuses on strengthening social networks and family support systems disrupted by trauma. While single-patient therapy is important for some, I found that a social approach is essential for the wider community.

From the start, ITSP was committed to applying our experience in the international humanitarian field to our local context of New York City. We would attempt to develop a community-oriented program that would also support the local providers. Our preventive approach would make us far more effective with whatever funding we could muster.

Meanwhile, broader healing was already taking root throughout New York City. Most theorists, according to anthropologist Helen Fisher, would probably agree that humans are biologically programmed to lower boundaries in crisis situations to more effectively bond and work together (H. Fisher, personal communication, October 2012). This theory was borne out in New York City for anyone to see. There were spontaneous candlelight vigils in Washington Square Park and Union Square, ad hoc memorials on many streets around the city, and fences covered with pictures of missing people. The outpouring of support in the week after September 11 was unmistakably people "practicing interdependence."

These organic efforts to promote recovery, much as in international contexts, were undervalued by response organizations and received very little direct financial support. As we anticipated, a great deal of funding was directed toward treating individuals suffering from post-traumatic stress disorder. The grassroots efforts of local professionals, community organizations, and residents rarely gained the attention of private funders, relief organizations, or government agencies.

It is all too easy to assume that an initial outpouring of altruism signals a healthy recovery from a catastrophe. In reality, healing is more complex and is not achieved so quickly. People tend to work hard and selflessly and then burn out after a disaster. But is that exhaustion inevitable? Can sensitive programming and relevant support mitigate it? It seems possible that the conditions most responsible for burnout are the lack of support—or even obstruction—of local recovery efforts. The ITSP, however, wanted to strengthen the altruistic spirit of volunteerism that people *already* possessed.

Within two weeks, Jack Rosenthal of the New York Times Company Foundation contacted me to discuss the mental health implications of the terrorist attacks. The *New York Times* had been receiving donations that would eventually total more than $50 million for New York's Neediest Fund. In my first meeting with Mr. Rosenthal, I spoke about the work I had done in Kosovo and in New York's refugee communities, and what we had learned about trauma responses to war in Yugoslavia. I emphasized the emerging trauma model as I had come to understand it, that efforts would be better spent building resilience rather than focusing primarily on pathology.

Rosenthal was convinced that we could do good work. My colleagues and I at ITSP developed an initial proposal to fund work to identify needs and develop approaches to engage the Lower Manhattan school community parents, school staff, and teachers. With the help of Dr. Judith Landau, my colleague from the American Family Therapy Academy and from Kosovo, the proposal also specified services for immigrant and refugee populations affected by 9/11. We initially received a small grant from the foundation to support the "Ground Zero Community Initiative," a school community-based project that convened forums to address the current needs of the community members and which is discussed at length in Chapter 5.

A Toxic Environment and a New Reality

At one of the first Parent Association meetings of PS 234 (which was temporarily based out of PS 42 in Greenwich Village), hundreds of parents gathered to voice their concerns. One major issue was the toxicity of the environment. Pressed in by a haze of smoke and an ever-present putrid stench, we wanted to know what particles and pollutants were in the air we breathed. What was the source of the smells and the smoke? And who was qualified to say whether it was safe to breathe? Parents wanted to know what was being done to clean the pervasive dust from schools, apartments, and neighborhoods and, ultimately, if we could move back to our homes, businesses, and schools and stay out of harm's way.

A number of parents from PS 234 took the initiative to form an environmental group for the community to address these concerns head-on. At weekly parent–teacher meetings, they presented reports about the environmental contamination. The parents on this committee did not have faith in the government's response to the environmental issues, and eventually they raised enough money to hire their own environmental firm to assess air quality.

Even with experts hired to test the air quality, there were still endless debates about various atmospheric measurements—so much so that our community probably became one of the world's most knowledgeable groups on environmental pollutants.

In many ways, this very tangible concern was a metaphor for the toxicity of the 9/11 experience. Were we and our children being damaged by what we were enduring? Was this going to make us sick, physically or mentally, in the future? Technical discussions about toxicity soon became emotionally charged, with feelings channeled into an unspoken question: "Were we breathing air tainted by burning corpses?" Many people living in downtown Manhattan came from a social class in which the locus of control resides in the self. For these people, the unknown future consequences of the air quality indicated a loss of control that was deeply frightening to community members.

The events of September 11 led many New Yorkers—and Americans—to feel simultaneously more connected to and more isolated from the rest of the world. On the one hand, they suddenly had a sense of what it must be like to live in war-torn parts of the world; on the other hand, they were bewildered by the cause of these events and they were forced to re-evaluate America's standing on the world stage. Seeing themselves as "good people," as "free and democratic," they wondered, "How could this happen to us? How is it that *we* are now living under threat?" As our country became embroiled in the Afghan war, many in the politically liberal community of downtown Manhattan felt that innocent Afghani civilians should not be killed in response.

In private therapy sessions and in the community, I was struck by the fact that many people who came to speak with me in the first few weeks were people who had previously experienced terrorism in another country. Downtown Manhattan comprises many ethnically and racially diverse communities, many of whose lives had been touched by trauma, displacement, political upheaval, and even terrorism. There was the Haitian parent who remembered running from Papa Doc Duvalier when she was the same age as her children, who now had fled from collapsing buildings in New York; there were the Argentineans who had escaped from the junta and remembered their own "disappeared" family members who had been less fortunate; the Israelis, some of them recent arrivals, trying to break free from Middle Eastern violence; and the Pakistanis, who remembered the days of the Partition and ensuing conflict. It seemed to me that these people who had experienced large-scale violence in their lives had a different motivation to reach out than those who had not. Members of these communities and many others would observe the effects of 9/11 on non-immigrant families and say, "They don't know what's happening to them yet." For those who had previously experienced trauma, there was a sense of continuity in the midst of disruption—this was the world as they had come to know it. Their innocence had been lost a long time ago.

For many foreigners, as well as African-Americans, the political dimension was often palpable in their discussions. In one disaster-response workshop, it was the foreigners and African-Americans who found perfect sense in the idea that problematic political alliances, like support for Duvalier, Pinochet, and bin Laden, might one day return to haunt Americans. These parents were not as reluctant to expose their children to the hard facts of 9/11. For them, this was already reality.

A Meeting of Professionals

While working with the downtown schools, I also wanted to support the myriad local mental health professionals who were devoting themselves to the recovery. The International Trauma Studies Program was connected to a network of faculty, alumni, and others who had attended programs over the past three years. Soeren Buus Jensen, the Program's co-founder, arrived in New York the week following 9/11 to teach the first workshop in the ITSP trauma-training program, as he had always done. Rather than wait for funding to materialize, we began our work.

Dr. Jensen and I, because of our experience in the trauma field, were asked by a number of organizations to speak about how clinicians should work with individuals reacting to the terrorist attacks. Many practitioners felt insecure about the tremendous amount of focus on "evidence-based" trauma treatment. Dr. Jensen stressed that they should remain confident; as therapists, they already possessed much of the clinical knowledge needed to support people experiencing trauma. He told them about his experience in former Yugoslavia, when groups of American mental health professionals presenting about PTSD urged the Yugoslavian professionals to learn what were supposedly the only effective techniques. The Yugoslavian professionals courteously attended their fourteenth presentation about PTSD and listened to incorporate new ideas into what they had already been practicing effectively with their clients, and what made sense within their particular situation and cultural context. Just as we were committed to supporting the pre-existing resilience in the local communities, we also wanted to reinforce the pre-existing competence of mental health practitioners.

In the first week after the attacks, we organized an all-day forum for a group of 80 to 100 mental health professionals to support one another and brainstorm how to best approach the challenges posed by 9/11. The professionals discussed the types of populations they were working with, how organizations were beginning to respond and the new training needs they faced. We wanted to provide a space for professionals to share what they had seen in their own contexts of providing care.

Dr. Jensen's trauma experience abroad was crucial in helping local therapists to validate their own skills and feel adequate under the circumstances. He presented the WHO regional model, and explained how we could learn from the framework and apply it to our local context. As seen in Table 4.1, Dr. Jensen's framework is broken down into seven conceptual headings for structural analysis and a present plan of action for mental health interventions in developing countries and emergency assessments/interventions in conflict/post-conflict situations. Dr. Jensen referred to these as the Seven C's: cultural sensitivity, coordination of services, community orientation, capacity building, clinical services, care for caretakers, and collection of data (Jensen, 2001).

Dr. Jensen then presented an inverted pyramid schema that delineated levels of humanitarian response in emergencies. In it societal interventions designed for an entire population are at the top of the pyramid. Descending the pyramid, interventions target progressively smaller groups of people. At the top level, the efforts comprise survival and the provision of basic needs such as food, shelter, security, and medical supplies, including a psychosocial sensitivity to such provision. Political/policy interventions at this level promote human rights, peace, democratization, and conflict management. The next layer includes community-level interventions that promote empowerment. The third layer comprises training and building capacity of local psychosocial and mental health providers. The fourth layer focuses on family interventions, with individual family members and strategies to promote well-being of the family as a whole. The fifth layer denotes the building of self-help groups around shared problems and challenges. The bottom layers of the pyramid concern interventions designed for individuals, families, or groups with psychological symptoms or psychiatric disorders. These include psychiatric, medical, and psychological treatments that can be the most expensive and labor-intensive, requiring highly trained professional staff (Baron, Jensen, & de Jong, 2002).

We've already mentioned how many mental health resources focus on therapeutic rather than preventive services. The ineffectiveness of this type of resource allocation is often compounded because many who do need specialized therapeutic support will need it later on, not in the early phase of response. The World Health Organization recommends that, in the early phases of a crisis, mental health workers offer psychological first aid, covering both social and psychological support. This involves the provision of humane, supportive, and practical help to people suffering from serious crisis events (WHO, 2011). The problem lies in the fact that funding for therapeutic support is often diminished by the time people exhibiting serious symptoms of distress find their way to treatment.

Participants in the seminar broke into small discussion groups to share what types of reactions they had seen during the past week in New York. Many shared the view that New Yorkers had different cultural styles for responding to crisis and seeking help. In a society like New York's, where many people live alone, how could we create alternative communities for healing? How could we reach out and engage families when they were so used to therapy as a means to address problems rather than prevent them in the first place? How could we help reach the immigrant population, some of whom had difficulty seeking services, and might be retraumatized due to their past experiences?

Some professionals at the forum reported that people at their workplace felt at a loss about how to respond. Others spoke of over-volunteering and how unrealistic limits had led to exhaustion even at such an early stage. A senior psychiatrist spoke about how more experienced staff offered support for those less experienced in a trauma context. Others were looking for practical frameworks to work with corporations that had lost staff members.

Yoel Elizur, an Israeli psychologist who had arrived in New York on vacation on September 10 and stayed to help, offered another important perspective. One of the major principles of response to mass trauma and disaster is known as the "continuity principle" (Omer & Alon, 1994). Omer and Alon theorize that because trauma results from a disruption in how we conceive of and live our lives, social support efforts should impose the least amount of external processes and frameworks as possible. Instead, these efforts should focus on restoring and maintaining continuities of personal function (health, professional, parental, etc.), interpersonal relationships, and historical narrative (understanding of self, family, and community over time). Based on these principles, effective social support should draw on and bolster pre-existing networks at every level of the community and these efforts should remain local across all stages of disaster recovery (Omer & Alon, 1994).

TABLE 4.1 THE SEVEN C's FOR MENTAL HEALTH RESPONSE IN COMPLEX EMERGENCIES (JENSEN, 2001)

1. **Culturally sensitive and contextually appropriate interventions**
   - What are the culturally specific elements of NYC relevant to planning a sensitive emergency response?
   - What resources are available within existing health and social welfare structures and families and communities?

2. **Coordination of all services**
   - Is there a coordination body with a clear, authoritative leadership for the psychosocial/mental health response that involves all major players?
   - Are there clear maps of needs, resources and gaps?
   - Are the planned interventions cost-effective?
   - Will the emergency interventions lead to effective mid and long-term plans?

3. **Community-oriented public mental health approach**
   - Do interventions mobilize family and community resiliency and self-help?
   - Are existing community support structures (i.e. community or religious leaders, local institutions, etc.) optimally utilized in the emergency and ongoing self-help? Are grassroots organizations for family and network support (i.e. Rotary Clubs and church groups) mobilized?
   - Is the media systematically involved in providing community education and appropriate information more than sensationalism?
   - Do clinical interventions promote a comprehensive public mental health and human rights perspective?

4. **Capacity building; training support and supervision**
   - Is training available in advance about the mental health issues of emergency response to health professionals, support helpers like school teachers, religious and other community leaders and firefighters, policemen and other emergency service workers?

- Is systematic training available in universities and professional schools so that all mental health professionals are prepared to provide effective crisis interventions in an emergency?
- Is specialization training available to interested mental health professionals for the treatment of trauma?

5. **Clinical services**

- Are mental health professionals encouraging public understanding about normal responses to trauma, natural resilience and the necessity of using family and community systems for self-help?
- Are they avoiding pathologizing what are normal responses to trauma?
- Is mental health crisis intervention available to the severely affected survivors?
- Are existing mental health clinics and private practitioners trained to provide the needed service in this context rather than just do what they always do?

6. **Care for the caretakers**

- Is there a mentality that recognizes the personal vulnerability of helpers and encourages them to seek support when needed?
- Are mental health crisis and ongoing services accessible to relief workers?
- Is there sufficient support, supervision and training for mental health professionals?

7. **Comprehensive data collection, analysis and evaluation**

- Is there an ongoing system for collecting information?
- Is there ongoing systematic monitoring of needs, resources and gaps?
- Are quality assurance systems integrated into interventions to assess effectiveness from the beginning?
- Are mechanisms established to ensure that future research honestly portrays the problems and the interventions?

Like Dr. Jensen, Elizur cautioned that the most intense therapeutic services would be needed later in the recovery process. Research has shown that certain factors increase the likelihood of later difficulties—such as the magnitude of the reaction and degree of dissociation. Bereaved families, for instance, will need a great deal of support, including long-term care and economic assistance. In these cases, it is not enough to be empathic and provide grief counseling; a parent leader (the mother, in many cases) will need to organize the family—this will be the main predictor of how well the family will deal with the situation.

Dr. Stevan Weine, with whom I had worked in Kosovo, emphasized the importance for leaders in the professional community to articulate unspoken needs of the population in general, not just at-risk populations. He emphasized that we must discern those more widespread needs—something mental health professionals have not done well in the past. He said:

> Most of the people who survive this will not come for therapy. They'll be in their families. There may still be a lot of suffering; you won't get to them from a therapeutic point of view. It is necessary for us to make a turn to family support and education. Think family.

In this first gathering of mental health professionals after 9/11, Dr. Jensen shared an important perspective for our work. "When you are working in large-scale disasters, it is important to think about topics such as truth, reconciliation and justice, but we rarely get to these," he said.

He noticed that Americans were starting to engage in a meaning-making process about the terrorist attacks, but based on his previous experience he recognized that this process often turns into a call for revenge; the political response might result in even greater disasters elsewhere. He asked:

> How do we balance forgiveness with vengeance? How do we promote a process of understanding why the perpetrators did what they did rather than turning them into the 'evil other' and de-humanizing them?
>
> If there is no revenge, then there's something about justice that doesn't quite work. But, on the other hand, if the response has too much power and it becomes an even greater violation, then we will be farther away from any reconciliation.

He cautioned us to keep the perspective of human rights at the forefront of our work, and to be cognizant of the mental health consequences of discrimination against Arabs, Muslims, and other immigrant and refugee populations in New York and the United States.

Close to the end of the meeting, Dr. Charles Figley, a prominent figure in the trauma and disaster field, arrived at the meeting dressed in Florida pastels—a startling contrast to the usual dark attire of New Yorkers. He told us that his heart went out to us, and his genuine sympathy triggered an emotional response in the room. He told us that as locals we were the real experts and that the outside responders were here to support us as mental health professionals, not undermine our expertise or competence. His affirmations as an outsider were very moving and his words served as a striking example of the power of external support used in a helpful way.

By listening to my colleagues, I was able to regain perspective. I gradually began to reconnect to lessons I had learned in Kosovo, and to the principles we'd been teaching over the last three years of the trauma-training program. Chiefly, I recognized that the communities in which we live are in themselves important resources to their members, especially to children. We would need to meet with families in the community when distressed, find ways to speak with the children, and support teachers in their work. Many of the children had had very disturbing experiences on 9/11. We realized that we needed to come together to support families so that parents could process what was going on and better help the children. We decided that the International Trauma Studies Program would have a dual mission—to support the community downtown and also to support a community of mental health professionals by offering an ongoing disaster-response workshop series built upon speakers that were already scheduled to come train students at ITSP during the year.

The New York Experience

For many of us living in New York, particularly those of us living in Lower Manhattan, the terrorist attacks raised tremendous concerns about whether life would ever be the same in our city. Had our sense of safety been destroyed forever? Would we have to live with constant threats and brace ourselves against ongoing attacks? People who I knew, as well as people who came to see me in my clinical practice, often expressed this sense of dread—a sense that very competent people in the world were determined to destroy our way of life, and perhaps eventually destroy our species.

At the time, these thoughts reminded me of the work of Robert Jay Lifton based on interviews with Hiroshima survivors. In the aftermath of the nuclear attack, they not only reacted to the devastation in front of them, but also wondered if this kind of destructiveness could lead to the end of humankind (Lifton, 1968, 1979).

I realized that I was in fact living amidst this kind of apocalyptic dread when I left New York for the first time after 9/11. At the beginning of October, I attended a conference in Minneapolis for organizations working with survivors of torture, attended by people from all over the country. It was then that I experienced the sensation of emerging from a war zone—I felt distinctly separate from the people who had not been in New York City, who only witnessed 9/11 from afar through the media. Many people who live through a disaster or traumatic event tend to feel this way early on, that they are markedly different from others due to their personal experience. Having been in such close proximity to the destruction of the WTC, I had felt firsthand the fragility of life and of national security in the face of terrorism. Outside of New York, I was more aware of this vulnerability and that others were less sensitive to the dangers we faced. At the same time, I was reminded that the United States was more than just New York City, which gave perspective to our vulnerability.

During the first few weeks after 9/11, before the war in Afghanistan, people were concerned about how things had changed for us and what those changes would mean. When the U.S. government decided to go to war with Afghanistan on October 7, 2001, it felt as if there was no longer anything to speak about. Discourse on processing 9/11 was abruptly displaced by the new national narrative of the War on Terror.

A colleague of mine, Peter Fraenkel, coined the term the "new normal" (Fraenkel, 2001). We know from other major traumatic events that meaning-making out of destruction and disruption is experienced on both a personal and a collective level. This can be a long-term process, and may never truly end.

During the first weeks after 9/11 my children began their adjustment to the new reality, though both were plagued by memories of having seen people jumping or falling from the buildings and by fears that bin Laden would strike again. Noam, like other children in kindergarten, drew pictures of people jumping from the towers to trampolines provided by firemen below. He and his nanny, Fatou, an artist trained at the Beaux-Arts in Paris, worked together creating paintings and collages to make sense of the unfolding events, an activity that was beneficial to them both. My son Adam, who speaks French, became a child spokesperson on CBC French-Canadian radio and TV within days after 9/11 and has been interviewed numerous times since about how the events have shaped his view of the world.

5

School and Community

Forging Collaboration

In this phase of disaster, unlike the prior phase where everybody feels like "united we stand," what happens is people move into fragmentation. They move into groups they feel safer with and those groups tend to see other people as not necessarily understanding things. At its most extreme, remember that "looking for the tiger" threat detection system I talked about ... we start to see each other as potential enemies. And it takes a very conscious effort because of that exhaustion, thin skin and fragmentation dynamic to listen very carefully past the minefield and understand that there is a bias to be offended and to fragment for safety, and [we need] to really make an effort to build a common purpose. The good news is one of the things that people are wired to build a common purpose for is children.

Dr. Claude Chemtob, from *A Partnership for Kids: Post 9/11 coping strategies for the school community* **(Saul & Ray, 2002)**

Organizing to Support Families

The World Trade Center attack was only the beginning. Lower Manhattan, particularly the neighborhoods of Tribeca, Battery Park City and the Financial District, faced a series of unparalleled stressors in the coming months. Workers and residents in these areas, including parents, children, and teachers, experienced the most direct exposure to the events of 9/11 and thus bore the greatest emotional brunt. They endured the deaths of friends and relatives, direct threats to their own lives, and emergency evacuations. They found themselves in physical danger from debris and environmental contamination and were displaced from their homes and businesses. Furthermore, they would share other burdens felt by all New Yorkers: the plane crash in the borough of Queens, the wars in Afghanistan and Iraq, anthrax threats, and heightened terrorist alerts.

Two weeks after September 11, the 600 children of PS 234 in Tribeca were transferred to another public primary school in Greenwich Village. The children spent a little more than a week there, but it was clearly overcrowded, sometimes with 60 students to a classroom, and too little space to store all of their backpacks. With weeks or months ahead of us before PS 234 was again habitable, the Board of Education rented an unused Catholic school in the Village called St. Bernard's. It became the home of PS 234 for more than four and a half months. Parents and teachers collected and transferred the kids' belongings that had been abandoned at PS 234, even lunch boxes with old sandwiches. They brought furniture and materials from the old school to the new. In one weekend they completed the move and painted St. Bernard's. The school was ready the following week.

> The sense of togetherness and of taking action in the context of practical activities were repeated numerous times during the year and were seen by many parents as some of the greatest contributors to a returning sense of well-being. By doing for the children, the parents were able to reassert their own agency and thereby regain some sense of power and control.
>
> **Fullilove and Saul, 2006**

Our family support group continued to meet every week. This group consisted of PS 234 parents interested in their children's emotional well-being. Some of these parents were also mental health professionals like myself. In this unique position as both insiders and practitioners, we hoped to act as a bridge to outside resources. We asked, "How can we work together with teachers and school staff to address the challenges we face? And how do we actively collaborate with city agencies and outside groups to effectively respond to crises?" At this early stage, we recognized that our parents and teachers had enough expertise and agency to complement the external support we expected to receive. With the support of the school principal Anna Switzer, our group began to meet at St. Bernard's one morning each week. Because I was running a trauma studies program at New York University I was able to draw support from colleagues in the trauma and disaster field and contribute my own knowledge of community responses to catastrophes.

First, we agreed it was crucial to drive home the importance of taking care of oneself to the adults in the school community. With permission from the principal we organized a meeting to introduce teachers and school staff to the concept of self-care in a disaster context. Donna Gaffney, a faculty member at the International Trauma Studies Program, spoke to teachers one afternoon about common reactions to traumatic events, including symptoms of stress and exhaustion. Her message's core was the crucial importance of self-care: to do one's job under trying circumstances, one must take breaks to avoid burnout. We emphasized that one of the most effective means of stress reduction was the ability to enjoy regular activities and old routines. If a teacher stopped his or her usual yoga lessons or jogging habit after 9/11, we encouraged them to recover some of those activities. Afterwards, the teachers discussed what they could do to reduce stress among themselves. We encouraged them to meet regularly to discuss new teaching challenges under these trying circumstances, and also to monitor how they were coping with their new reality as a community.

As our group moved forward and brainstormed how to help the school, our involvement became a balancing act: how to engage the community and contribute to recovery without overly disrupting how classes were run. In these first few months, parents and teachers frequently met for dinners at each other's homes, not only to socialize, but also to explore ways to integrate parental contributions to the classroom. My son's kindergarten teacher, Kara, was very open to parental involvement and even developed a schedule for parents to help on different days. In these first months, parents visited the school every few weeks for morning presentations of schoolwork. These meetings became meaningful for our community, a place where parents could meet with each other and also get to know other children in the class.

We were not alone, however. Family support groups began to form at displaced schools all over Lower Manhattan and we soon created a network to share helpful information. Soon, this collaboration had a name: the Ground Zero Community Initiative. The project, funded by the *New York Times* 9/11 Neediest Fund, drew on research and experience from other humanitarian crises and terrorist incidents to assess the needs of downtown schools and develop a comprehensive agenda for recovery. In these cases, family and community played a crucial role in the recovery process and in the prevention of later mental health problems (Norris, et al., 2002; Padgett, 2002). We hoped to apply this research to the downtown school community.

While we were responding at a community level, the New York City Board of Education presented an alternate approach to address the schoolchildren's needs. After much struggle between researchers, an intended needs assessment by the Board of Education was shifted to an epidemiological survey of mental health symptoms and disorders in school children (M. Cohen, personal communication, January 20, 2012). The Board of Education's approach revolved around screening children for problems and then offering therapist services provided by outside mental health agencies and hospitals in Manhattan. Not only had very little attention been paid to the impact of the events on parents and teachers, but neither group had been engaged in giving input into the evaluation process (Fullilove & Saul, 2006).

The process unfolded as follows: The NYC Board of Education divided the schools among different mental health agencies in the city. Professionals screened children for signs of traumatic stress and other mental health difficulties, and based on these screenings referred students for treatment. While some schools welcomed the psychologists, others saw them as an intrusion, treading on ground already well trod by school psychologists and guidance counselors who both knew the families and were familiar with the school's culture. Public School 234 was one such school that preferred to handle the mental health response with its own staff, a psychologist, and a special education teacher.

I received a call one day from a director of a mental health agency, concerned that I was providing mental health services to children when his agency was the one chosen to provide those services. I assured him that my motives were solely as a parent; I was working with other parents to address the children's needs and thus we were not in competition.

What distinguished our school community's method was our principal assumption, namely that our participation in a collaborative process was more potent an approach than a limited clinical intervention. We planned to address psychosocial and mental health needs as a community by recognizing and enhancing existing social capital. Over the next four months, we held meetings in the community to promote recovery and accomplish this goal.

This approach was not a new one. Israel, for instance, had well-established integrated school-community programs to respond to crises. Fortunately for us, Dr. Esther Cohen, chair of the educational psychology department at Hebrew University, had just come to New York for a sabbatical year. Dr. Cohen was very experienced with developing school-based mental health programs following terrorism. Her methodology turned out to be very applicable to our situation, stressing that support of parents and teachers was extremely important in crises. The programs developed in Israel did not just target children with symptoms, but provided supportive services to all children in the class or school when traumatic events affected the school community. These programs were preventive as well as curative, allowing for all children to participate and express their concerns. In this context, children with ongoing needs could be identified more easily and extra support services could be offered to children who exhibited such difficulties.

When I met with Cohen, she stressed that the school can represent a vital structured routine which children can share during upsetting events. Teachers not only observe children every day but may also be able to help sensitize parents to changes in their child's behavior. The school can be a natural support system for parents. Of course, a prior investment in building school–parent relationships will enhance children's coping in an emergency. Crises themselves offer opportunities for schools and parents to strengthen collaboration and a sense of greater communality (Klingman & Cohen, 2004).

Without a previously existing trauma response program at PS 234, we were left to create one ourselves, drawing on the different skill sets available in the community. We found that the expertise needed to promote a social process of recovery was present not just in the mental health professionals among us, but also in businessmen, artists, educators, journalists, and other leaders. Everyone seemed to have something considerable to contribute and we wanted the chance to respond to this crisis with our own resources before being displaced by outsiders coming in to provide services.

Documentary filmmakers, for one, became a significant resource within our community. Several projects developed simultaneously, telling the story of our school. We came to realize that this spontaneous documentation could become a tool for education, advocacy, and project development (and, even later, provide significant data for the writing of this book). One parent filmmaker, Linnae Hamilton, interviewed school staff and teachers about their experiences and responses in her film *Our School: PS 234 on 9/11*. Our family support group allocated funding for another parent filmmaker, Jude Ray, to track perspectives among parents and teachers and document ongoing community activities—such as large group forums. The videos of these forums would become integral to our approach.

Communal Tensions Emerge

Tensions inevitably develop in a community after a disaster, leading to feelings of mistrust. During a crisis, a community may experience an influx of outside responders to assess the damage and offer assistance. But community members might feel this as an intrusion upon their communal space and a violation of privacy, a disruption to the natural process of healing rather than aid.

Our family support committee in Lower Manhattan was no different. Parents were uncertain about where to go for additional mental health services. Initially, only providers at local mental health clinics were free, and the bulk of their cases were those of affected family members. Only later would residents be able to seek reimbursable mental health services from providers of their choice.

Another source of tension in the first three months arose over the appropriate time to safely send students back to their schools in Lower Manhattan. Some parents and teachers even wondered if it would be safe to return at all. They were concerned not only about the emotional toll of such a quick return, but also about the possibility of a toxic physical environment; many community members did not trust government assertions about air quality. As we would later learn, the U.S. government had indeed misled the public concerning air toxicity in order to mobilize people to return to work in Lower Manhattan as soon as possible (Gonzalez, 2002).

Public School 234 had been covered with debris, and toxic dust had infiltrated the entire school. There was a pressing need to clean it up, install air filters, and fix the intercom system, which incidentally had not been working on September 11. As smoke continued to rise from Ground Zero, a mere two blocks south of the school, many parents were hugely concerned about the safety of the school environment and the health of their children. If the air was contaminated, could children even go outside for recess? How would they react when they saw the destruction?

Others argued that it would actually benefit children to see the new construction in the neighborhood, as many families had moved back to the area near the school. To some, it seemed as if those children were already coping with the changes. But a barrage of media attention and the subsequent anthrax scare only further exacerbated the level of fear.

On December 5, parents gathered at the St. Bernard's school for a PTA meeting with representatives from the New York City Board of Education. They discussed the idea of returning to their original school.

Parents soon became pitted against one another. Families who had remained in their homes downtown felt the kids were resilient and could return. Some felt that the anxiety of certain parents was trickling down to their children.

Other parents expressed that their kids actually wanted to go back, seeing the old school as a comfort.

Still others were dissatisfied with the way the Board of Education was handling the situation. Many parents expressed dissatisfaction and frustrations toward the Board of Education, feeling as if the parental input and collaboration were meaningless in the Board's decisions. One parent felt the mistrust stemmed from the U.S. Government's desire for everything to appear "back to normal."

A city representative announced that the Board of Education wanted to establish a date in early January 2002 to move back—which meant that the teachers would have to forgo their winter vacation to prepare. Teachers began a heated discussion, expressing their need for a long-overdue vacation after working under very stressful conditions for weeks without reprieve. In fact, the children's well-being was at stake if they didn't have the time off to recuperate, they said. I recall a Board of Education representative responding: "Don't worry about the children; if they have difficulties later, we have a team of therapists waiting to treat them."

More than just two opinions, two perspectives for recovery were once again at odds: caretaker support and community-based prevention versus screening and treatment. Parents supported the teachers' decision not to cooperate with the Board of Education—they would take their vacation. The teachers had embraced the idea taught in the self-care workshop: to take care of the children, one must also take care of oneself. And the Board of Education got the message; they postponed the decision about when to return.

A Series of Community Forums

Shortly after the PTA meeting, the Ground Zero Community Initiative organized a series of community forums to discuss ongoing concerns about children's well-being and community response to disaster. On December 10, we held the first forum at St. Bernard's. This first forum addressed the emotional and psychological stages experienced by communities during disasters. We invited Dr. Claude Chemtob to give a presentation entitled "Post-Disaster Reactions of Children and Parents." A child psychologist based out of Honolulu working for the National Post Traumatic Stress Disorder Center, Dr. Chemtob was an expert in disaster relief and had worked in different contexts on the process of disaster recovery. Dr. Chemtob had been teaching in New York for the past two years and was familiar with the local culture and school system.

Much of the discourse in New York City at the time was focused on individual stress reactions and PTSD. The media in particular had embraced the framework of PTSD to illustrate the psychological effects of 9/11. I was asked to participate in a number of interviews for newspapers, radio, and television about the prevalence of PTSD. However, I felt the need to shift the discourse by educating media professionals about the complexity of reactions to such events and the limitations of a perspective that focused exclusively on PTSD symptoms (see *New York Voices* interview, "Coming Together to Heal": www.thirteen.org/nyvoices/transcripts/saul.html).

Our forum, however, presented a broader framework to understand reactions to the terrorist attacks. The phases of this framework normalized rather than pathologized people's experiences, which helped many community members organize their individual and community-wide responses.

The stages began with "United We Stand"—an initial period of shock, followed by a sense of coming together, sharing, and letting one's guard down. The intermediate stage was known as "Molasses and Minefields."

"In this stage people feel as if they are moving through molasses from exhaustion," Dr. Chemtob explained. By this interval, people start to tire as stressors accumulate, and a once cohesive community may become irritable, and retreat into smaller groups to feel "safe."

And if people are constantly focusing on safety, always trying to see where danger might present itself, they become more sensitized to possible threats, even if one isn't actually present. "Various things will then trigger them off and they get offended when one never had the intention of offending," Dr. Chemtob said.

In the final stage, a community may create a positive vision of recovery. Recovery, Dr. Chemtob emphasized, is not a passive process but a consequence of the community actively coming together for a common purpose.

More than a hundred adults attended each meeting—predominantly parents, but also teachers, principals, and other school staff. The format usually consisted of a presentation followed by breakout groups for discussion on relevant topics. The groups then reported back to the larger group on what they had discussed and asked questions of the presenter.

One group of parents raised the concern that tensions were rising in the community and noticed that there was a great deal more parental bickering. Dr. Chemtob highlighted that we were now moving into the second stage of community response, in which tensions develop. Therefore he urged participants to take extra care to modulate some of their reactions that may be due to exhaustion, thin skin, and increased irritability.

One particularly useful concept Dr. Chemtob introduced was that of "Survival Mode." Faced with a threat, people tend to react with a set of two specialized survival mechanisms: heightened threat-detection, which is a readiness to assess danger, and a tendency to strive for social bonding. A heightened sensitivity to threatening environmental cues is beneficial during a disaster, and, as social animals, we seek safety in numbers. We not only feel the need to check for danger, we become aware of who is with us and who isn't. In situations such as these, we tend to have a threat confirmation bias. We fill in information gaps by looking for the evidence of danger. When the disaster is over, we have to actively restore our perspective.

In our case, people rallied together spontaneously after 9/11, and this outpouring of altruism helped them to feel less vulnerable. The community became more interdependent, and boundaries between the self and the group shifted during this phase. But as time would tell, the groups began to find fault with one another and fragment. Dr. Chemtob emphasized the importance of communication and awareness of tension in an effort to prevent this reaction, which does not have to be automatic.

Disaster specialists often speak about how this initial honeymoon period of cooperation and collaboration inevitably diminishes. My experience indicated that this spirit could have been sustained for a long period; it began to diminish in large part because authorities didn't recognize it as an important resource for recovery. While this phase is often nostalgically remembered in the life of the community, the spirit of interdependence is not currently encouraged by our health and mental health system, oriented around individuals. After 9/11, some of us asked whether we as a society need to recover some of this collaborative spirit as part of our everyday lives.

To diminish periods of tension, it seemed important in our forums for both children and adults to allow themselves to relive, in small doses, what they had been through in the weeks following the terrorist attacks. Achieved through conversation or other types of expressive activity, such as art and play, especially for children, it is important to find ways to grow comfortable with memories of the disaster while not avoiding them altogether. Our groups also discussed the importance of monitoring reactions to danger. Therapists have long observed that trauma survivors may experience a disruption of their cognitive schemas after living through an unusually dangerous set of events (McCann & Pearlman, 1990). This disruption might cause someone to react to a sense of danger when none exists, or miss signs of danger when they are present. Effective recovery, we determined, is about reclaiming one's sense of agency by actively choosing to modulate one's reactions.

The forum participants spoke of having a range of reactions in the wake of disaster; some became more easily aroused, others more withdrawn and numb. We know from the humanitarian response field that many activities can restore a sense of safety and predictability for children and families, such as quickly re-establishing recreational activities, and creating opportunities for togetherness and greater involvement in normative activities. The groups shared techniques to combat arousal, such as deep breathing exercises, massage, and physical affection.

Parents spoke in small discussion groups about how some of their children showed signs of distress in the form of regressive tendencies—wanting to sleep in bed with parents, fears of going alone to the bathroom, and other behaviors that had been more appropriate at an earlier age. We encouraged parents to interpret this behavior as a need for extra attention and nurturance, and to respond just as they would have to the same distress when the child was much younger. While allowing their children to engage in some regression, parents also needed to set expectations in order for the child to quickly return to age-appropriate behaviors.

When parents and teachers have their sense of safety challenged, as in a disaster, they often forget their basic competencies. Their competencies are there, but some people have difficulty figuring out how to use these skills in the new situation. One cognitive effect of disaster is the sense that events meld together, necessitating time to sort out events and reflect on successful experiences of coping with the change. Sharing stories about the events can often restore perspective. The community was still making sense of this unprecedented disaster. By creating cooperative groups, people felt stronger, regained prior capacities, and felt their sense of self-efficacy restored.

Families were not only evacuated and dispersed to different parts of the city for weeks and months, some families permanently moved away. This was a painful loss for many kids. In one of the smaller discussion groups, parents raised concerns regarding how to answer children's questions about why their friends' families had moved away, why they remained, and if it was safe enough for them to stay.

In mid-December, the Board of Education finally decided to delay the return to schools in Lower Manhattan until the end of January 2002, allowing teachers to have their well-deserved vacation.

Preparing to Return to Ground Zero

In January 2002, with the plan to return the children to their home schools by the end of the month, many parents felt anguish about going back for the first time to the place where they had experienced horror four months earlier. While some families had moved back long ago, others were still displaced from their homes. Hence, some parents were less ready than others to have their children return to the school.

In one school, discussion about returning had become very inflamed and sparked tremendous conflict between two groups. The conflict was so great that insults were hurled through emails between the two sides. This community was also more transient than Tribeca, so many people decided not to return to their apartments in Battery Park City. Instead, they stayed outside the city, in their country homes if they had them. Since many people worked in the Financial District and had lost their jobs, many of these people left New York. There was an attrition of kids returning to the school. The community experienced a tremendous loss of families, exacerbated by the conflict between the two factions, which led more families to decide not to return. It was very difficult for this school community to contain the feelings about their concern for their children, and for their health, and to reach some resolution that was acceptable to the school community.

The January community forum opened with remarks by the chair of PS 234's Family Support Committee, Andrea Robins. She acknowledged that we had truly built a community over the past four months, and that our mutual support of one another was extremely important in our children's lives. The focus of this forum was to examine what kinds of reactions parents should look for in their children as well as how best to handle the transition back to the school. As few of the attendees had been at the previous forum, Dr. Chemtob, the guest speaker once more, first asked parents and teachers to acknowledge their own merits and think about all the good things that had happened over the past four months.

He presented a new framework on how to restore perspective after a disaster, recognizing that danger is no longer imminent. Some children thought that Osama bin Laden was hiding in the school. Rather than staying on automatic response as we do in survival mode, Dr. Chemtob said, we needed to switch to manual response, and make an active effort to restore control, and to separate stimuli into "then" and "now." When we think of returning to the school, we have a tendency to think of how we felt at the time of the traumatic event and to feel those emotions all over again. Dr. Chemtob suggested that one solution might be rehearsing going back, both internally and with our families, as a way of restoring a sense of safety. Key to the process, he said, is the recognition that recovery is a long-term process, taking as many as three to five years to bounce back from disaster. In rehearsing with children, Dr. Chemtob encouraged parents to teach self-talk to help differentiate between current and past feelings. These rehearsals offer a chance to revisit the experience in a safe way, without going into survival mode. Furthermore, he said, by mentally going back we need not experience our memories as a fresh sign of danger.

An excerpt from the video produced about the forum, *A Partnership for Kids: Post 9/11 Coping Strategies for the School Community* (Saul & Ray, 2002) illustrates how our groups each perceived different reactions in themselves and their children:

DR. CHEMTOB: The task is to have a discussion among yourselves about what you have observed in your children, what concerns you may have, what questions you may have and then when we come back together, we'll hear from each recorder what the group discussion was about and then we'll address these altogether.

[Parents divide up into groups according to their children's age level.]

A MOTHER: You know just the other day, it seemed like they had the picture of the towers burning again on TV. It's one thing to get past it, especially for us, but it's in your face all of the time, not just one time a day but several times a day.

A MOTHER: I don't want to create a problem for my daughter if there is none. The fear I have is that she gets there and she expects it to be exactly the same and it's not.

FEMALE: That's what she said?

A MOTHER: I think that's what she does expect.

FEMALE: Why?

A MOTHER: Because that's what I expect.

A FATHER: That's why I went down to 150 [the elementary school] yesterday to see the state of the school. And we're on Independence Plaza that has been totally gutted. So what he's looking forward to, he won't even get.

A SPECIAL EDUCATION TEACHER: I think everyone is running to their parents' rooms and wanting to sleep with their pets. So this is a lot of what's going on: support of kids in groups at the schools where we talk and try to help each other.

A MOTHER: I'm not saying it's not on his mind, because he draws cartoons and the word rubble comes up plenty, but for him I think all of this talk is really torture to him and I understand the need for rehearsal because I could use another one, but he would really do better to not go back, just shut up, let me just live my life. And he has little methods that he works out himself. He's not empty inside. He is just not a sit and talk about it in a little family meeting kind of kid.

A MINISTER: It just seems to me that it's real. That we're not going to see exactly eye to eye with our spouses.

FEMALE: Or the Board of Ed[ucation].

A MOTHER: She had a lot of fears and worries about going back and I said, "Maybe you should let me worry about the safety of it," and at one point she just allowed me to worry for her. She checks with me and says, "You won't let me go back unless you are sure, right?"

Another concern we addressed was how to strengthen the confidence of children returning to the school near Ground Zero. With so many families moving away permanently, it became important to explain why some children would not be returning. My son's best friend and his family abruptly left for an island off Vancouver.

Parents were particularly concerned about how the school could provide space for the less vocal students who might be internalizing problems and how to deal with reminders of 9/11. Dr. Chemtob urged parents to give meaning actively to these reminders, and not to dismiss them. To put things into perspective for the children, he emphasized the importance of group interaction in the community. As an example of the corrective perspective, Dr. Chemtob suggested using the heroism of firefighters; some parents were reticent to use this example for fear of reminding children that many firefighters had died.

While parents were uncertain about how to confront ongoing threats, they decided that it was beneficial to speak of the positive steps being taken to increase security. Many parents in the group felt that they lacked agency—that things were happening to them rather than being decided upon. And foremost, they felt pressure to return to normal. We discussed how people have different rhythms and some families may need much more time to resume normal activities after a crisis than others.

Responding to Emerging Needs

The community forums became an important site where needs assessment could take place through informal surveys and focus groups. First and foremost, groups reported a strong interest in finding ways to keep the community together and to continue to build on the spirit of camaraderie they had felt since the terrorist attacks. Because of our presentations, people were aware of the need to prevent the community from fracturing. I felt frustrated trying to alert the city to the need for a community approach to recovery, particularly because we would need to sustain tremendous momentum toward positive recovery despite a lack of acknowledgment for this process. For me, this raised the question of how to creatively sustain our cohesion without overt support.

Other family support groups expressed the need for clear communication from the city, and irritation over how little there was. They felt a need for a community meeting place, where adults and children could come together to engage in activities, meet other residents, and access important information on developments in the city and recovery efforts. Overall, there was a strong need to develop a community space. Previous public meeting spaces, such as the school playground and Washington Market Park, were closed. Spontaneous meetings people had with the community members, exchanging information, checking in on one another, and speaking about emerging concerns was a very important part of the ongoing processing of our disaster experiences. But this everyday organic process is very much influenced by environmental parameters—people need access to one another, they need a physical place to be able to stop and spend time together and mutually restore perspective, as described by Dr. Chemtob.

It also became apparent that people wanted more opportunities to come together as a community of schools. Hindered by displacement of the schools to outside the community, the area schools had not often met in the months since 9/11.

Parents also voiced the fear of transmitting their own anxiety to their children and how to answer questions truthfully and still provide assurances. Dr. Chemtob acknowledged the need to tell children the truth, but also noted that there are different ways to talk about issues at different stages of a child's development. He used the example of speaking about sex with children and how we need to give different honest information depending on the age of the child.

We compiled a list of needs and concerns from surveys conducted in the community forums. This list was distributed to parents and teachers through the school's website. The needs fell in to four categories as follows:

1. Needs to monitor environmental safety and respond to risks that may arise.
2. Needs to monitor and respond to emotional reactions in children and adults.
3. Needs to promote social cohesion, and establish a public space for activities, discussion, and play.
4. Needs to provide clear and useful information on emotional reactions and recovery skills.

This list of needs became the basis for discussion of the next phase of the Ground Zero Community Initiative. It also informed a grant proposal to the New York Times Foundation to create a Lower Manhattan resource center to promote collective efforts toward psychosocial recovery.

The School Develops a Plan

The PS 234 principal Anna Switzer also used the forums as a place to raise concerns about how to address particular needs of children in the school. Switzer very much liked the metaphor Dr. Chemtob used to describe how children look to their parent(s) to assess a threat rather than at the threat itself. He called the threat "the tiger," and explained that a parent doesn't wait to see the whole tiger before responding; rather, a glimpse of the tail is enough. At the time, PS 234 held discussion groups for the children led by the school psychologist and special education teachers to monitor the children for signs of distress. Dr. Chemtob cautioned that these groups could be helpful for some children but not for others. He warned that there is often a bias to target only those children who exhibit overtly problematic behavior and to underestimate distress in the quieter children. Dr. Chemtob's previous study found that females in particular were more susceptible to falling into this category, and thus it was also important to administer screening and self-reports. Principal Switzer countered, however, that in this particular school environment the teachers were very sensitive to the children and gave them many opportunities to express themselves. In their school setting, she felt the teachers were more primed to pick up on a quieter child experiencing distress. Rather than primarily relying on screenings, addressing the culture of the school may be a more effective and preventive approach.

Principal Switzer then went on to describe how they had provided assemblies to allow the children to speak for themselves about what had happened after 9/11. But at one of the first PTA meetings, a group of parents had urged the school to actually ban talking about 9/11 as a way to protect their children from hearing or learning more about the events. Over time, Switzer stressed the importance of moving on—enough talk and pictures of falling buildings—which Dr. Chemtob would also echo.

While screening is very important, the field of child traumatic stress tended to under-emphasize the need to support and strengthen the capacity of teachers and parents to recognize and positively respond to children's needs. It's important to note the two perspectives embodied by Switzer's emphasis on the school community's capacity to sensitively respond and by Dr. Chemtob's child trauma perspective that emphasizes screening. Ultimately, it is important to incorporate both strategies.

As a family therapist, I and many of my colleagues were concerned about the strategy of focusing on symptoms and therapy without attending to the larger system of the school community. One thing that struck me as a parent in this disaster context was how seemingly little attention the mental health professionals paid to parental authority and their competence to address their children's needs, or at least to be complementary partners. The rush to come in and "rescue" children from the possible adverse affects of trauma was driven partly by the competition for funding, and perhaps because of a bias in the child trauma therapy field.

Parental emotional reactions after a traumatic event are a powerful mediator of the child's psychological well-being. Norris et al. (2002) show that poor child outcomes are associated with higher rates of traumatic stress symptoms, anxieties, and other mental health difficulties in either parent, as well as parental conflict and irritability, and poor family cohesion. Parents may play a number of roles in their children's recovery. According to Klingman and Cohen (2004), these may include offering their children any or all of the following: emotional support and soothing, a stable and regulating environment, empathic communication about their reactions to traumatic events, help in making sense of the experience and correcting misconceptions, exploring and promoting family strengths, increasing family cohesiveness, ongoing monitoring for problematic reactions, and seeking help for persistent difficulties.

Consequently, Klingman and Cohen (2004) state: "Parents constitute a major resource for children's coping and should be proactively helped to remain so, even when their parenting capacities are threatened or temporarily diminished by trauma" (p. 64). They note that this coincides with the U.S. National Institute of Mental Health recommendations (2001), which suggests that the family should be the first resource for helping children deal with catastrophe in order to promote a faster and better adjustment. Their conclusion was that children's resilience is supported by secure and stable families, which can act as a protective shield for children against traumatic events.

According to Principal Switzer, PS 234 from its beginning had developed a culture based on collaboration between parents, teachers, and school staff. Parent involvement had been a part of its day-to-day culture; parents were invited in to give their opinion and their cooperation was welcome. The collaborative actions taken in the first months following 9/11 strengthened the school's determination to continue to address the crisis as a community.

What was Accomplished?

The community forums accomplished several goals: they deepened participants' understanding of the process of disaster recovery, they offered an opportunity to talk through concerns, and they also provided data on community needs. The forums simultaneously helped to heal, problem-solve, and assess needs. Through its activities, the Ground Zero Community Initiative demonstrated that disaster victims could in a sense treat themselves by engaging actively and collectively with the challenges that had descended upon them. With each action of empowerment, engagement, agency, and initiative, the group gained clarity and sanity, pulling a new basis for order out of the chaos of disaster (Fullilove & Saul, 2006).

Bruce Arnold, the school psychologist, felt that age-specific parent groups provided a useful model to organize weekly parent support meetings in the school. Parents knew that they could attend a group and meet parents of other students who were in the same grade level to raise developmentally appropriate concerns. Many parents attended these groups for two years, through the end of the 2003 school year. Simultaneously, the special education teacher ran widely attended discussion groups in each grade level for children to voluntarily talk through 9/11 concerns. These groups engaged in modalities of expression through the arts. I remember seeing dream catchers hanging from my sons' beds to help prevent them from having nightmares. Furthermore, the psychologist and special education teachers continued to closely monitor children who might be having difficulties.

Our group produced a 50-minute edited videotape of one of the School Community Forums for distribution (Saul & Ray, 2002). Over 100 copies were given to classrooms in Lower Manhattan so that parents who had not attended the meeting could view our discussion on how to confront children's needs. We also made a seven-minute version, which highlighted the importance of parents and school staff working together to address the needs of the children and the school community.

In January 2002, I brought the shorter video to a meeting at the New York City Department of Health and Mental Hygiene. It was useful as a graphic visual example of the importance of a community approach to recovery. Images of parents vigorously participating in discussions drove home the idea that a community focus was a necessary part of recovery; the video among other efforts eventually led to a city-sponsored conference on community healing and to New York City's Department of Health and Mental Hygiene's funding for community-driven recovery efforts.

6

Promoting Collective Recovery

Shifting the Discourse

As presented in previous chapters, New York City's mental health response after 9/11 at first focused primarily on individual therapeutic interventions. Many mental health professionals from Lower Manhattan felt compelled to more broadly address needs at the community level. To achieve this end, we appealed to city and state agencies for a community recovery approach, we gave media interviews to spread awareness about the mental health impact of 9/11 and subsequent events, and we worked to connect our local projects to citywide programs. We continued to provide workshops for mental health professionals to address ongoing issues they saw in their daily work and to help them put clinical work within a community context.

Following the same principles, a core group of parents and mental health professionals, known as the Ground Zero Community Initiative (see Chapter 5), negotiated a contract with the Federal Emergency Management Agency's (FEMA) Project Liberty to develop a community resource center in Lower Manhattan. This center would be a site to engage interested community members in planning and supporting local recovery initiatives. The long process of negotiation with different stakeholders defined the project's growth, and indicated the overarching bureaucratic issues that plagued community-based groups hoping to receive funding.

In February 2002, I attended a meeting on community approaches to disaster at the office of Martha Sullivan, deputy commissioner of mental health at the city's Department of Health and Mental Hygiene. Dr. Sullivan was a social worker at the forefront of mental health work in New York City; her particular focus was on community approaches. We had met as former students of Dr. Salvador Minuchin at his family therapy training institute in New York and as members of the American Family Therapy Academy. The meeting included prominent people in the field of community mental health;

my colleague Judith Landau was on the phone from Colorado, and Bruce Dohrenwend and Mindy Fullilove from Columbia University's Mailman School of Public Health were in attendance. We discussed how disaster and mass trauma affect communities and what approaches could best promote their psychosocial recovery. Our goal was to come up with a set of conclusions to present to the New York City Health Commissioner, Thomas Frieden, at a meeting later that day.

At the meeting, I showed the short video about the school community forums that the Ground Zero Community Initiative had made to illustrate the positive impact of community-oriented post-9/11 mental health responses. The Department of Health agreed to support a public conference that Dr. Fullilove would organize on community approaches to healing in the spring. The International Trauma Studies Program at New York University partnered to sponsor the conference and to find ways to coordinate with a regional project called NYC Recovers, run by Dr. Fullilove and her community research group at Columbia University.

NYC Recovers: Strengthening the Mesosystem

By developing NYC Recovers, Dr. Fullilove and Lourdes Hernandez-Cordero sought to replace the "weak ties" among the thousands of people who traveled to and worked in the Twin Towers. Weak ties are the relations that take place on a daily basis between people who work or live in proximity to one another. For example, the cashier at the deli says hello to the man who buys his breakfast each morning; it's "familiarity among strangers." These weak ties are formed by routine and depend on place, as opposed to the strong ties that connect people to work, family, religious organizations, and school. Weak ties create linkages across groups—the so-called six degrees of separation.

The World Trade Center can be seen as both a neighborhood, i.e. a central business district, and a keystone. A keystone is an entity that gives stability to a complex system, like the keystone in an arch. Urban ecologists see some neighborhoods as "keystones" that are important for the well-being of the city as a whole and even to the well-being of the region (Fullilove & Saul, 2006). Each day more than 50,000 people went to work at the WTC, which was also the crossroads for an additional 100,000 people as a transportation hub. In many ways, the towers symbolically represented New York City. When this large vertical neighborhood was destroyed, it severed tens of thousands of weak ties, which are important to a city's functioning. Fullilove and her team believed that recreating these linkages was crucial to the process of collective recovery. According to Fullilove and Hernandez-Cordero, the sundering of social ties at the neighborhood level breaks connections between groups. Repairing this system of connections required reconnections among groups and people that have lost their common network.

The central thesis of NYC Recovers was that the wisdom to implement effective recovery lay within and between organizations as opposed to directing efforts primarily to individuals. Organizations, which were integral to the various communities that comprised the regional ecosystem, had the ability to assess the needs of their constituents and institute appropriate remedies. Furthermore, organizations had the capacity to form linkages with other organizations, thus recreating the social and organizational framework damaged by 9/11 (Fullilove & Saul, 2006).

The spring conference was called *Together We Heal: Community Mobilization for Trauma Recovery* (Fullilove, 2002). It brought together 200 people from community-based organizations of all kinds to discuss how these organizations were working with groups, families, and individuals at the grassroots level. Conference participants planned for the first anniversary of 9/11, and originated the concept of "September Wellness," an effort to embed the anniversary in a larger period of healing the mind, body, and spirit through wellness activities. It was planned that NYC Recovers would reach out to people in the metropolitan area through a network of more than 1,000 organizations linked together with the goal to mourn losses, to learn what caused the 9/11 disaster, to rebuild social connections, and to prevent scapegoating and prejudice. Their motto was "Remember, respect, learn and connect" (Fullilove & Saul, 2006). One of NYC Recovers's innovative strategies was its focus on how organizations planned seasonal events and holidays in the first year after 9/11. During these periods people tend to have more difficult feelings after a tragedy, and thus will feel conflicted about celebrating. These times present opportunities for organizations to offer extra support to members for the distress and dysphoria they may feel and to plan activities and programs in which people can acknowledge and express these feelings. The many programs promoted by NYC Recovers emphasized that unselfishness, temporary sacrifice, and expressions of interdependence and mutual concerns were necessary for collective recovery.

The work of NYC Recovers strengthened the mesosystem—the level of community organizations in an urban social system that mediates between the macrosystem of funders, planners, and policymakers and the microsystem of individuals, families, and small, informal groups. All parts of the community are touched by organizations in the mesosystem—it encompasses the entire population. These organizations truly know their constituents' needs because they have regular, direct connections; as a result they can reach a diverse population throughout the region. In this model, these organizations often know how to best respond and offer comfort to their members.

The mesosystem plays a central role in supporting collective recovery; one of the greatest challenges is connecting the community from the individual level to top policymakers, who are determining where and how to allocate resources. This presence of a mesosystem allows for synergy between groups—which may lead to greater access to information, shared knowledge, creative ideas, and problem solving. This approach is based on Louis Wirth's urban ecology theory (1938) that organizations mediate between policy and people. After 9/11, as is likely the case after many disasters, certain segments of the population did not have any connection to policymakers. Consequently, their needs were not addressed, and resources were not made easily available to them.

Because organizations in the mesosystem are already engaged with their constituents, they can more easily identify their constituents' needs. The mesosystem can offer them support without additional cost to themselves. By providing structure and support for community organizations, NYC Recovers was fulfilling one of the most important principles of community recovery—strengthening existing natural support systems of organizations, which in turn strengthen the natural support systems of families and communities.

The collaboration with the International Trauma Studies Program and its Lower Manhattan community project facilitated the responses of a range of different types of organizations and groups to post-9/11 psychosocial needs—see Table 6.1.

Building Clinical and Community Capacity

Within a week after 9/11, the International Trauma Studies Program at New York University initiated a series of workshops on disaster response. These workshops were intended to provide a regular meeting space for mental health professionals working therapeutically with clients who were affected by 9/11. This would be a place where professionals could address mental health concerns that emerged over time as well as enhance our collective capacities for networking, sharing ideas, and mutual support. The goal was to build

TABLE 6.1 ORGANIZATIONS IN THE NEW YORK CITY MESOSYSTEM

1. Pre-existing groups that would normally get together on an ongoing basis. Ex: Church groups, school groups, youth-activity groups, food co-ops, etc.
   a. They understand needs of constituents, and can attempt to respond in an appropriate way. They are exposed to the diverse needs of the existing community.
   b. Tenant groups already existed and were very well organized so they were in a position to become a very active and supportive disaster-response team; they were well-organized to respond to the vulnerable (see Chapter 7).

2. Spontaneous emergence of groups; people who recognize particular needs as a result of a catastrophe.
   a. Ex: Group that responded to the environmental toxicity; a number of parent-initiated after-school programs; school/community forums; parent-support and children discussion group at school (see Chapter 5).
   b. Initiated by community itself.
   c. We (downtown community group) could provide structure and support for emergence of newly formed peer groups.
   d. Peer groups coming together out of communities of interest/shared-discourse (artists and journalists groups; see Chapter 7).
   e. Loosely affiliated groups that needed to gather.

3. Organizations that target marginalized populations.

4. Organizations specifically organized around emergencies; they are formed before disasters but get mobilized after, and are able to focus on getting access to resources.

5. Downtown community group: aimed to provide resources for community members; had goal of supporting different contingencies in community that recognized recovering needs and helping them be able to come together to address those needs.
   a. Role that either inside or outside group could perform.
   b. Providing structure and support for newly formed groups.

6. Outside groups formed after disaster that come in and offer services to members of community.
   a. Not a natural group in community; coming into the community to look for participants rather than arising out of organic needs.
   b. Usually access those participants through working with already existing groups.
   c. May be able to provide support in ways locals cannot.

7. Samba school: example of network of people who knew each other through sports/athletics who then came together to create a different activity that they found would be good for youth (see Chapter 7).

8. Separate groups that pop up to create sites for narration and public discourse (like Archives and Theater; see Chapter 8).

9. Sites for memorialization – also emerged spontaneously.

community and collective resilience among clinicians that could provide some protection against the often emotionally challenging work they were providing for severely traumatized survivors and mourners.

We supported community projects in Lower Manhattan with donations and low-fee workshops led by altruistic experts in the disaster and trauma fields. The workshops presented various approaches to treat individuals, families, and groups within a multisystemic resilience framework. They ran once or twice a month for two years and were attended by hundreds of mental health professionals. Unique to these workshops at the time, many presenters were internationals who had experience working in contexts that addressed the impact of war, violence, and terrorism. This included Palestinian and Israeli mental health professionals, as well as colleagues from Kosovo, Africa, and Latin America. Dr. Nancy Baron presented a workshop titled: "Turning the Tide: Working with Violence Affected Families from the Field in Africa." It examined comprehensive community-based psychosocial and mental health intervention developed in Uganda, Sudan, and Burundi to help those affected by political violence. Similar to the community resilience approach we had implemented in the school community in Lower Manhattan, these projects relied upon the strength of the local culture, trained local practitioners, and empowered families and communities to address the psychosocial concerns of community members.

Six weeks after 9/11, Dr. Bessel van der Kolk presented one of the first workshops on the essentials of trauma treatment. For some people, the impact of trauma can be so severe that the lens of trauma clouds their entire worldview; they have difficulty processing new information, he said. The mind tends to remember traumatic experiences through sensory modalities instead of verbal narratives, and these memories may be experienced vividly, as if the occurrence were happening again. When using theatrical and artistic approaches to work with trauma survivors, we recognized that they often had better access to difficult memories through sensory and kinesthetic exercises. In a safe, supportive environment, survivors could calm the distressing physiological reactions these memories evoked, enabling them to externalize and communicate their experiences to others.

Dr. Peter Levine, who developed the "Somatic Experiencing" body awareness approach to the treatment of PTSD, presented his work with a woman who was in one of the towers as the plane struck it. He showed a video of his work with her. As she told her story, Levine brought attention to the reactions she expressed with her body: the tension and constriction in her movements, how she swayed her body as she described the building being hit by the plane, how she turned her head to the left as she recalled hearing someone on her left scream "Run!" The woman's body performed a parallel narrative to the one she was speaking. Levine helped her track these physiological responses so that she could better integrate the broken sensory fragments of the event, a process he calls "creative self-regulation."

Dr. Judith Landau presented the LINC (Linking Human Systems) Community Resilience Model. This collaborative strategy sustains the view that communities are inherently competent to implement positive change during times of rapid and untimely transition, trauma, or loss. She defines resilience as the "capacity, hope, and faith to withstand trauma, overcome adversity, and to prevail and survive" using resources, competence, and connectedness. The model assumes that communities can access both individual and collective strengths to overcome loss and trauma with appropriate support and encouragement. The LINC Community Resilience Model evolved from a family system approach, and is based on utilizing surrounding systems and map techniques to access community history and structure, and to identify natural change agents from the local population, called "links," to promote community recovery (Landau, 2010).

The LINC model has three stages. The first entails holding town meetings to map the community's strengths and resources and establish goals and work groups. In the second stage, an outside consultant facilitates weekly and monthly work group meetings. In the third stage, the community works to build a model that can respond to the immediate crisis, offer various interdisciplinary programs and services for trauma intervention, develop long-term family and community services to prevent the sequelae of trauma, and create exportable plans in case of future crises (Landau-Stanton, 1986).

Dr. Landau facilitated discussions with mental health professionals in her workshop, who role-played community members to demonstrate how the model could be responsive to traumatic events. Kelly Ryan, director of disaster planning with the New York City Department of Mental Health Mental Hygiene, attended the workshop. She presented her view on community resilience:

> I use the analogy of a sheet and the thread-counts of a sheet. If you have a sheet hanging fully taut with a very low thread-count and something is thrown at it, chance is there will be a hole. The size of the hole will be greater the lower the thread-count. But the

> higher the thread-count is ... [the] more resistant it is to damage.
> Each thread represents something that we as individuals or as a
> group pull upon to make us feel safe, to make us feel happy, to
> express when we don't feel eager to.

In Ms. Ryan's analogy, the LINC model increases the thread-count by
incorporating all members of the community—individuals, families, schools,
neighborhoods, local authorities and political leaders, and professionals—to
strengthen resilience by taking advantage of the community's special skills and
leadership. Ms. Ryan became an advocate for incorporating such community
resilience approaches into New York City's disaster planning and response
efforts.

The LINC model's key benefits lay in its use of natural change agents to
build support, rather than relying on the "artificial support systems" only
engaged in times of crises, such as emergency services, medical specialists,
therapists, social services, and legal services. Consequently, it is also a more
cost-effective model.

In my work with Dr. Landau on a community resilience approach in Lower
Manhattan, we incorporated a multisystem map that I originally developed
with Steven Reisner based on Talcott Parson's general systems theory (Parsons,
1951) The map presented the different levels of human systems from physiological, to individual/psychological, to various levels of social systems (families, communities, organizations, and helping systems) to cultural, political,
and economic systems and the physical environment.

According to general systems theory, each systemic level has its particular
function. The function of the physical organism is survival. Similarly the
function of the psychological system is goal-oriented behavior, the function of the social system is integrated social process, and that of the cultural
system, pattern maintenance. Traumatic events may impact each or multiple
levels of the system; if a function of one system is compromised, it affects the
other systems. Various impacts of traumatic events can be mapped to corres-
pond to each systemic level—e.g. sources of resilience, symbolization and
narrative capacities, problematic reactions to events and long-term sequelae,
and therapeutic and preventive interventions. It should be noted that the
map is a snapshot and does not capture the dynamic processes within and
among systems that evolve over time; the map does not reflect interventions
that target multiple systems. A multisystemic map of post-9/11 Lower Manhattan is presented in Table 6.2 (Saul, 2000).

The Lower Manhattan Mental Health Providers Group, sponsored by the Mental Health Association of New York, was attended by representatives and directors of various mental health clinics and community organizations that provided mental health services. The meetings were also attended by members of the NYC Department of Health, who made recommendations about the kinds of services that Project Liberty should support. People working with or representing community members could converse with policymakers about mental health service decisions; this setting was a prime example of mesosystem support

Funding generated by Project Liberty was first directed to existing licensed mental health clinics capable of providing one-on-one therapy by licensed practitioners. We soon discovered that these clinics had enough funding and resources to provide therapy, yet relatively few people utilized the clinics. Despite being located in Lower Manhattan, these clinics lacked effective means to reach out to community members and advertise their services because most of the practitioners were not from the community. In parts of Lower Manhattan, social workers went door-to-door to speak to people, give information, and spread awareness of available mental health support services. Simultaneously, community members working to address psychological and social concerns within their own networks found themselves lacking resources and exhausted. Community member volunteer work requires a different model of funding. As co-leader of the providers group, I was struck by this disconnect between the funded clinical one-on-one services and the needs of community members who were disinclined to seek therapeutic services but instead were looking to engage with non-stigmatizing activities to promote their emotional well-being. An idea emerged to fund community members' outreach and community-based recovery efforts, a win–win proposition for both the community and clinical services. This funding support could simultaneously help reticent community members find a pathway to services and provide referrals for those who needed professional counseling and therapy. Community members were more likely to recognize people in their network who were suffering and give them the appropriate aid. This notion led the Ground Zero Community Initiative to seek funding from the city for our community resilience efforts and for development of a physical space to promote community-run activities: a community resource center.

TABLE 6.2 A MULTISYSTEMS MAP OF POST-9/11 LOWER MANHATTAN (SAUL, 2000)

Multi-systemic levels map: Terrorist Attacks – New York City – 9/11/2001

Systemic Level	Traumatic Event(s) Impact (Severity and Duration)	Protective Factors Resources and Resiliency	Symbolization and Narrative System	Problematic Reactions to Event(s) and Long-term Sequelae	Interventions and Prevention
Biological System • physical • nervous system • endocrine	Death, injury, central nervous system response, respiratory reactions to toxic air and dust	Levels of physical fitness, and health, youth, stress inoculation, mind–body–spirit practices	Somatic expression, dreams	Somatic symptoms, respiratory and health problems	Pharmacological agents, mind–body–spirit regulatory practices and intervention, physical self-care
Individual Psychological System • cognitions • emotions • behavior • relations	Loss, insecurity, disruption of routine and role, fear and anxiety, dissociation, sense of altered time	Personality and coping skills, identity, self-image, cognitive skills, relational behavior, affect regulation	Recall and constructions of dreams and intrusive memories, and multiple personal meanings	Anxiety, depression, acute stress symptoms, PTSD, grief reactions, aggression and suicidality, alcohol and substance abuse	Individual counseling and therapy, stress-relieving interventions, psychoeducation, enhancing intrinsic strengths, facilitation of post-traumatic growth, psychological and emotional self-care, recreational, physical and artistic activities
Social Systems • family and intimate relations • natural support system—local community—church, neighborhood, school, work, other groups • ethnic/national/global • ancillary support system—emergency; hospital, welfare	Separation and loss, change in relational behavior and bonding, stress on family and other social groups, displacement, disruption of role and routine, increased connectedness and bonding, communication breakdown, media response, activation of ancillary support system	Family support, competence of natural supports, community organization and support, history of family and community, community self-mobilization, organization and support, national and international support, ancillary support	Collective narration with family friends, neighborhood and community, national and global narratives	Disruption of family life cycle, neighborhood relations, flight from city and severing of social attachments, displacement of families and work organizations, stress due to loss of income, housing, employment, intrusion of ancillary support systems	Family, group, and network counseling and therapy, mobilization and facilitation of natural support systems by ancillary support systems, peer support networks, building on long-term preventive groups and methods, organizing community forums; enhancing social connectedness for communication, problem solving and resource accessing

Cultural Systems • meaning systems • knowledge systems • language and symbols • identity • rituals and practices	Shattered world assumptions, sense of invulnerability and safety	Creation of rituals, religious and spiritual solace, patriotism, sources of coherent worldview, arts and literature	Interpretation of collective narration, of old and new rituals, contextualizing and memorializing, creation of new symbols, 9/11 as a temporal marker	Increasing rigidity and resort to primitive belief systems, discriminatory responses to Arab and Muslim minorities	Changing cultural belief systems from vulnerability to resilience, facilitation of new rituals and practices focused on communal grieving, revitalization, and conciliation, cultural legacy and mission
Eco-systemic Environment • physical and natural world • economic and political context	Environmental destruction and hazard, mobilization of rhetoric	Economic and political resources, physical and environmental resources	Impact of environmental, economic, and political change on symbolic systems	Disruption of utilities, transportation, and communication, exaggerated political responses (Patriot Act and curtailment of civil rights)	Clean-up of environment, plan for reconstruction, war on terrorism, pre-emptive strikes

The Downtown Community Resource Center

In the winter of 2002, we held a community meeting in an art gallery on Reade Street in Tribeca on a very rainy evening. Dr. Landau, the consultant on our downtown project, was a guest speaker at this meeting aimed at promoting community resilience in Lower Manhattan. An installation covered an entire floor of the gallery, and we had to place our chairs around the art pieces and do our best not to step on the art itself. We essentially became part of the installation.

Not many people showed up because of the torrential rain, but we were joined by the Deputy Commissioner of Health, Lloyd Sederer, and his associate, Kelly Ryan, at the Department of Health, who was closely following the work that we were doing. During this meeting we had the opportunity to bring community members together for a discussion. Dr. Sederer's presence conveyed the city's openness to promoting preventive community-based mental health programs. At the time, community members were looking to address needs identified in the community assessments gathered during the school forums in December 2001 and January 2002.

Dr. Claude Chemtob and I requested funding from Jack Rosenthal of the New York Times Foundation to create a Downtown Community Resource Center on the West Side for the neighborhoods of Tribeca, the Financial District, and Battery Park City. Our proposition was based on information from the needs assessment, in which people asked for a space that would be a focal point for people to get information and access resources. We also advocated that the East Side of Lower Manhattan set up a resource center, and invited the director of the Hamilton-Madison Community Mental Health Center, which ran programs in Chinatown, to create something similar in those neighborhoods.

We met at the office of Madeline Wills, chair of Community Board One of Lower Manhattan, to present our idea of what a resource center could accomplish. The director of Hamilton-Madison also spoke about the importance of the project to promote mental health services. As a result of the meeting, Jack Rosenthal awarded us grants to create resource centers on both the Lower West and East Sides. Hamilton-Madison eventually set up the Chinatown Resource Center (CRC), which provided information on entitlements and economic compensation, as well as information about emotional reactions to 9/11 and resources to address psychosocial needs.

The CRC was a focal point of Hamilton-Madison's effort to meet the psychological, economic, and social needs of area residents, workers, and businesses that were affected by 9/11. The Center worked to empower the community and to promote its recovery through a holistic approach by offering behavioral health services, consultation, education, workshops, and advocacy.

Based on the previous needs assessment, our West Side center took shape: the center's programs and activities were initiated and developed by community members and a small group of center staff supported their efforts by providing space, stipends, administrative support, technical assistance, and funding development.

With a green light from the New York Times Foundation, we hired a managing director—Carol Prendergast, a human rights attorney with experience working with communities affected by trauma. She negotiated with the city in more concrete financial terms about support for a downtown community resource center. New York University would act as the center's financial conduit. At first, we at ITSP worked closely with Project Liberty to come up with a proposal, and by the summer of 2002 Project Liberty decided to give us a contract to develop a community resource center on the Lower West side.

We were involved in the process of writing and re-writing the contract from September 2002 through February 2003. This presented a challenge: the structure of funding post-disaster mental health services was based on a supportive counseling model. Our project was about promoting community development and facilitating community-run recovery projects. As this process dragged on, we became concerned that it was taking attention away from the momentum of community members' voluntary spirit and their interest to develop the resource center. We kept putting them on hold as we waited for the contract to go through.

By the fall of 2002, we began to feel that we had lost our drive. In the meantime we were searching for a space for the resource center. One year after 9/11, it was still possible to get a space in Tribeca in which rent was not too exorbitant. We identified a space on Reade Street, a street-level storefront loft, ideal because of its visibility and accessibility to neighbors from all three of the West Side communities. It was also ideal in that it had a space that was large enough for community meetings, with additional room for informational, classroom, and other meeting spaces. An architect from the community drew up a plan to transform this long-vacant spot. Ms. Prendergast located the landlord, living in Hong Kong, who was willing to support the center by making the space available for a minimal rent.

However, when the funding finally came through in March 2003, we ran into unexpected red tape. Despite our contract that assured funding for the year, New York University decided not to take on the responsibility of signing the lease. As a result, we had to drastically adjust the vision for our resource center. Our services were relocated to university offices, quite a distance from the community and not as readily accessible. We were no longer able to have a physical presence in the community, but instead had to operate like a community foundation to promote our community resilience. The goals of the Downtown Community Resource Center were:

- To recognize and strengthen existing skills, resources, and resilience in the community;
- To enhance connectedness in families, neighborhoods, organizations, and occupational groups;
- To promote mental and physical wellness in youth, adults, and families; and
- To create forums for public discourse and the expression of the multiplicity of community voices, viewpoints, and histories.

Five weeks after we received funding in March, along with the 80 other funded organizations around the city, Project Liberty told us that we only had until the end of August 2003 to carry out our work. Our long journey had come to a frustrating end. In hindsight, many community members involved with the project felt that if they had known that it would take so long to negotiate a six-month contract, they would have used their own private funding and better focused energies elsewhere. There has yet to be an assessment of the enormous cost to the 80 programs that had a similar experience or an explanation of where tens of millions of dollars to support these projects ended up. Nevertheless, we got ourselves in gear to implement the projects proposed by community members, although they would be cut short. The community members chose two types of programs to pursue—those that focused on peer and family support, and those that developed public sites for narrating and hosting conversations about their concerns, their experiences as a consequence of 9/11, and what those experiences meant.

Challenges in Promoting Collective Resilience

After Hurricane Katrina caused widespread devastation along the central Gulf Coast in 2005, I met with Dr. Saliha Bava, a family systems therapist who had worked to provide community-engaged services to the displaced population that had moved to Houston. We discovered similar challenges in implementing a "community resilience" approach following massive trauma. In a joint article we highlighted a number of common themes from our respective contexts (Saul & Bava, 2009; Bava & Saul, 2013). Among the most salient were:

Tensions in clinical and community approaches: A clinical approach can be distinguished from an ecosystemic or community approach in that it focuses almost exclusively on the individual as the client and offers services. In a post-disaster context, this can be easily stigmatizing, People tend not to want to be identified as having a mental health problem, severely limiting the range of possibilities for healing. Frequently, clinical services are not specifically oriented to the stated needs of clients, but to the services the clinicians are interested in providing. The clinical approach puts a greater emphasis on enhancing the expertise of the providers and less attention on enhancing the competence of community members to recognize and find their own solutions. A clinical approach often pays little attention to the communal or relational nature of their difficulties.

In the ecosystemic, or community approach, the client is the social environment and the focus is on strengths, resources, and continuity of the community. One of the most important assumptions of this approach is that communities have the capacity to heal themselves and that the greatest resources for recovery are the community members themselves. The most effective activities are often those in which community members are already engaged, and thus non-stigmatizing. The connections between people may be enhanced, and as we have recognized both internationally and in New York, the communities themselves become the sites for sharing information, expressing emotion, and providing mutual support (Fullilove & Saul, 2006).

One of the common themes in our work was that we continuously had to explain the collective/community perspective to mental health practitioners, city agencies, funding organizations, and the media. In the years following 9/11, there appeared to be greater acceptance of community approaches, as well as an emphasis on promoting strengths and resources. However, the changes seemed more rhetorical than conceptual or concerned with implementation. There is certainly now a greater willingness to explore how individual clinical approaches, both pathology- and resilience-oriented, can be implemented in the context of broader social interventions that highlight engagement and collective resiliency. And there is a greater utilization of approaches after major trauma and disaster that address mental health needs in the context of family and community interventions (see Walsh, 2007; Boss, 2004; Fraenkel, Hamelin, & Shannon, 2009).

Insider and Outsider expertise and competing agendas: The IASC Guidelines recognize that an "affected community can be overwhelmed by outsiders, and local contributions to mental health and psychosocial support are easily marginalized or undermined" (Inter-Agency Standing Committee, 2007, p. 33). A community resilience approach requires the systematic identification of the various adaptive capacities of members within the affected communities. The process of recognizing local expertise enhances the resilience of the local population during disasters. There is an additional need to develop frameworks for working with displaced and disenfranchised communities, rendered further voiceless as a result of the break-up of their customary social networks. Bava raised a concern: since there are competing agendas in a post-disaster context, who keeps an eye on what is needed by the impacted communities? Landau's framework provides an alternative: the community rather than a single entity keeps the agenda accountable to the people.

In the LINC model, all parts of the community have to be present. But such a model was challenged by Katrina, as the community was displaced to multiple locations. Dr. Bava asked: "Who will bring all those people in? Such a practice is both resource- and time-consuming, especially in the aftermath of dislocation and in the midst of response when the individual family agenda might trump the community agenda" (Saul & Bava, 2009). But even in a non-displaced and well-resourced community like post-9/11 Lower Manhattan, outside forces could have potentially rendered us voiceless.

Another challenge faced in both the 9/11 and Katrina efforts to promote community resilience was having to answer to an accountability framework that required counting heads, i.e. face-to-face contacts, rather than tracking indicators of positive social processes. This mismatch between funding requirements and the basic principles of a resilience approach diverts attention and resources away from services and more appropriate evaluative measures. For a more comprehensive discussion of challenges to promoting community resilience see Saul and Bava (2009) and Bava and Saul (2013).

Four Themes in Community Resilience and Recovery

When it comes to effecting change, research has shown that community members are five times more powerful than outside providers. Local knowledge, combined with pre-existing resources and social networks, gives community members advantages in identifying efficient ways to have a meaningful impact. Driven by the community members' own priorities and preferences, programs are more likely to successfully build solidarity that is crucial to enacting sustainable programming.

Providers from within the community are often best suited to provide the most adequate framework to promote supportive social processes. Community-focused providers help connect new constituencies and enrich pre-existing resources for recovery. Mental health professionals often find it challenging to accept that, when disaster strikes, they are not the only help on the scene, or even necessarily the most important. On the road to psychosocial recovery, mental health professionals are but one resource among many.

Community members inherently possess a wide variety of skills to aid in the healing process. A diverse range of ages, occupations, and talents provide a distinct opportunity for healing that would be difficult to find in any single mental health provider organization. The recovery process in this context takes on synergistic properties, organically combining expertise to creatively process trauma as a group.

In the process of recovery, community resilience approaches address multiple levels and themes. Many trauma programs, however, focus their efforts too narrowly on the individual while overlooking larger networks in the community, such as family and work groups.

On occasion, the aftermath of a traumatic event may cause more harm than the event itself. Social fragmentation at work and school, and the ensuing conflict, was more painful and destabilizing for many New York City residents than the events of September 11 itself, for instance.

The following four themes are typical of a community resilience and recovery approach following massive psychosocial trauma: (Saul, 2007):

Building community and enhancing social connectedness. The core of community recovery, in this case, is rebuilding previously held connections and forging new ones. Dr. Landau refers to this as the "matrix of healing." Social networks disrupted by traumatic events find new incarnations as they become bolstered by information sharing and social support.

Collectively telling the story of the community's experience and response. One integral step to recovery is public acknowledgment, and therefore validation of, the communal story experienced by the survivors. Affirmation of a broad range of experiences is the most helpful for healing. Too narrow a perspective can marginalize members of the community and be damaging to the community at large. After 9/11, we saw evidence of this phenomenon when Arab and Muslim communities were discriminated against despite being deeply affected by the same tragedy. Their voices were pushed out of the collective narrative, and their experiences were deemed "invalid" as a result.

Re-establishing the rhythms and routines of life and engaging in collective healing rituals. Holidays and other annual events take on new meanings as community members must process feelings of loss during previously routine occurrences. These events present ideal opportunities to reconnect. One of the most important modalities for promoting collective recovery is that of a festival. A party-like event in the time of tragedy may allow for soothing and inspiring interactions and help people re-envision their way of living together (Fullilove & Hernandez-Cordero, 2006).

Arriving at a positive vision of the future with renewed hope. In the face of tragedy, communities ask themselves how to move forward. Many community-wide responses to 9/11 involved efforts to shape a positive, yet realistic future while wrestling with the troubling past.

The following chapter highlights several different collective responses that helped groups build community and re-establish hope for the future in the wake of disaster.

7

Community Initiated Recovery Activities

In the months following September 11, people naturally came together to address the needs of their neighbors and created support networks around shared activities and interests. The Downtown Community Resource Center facilitated a number of local projects by offering both structure and support. This chapter presents four community initiatives that evolved in Lower Manhattan: a tenants' organization that responded to the needs of vulnerable neighbors; a samba drumming and dance school for community youth; group support meetings for journalists; and a network of artists that met in each others' studios and developed into an international exchange project.

Neighbor to Neighbor

It just so happened that I had some keys to a house on the East Side, so we went down to the lobby with our cats and assorted animals and I look over and I see a bunch of tenants all huddled together, especially the senior citizens.... You know, a lot of people had nowhere to go. And I said to myself, "I can't leave." And then ... it was not like me before this, I always considered myself a follower ... I took over, and everyone agreed: Diane is in charge.

We had to fight for everything, food.... At times I thought I couldn't beg anymore, and then I'd be sitting in one of the tenant's apartments and the carpet is polluted and she's having trouble breathing and she would say, "I just took my last heart pill." I was at a meeting every single night: respiratory studies, the environmental EPA. ... You know what it's like when something like that explodes, the PCBs from the computers and the fluorescent lights. For God's sake, it was anarchy ... bureaucracy

... but I held off and I fought for the living and I challenged the system.

From "Everything's Back to Normal in New York City," Downtown Theater Group

Prior to 9/11, the Independence Plaza North Tenants Association (IPNTA) had organized an emergency action committee to identify the building's neediest and most capable residents in the event of an emergency. The former category included young children, senior citizens, the disabled, and those who needed life support medication. The latter were people such as doctors, nurses, architects, and mental health professionals. They collected each person's telephone number, and everyone had the number for the committee leader whom they would contact if an evacuation became necessary. At the time, they had no idea they would one day face an emergency that would require the evacuation of not only their building, but also the entire neighborhood. Diane Lapson and John Scott, two IPNTA leaders, took an active role in coordinating a community response to 9/11. What they and their organization exemplified was that in crises, "people naturally want to help each other, and that effective emergency preparation maximizes the benefits of this spirit of action" (IPNTA, 2003, p. 2).

The Independence Plaza Towers, just a few blocks north of the World Trade Center, comprise three 39-story buildings housing more than 1,500 families. Built in the early 1970s, this affordable housing complex is home to an ethnically and economically diverse population that has contributed significantly to the character of the vibrant and tight-knit Lower Manhattan neighborhood of Tribeca. During the weeks and months following 9/11, many people felt that the removal of debris from Ground Zero took precedence over recovery for the more than 35,000 local residents whose lives had been deeply disrupted. Fortunately, few Lower Manhattan residents suffered casualties, though the deaths of several local firemen were intensely felt. Nevertheless, community members often expressed in the first few months that there seemed to be more concern with the dead than with the living. Trucks transporting debris from Ground Zero to landfill barges traveled back and forth all day and all night. This constant rumbling of heavy trucks, loaded with seemingly endless remains of the catastrophe, exacerbated the stress of those unable to leave the neighborhood. The polluted air agitated in the removal process settled into people's lungs and apartments, and residents who hired their own investigators quickly discovered that the government had misled them about the toxicity in the environment downtown.

Recovery efforts were geared toward getting the site cleaned up and the financial sector employees back to work as quickly as possible. One Plaza North resident remarked that while senior citizens in their buildings were hungry and unable to secure enough food, an abundance of food was stored nearby for recovery workers. Neighborhood residents recognized early on that they would have to take full responsibility for their own needs and well-being, as the city provided them little to no support. Outside relief organizations like the American Red Cross eventually delivered some relief, but it was more effective for community members to take an active role in their own recovery than to wait for aid deliveries. Small groups of parents, residents, and others mobilized to address the most pressing needs they identified, and through this process exhibited a newfound capacity for leadership. In the wake of the disaster, they were forced to call upon their own resources and internal coping capacities.

As the months passed, the residents of Independence Plaza North realized it was important to assess and reflect on their community's response. They wanted to spread the word about what had and had not worked for them, and hopefully thereby provide a resource for other communities facing crisis and emergency. "Community is key," they said, "even long after difficult events." In the spring of 2003, the Downtown Community Resource Center helped the IPNTA tell their story. They worked together to create a pamphlet titled "Neighbor to Neighbor: The Downtown Solution, IPNTA's Guide to Community Healing" (Independence Plaza Tenants' Association, 2003). The pamphlet was printed and 5,000 copies were distributed in neighborhoods throughout New York City and around the country.

The process of acknowledging, concretizing, and sharing the community's response through the pamphlet enhanced the Plaza North residents' collective strength. They were able to teach others what they had learned. They also recognized the collective resilience they had displayed as a community, and how that resilience had come from capacities for organization, reconnection, and reconciliation within their own group. In producing the "Neighbor to Neighbor" pamphlet, they constructed a story of their resilience and told it in a way that would be helpful to others. They showed that a great resource for that resilience is simply being prepared: knowing who lived in their community, where they lived, and what needs and what resources they possessed was an invaluable asset. That kind of neighborhood information would have been extremely difficult to gather in the wake of 9/11, but without it the group's organizational efforts to support itself would have been severely diminished.

The collective response to 9/11 also helped prepare the Plaza North residents for a community threat they faced a few years later, when developers who owned the Independence Plaza Towers decided to end rent stabilization. By raising rents to market value, they threatened to displace the entire neighborhood, and with it the tightly knit community created across decades and solidified in the aftermath of 9/11. The developers knew that if rents were raised, most tenants could not afford to stay. Personal profit was pitted starkly against community interests. Studies of urban renewal show that dispersal and destruction—the loss of schools, friends, business relations, acquaintances; all of the relational strands that make up a neighborhood—is one of the most devastating instances of collective trauma, affecting entire populations for up to decades afterwards (Fullilove, 2004). The exploitation of traumatized populations following disaster is not uncommon, as they are often pushed out to make way for new development and reconstruction. The battle to protect affordable housing in Independence Plaza is still going on in 2012, and it may be that the leadership and collective resilience shown after 9/11 has given them the necessary resources to fight for their neighborhood's survival.

Battery Drumline: The Healing Power of Samba

A group of youths in yellow shirts stood in a clearing in Central Park. Among them small groups formed, each section with different musical instruments: tamborims, surdos, agogos. They were 20 percussionists in all, with ten dancers in the front. They stood in silence until Curtis, the group leader, played a beat on his drum. He played a solo call pattern, and suddenly the group of kids erupted: the jam session took off, the call-and-response pattern of student and teacher producing undeniable dance rhythms that drew people from all over the park. The group was the Battery Drumline, and they were having a samba session in the park.

The founder of Battery Drumline, Polar Levine, is a musician and graphic artist whose son was a student at PS 234. Curtis Watts, the head teacher, is a musician from the South Bronx. Both are native New Yorkers who met in the 1980s while studying Brazilian samba music in the city. In 2003, Curtis needed a replacement drum teacher for a summer camp he organized. He felt that Polar was the best person for the job. Polar loved it, feeling he had a particular gift for communicating with the kids, thinking like them, and motivating them. He had coached his son's Little League baseball team, experience he used to develop a highly engaged coaching style. He wanted to translate this into the drumming class, which he thought would be a particularly positive experience for the kids in coping with the tremendous stress they had experienced after 9/11. The towers had been only a few blocks from their school.

Polar knew that the school had been making a conscious effort to provide safe spaces for the students and their parents to talk about what had happened, but he wanted to create a space where they could engage in an activity that was not focused on the World Trade Center attacks. "It seemed like a good idea to have them resonate around something else that would be less self-conscious," Polar explained. He wanted the class's activity to focus not on the tragic events, but on learning to make music, on being part of a group, and on being attentive to other group members and group leaders. He believed it would build character. In 2003, with minimal funding from a Downtown Community Resource Center through a Project Liberty Grant, Polar and Curtis started the Battery Drumline.

The first meetings took place in the cafeteria of PS 234, and consisted largely of Polar's Little League team. Within weeks word had spread, and the group grew to 20 drummers and ten dancers. Meetings moved to a bigger space at the Borough of Manhattan Community College, and the kids were expected to show up on time, in uniform, and ready to work. Keeping up an energy of heightened excitement was critical to Drumline, Polar explained:

> As I used to tell the kids when we were playing ball, nothing else mattered. It was serious play. You are a ballplayer, and when you're a ballplayer, nothing else matters but winning the game. And then when it's over, you let it go.

At Battery Drumline, the jam sessions were serious. When they were playing music, the only thing that mattered was getting the audience to move. The students learned to follow and pay attention to complex rhythms, and to see themselves as serious percussionists with a deep dedication to their music.

When coaching Little League, Polar had used a blog and mass emails to give the kids feedback after games and practices. They would receive encouraging public acknowledgments for the things they were doing well, as well as gentle constructive criticisms for the things that could be done better. He would make a phone call to parents only if there was something particularly serious that needed discussion. Polar used the same feedback structure for the Drumline, and, as in Little League, helped foster the development of mutual expectations among the kids, and kept the parents involved in the process. Parental involvement was critical. Parents supported the practice sessions by transporting instruments, bringing snacks, and confiding in Polar if they had any concerns. Communication channels within the group were open and supportive, and this created a safe community space where relationships could be constructively explored and strengthened. For example, one mother was feeling disconnected from her son, concerned that he might have Asperger's. She went to Polar for help, who worked with the boy slowly and supportively, and realized the problem was not severe. It could be tempered, and through drumming practice and social support the boy became less self-conscious and more communicative. His mother credits Polar and the Battery Drumline with her son's transformation.

Even though the music program provided a safe space, Drumline was never about taking things easy. Playing samba, and playing it well, demanded tremendous discipline and character. The practice space, the practice time, the group members and leaders, and the instruments themselves, had to be respected. Polar and Curtis's goal was to use music to bring the kids into themselves, but that required a dedicated and rigorous process. Playing samba requires a kind of double-attentiveness where musicians listen closely to their neighbors in order to maintain rhythm while simultaneously playing their own independent pieces. In Brazil, samba is an especially important activity for the youth because it is both a form of discipline and an opportunity to engage as part of the community. Samba has many meanings in Brazil, and in a country divided by extreme social and economic inequality it has become a mode of resistance, a way of maintaining dignity in the face of crushing poverty. It also carries deep connections to Brazilian spirituality and history.

But even without this cultural backdrop, New York City kids experienced samba as something intensely visceral. It was a transformational experience, the core of which Polar explained was based in the universal connectivity that comes from playing intensely rhythmic music as part of a group. He explains that playing well requires "total engagement that puts you in communication with the universe. There's nothing else that can do that, it's a transcendent kind of experience." The transformative quality comes from creating a structure in which the kids can be highly attentive participants of the group, such that they are in tune with their own bodies as well as the bodies of others during the collaborative process of music making. As Polar explains it, when you play samba, you feel your body connected to the body of the group. During intense playing, people actually feel the sound waves of the rhythms and find that their bodies respond in unpredictable ways. If you are listening to everyone in the group, then your whole body is going to feel and be part of the experience. And when the musicians feel it, the dancers feel it; and when the whole group feels it, the audience feels it. The group knows it is playing good samba when people simply cannot help themselves from dancing.

When a community has experienced intense traumatic stress, people tend to be constricted in their minds, in their bodies, and in their relationships. Samba's power in this context is that it can free the mind and body from this constriction via phenomenological physical experience. The Battery Drumline was a powerful outlet for the adolescents living in downtown Manhattan in that it promoted movement, concentration, flexibility, and attention to others. This kind of creative, physical practice is a powerful antidote to trauma and has the potential to enhance both individual and collective resilience. The attunement to body and others that samba practice bolstered may be similar to other body-oriented techniques, like yoga, that have been found to be effective in reducing the symptoms of traumatic stress in communities who have weathered disaster or crisis.

Battery Drumline continued for about three years, and at one time functioned as a non-profit organization. They kicked off the Tribeca Film Festival, were named "New Yorker of the Week" on local Channel 1, and they performed at The Knitting Factory for *Time Out* NY. They were also featured in the city's Halloween parade for two years, where they played and danced for the hundreds of thousands of spectators lining the Avenue of the Americas. When asked if he would do anything different, Polar says that everything they hoped would happen, happened. His greatest influence on the project was to provide an understanding of where the kids were coming from, and a dedicated sense of where he wanted to bring them. With his devoted guidance, the kids far exceeded any expectations; they blew their audience away every time. And as Polar would laughingly tell them, "The score at the end of the game is how many asses are moving, that's how you know you've won."

Supporting Journalists as First Responders

Less than two weeks after September 11, David Hanschuh, a friend and photographer for the *New York Daily News*, called me to see if I would meet with a group of journalists and photographers. For this group, many of them freelance and international reporters, the experience of covering 9/11 had been traumatic, exhausting, and isolating. The handful that worked under the umbrella of mainstream news teams had something that resembled a support system, but even they described feeling overworked and mentally strung out. They needed a space to come together and share their experiences, but their community was dispersed after the crises, and many had not even identified their needs. They had covered trauma and given themselves as witnesses to narrate the trauma of others, but had not taken a moment to assess their own psychological state. No one was providing the resources to help them do that. After David called me, I gathered a few of my colleagues and we set out for the meeting to listen, to learn, and, we hoped, to help.

My interest in working with journalists began earlier, when I was the clinical director of the NYU/Bellevue Program for the Survivors of Torture. I discovered through working with this population that survivors felt a powerful need to tell their stories. One rarely reads about torture survivors living in New York City, despite the huge number of immigrants and refugees who are reckoning with traumatic histories. I invited some journalists to Bellevue to speak with therapists and other staff in the program, with the hope that we might come up with innovative ways to raise awareness about the experience of this unseen population. It struck me that journalists, with their skill for telling and representing stories to the public, could play an important role in my patients' recovery.

We gradually began to see journalists taking an interest in covering the stories of refugees who had been tortured. As mental health professionals, we recognized that working with people who had been through violent traumatic situations had had a strong emotional impact on us as caregivers, and we wanted to make sure the journalists were prepared to cope with the vicarious traumatic reactions they might experience. In my work on human rights, I had seen that it could actually be detrimental to both the survivor and the reporting process if a journalist did not effectively manage his or her own emotional reactions. I felt it was important to address this in the collaborative process taking place at Bellevue.

I first met David at the International Society for Traumatic Stress Studies (ISTSS) Annual Conference. We worked together teaching at a fellowship program for journalists sponsored by the DART Center for Journalism and Trauma. The DART Center was founded at Michigan State University in 1991 as a small program to support journalism students who were reporting on victims of violence. In the early stages, the program collaborated with the Michigan Victim Alliance and Dr. Frank Ochberg, a prominent psychiatrist in the trauma field who had been instrumental in the early identification and classification of PTSD. Ochberg was conscious of the need for journalists to be better equipped to deal with traumatic reactions. They needed to be better informed about the experiences of their informants, as well as the experiences to which they would be personally vulnerable in the circumstances of their reporting. He understood that journalists could play a very important role in identifying traumatic stress reactions, in directing traumatized individuals toward resources, but also in potentially exacerbating the stressful experience of the survivor if not adequately trained.

The meeting of journalists and photographers that David organized after 9/11 was a valuable opportunity to foster the kind of interdisciplinary support system that had been pioneered at the DART Center. The meeting took place at one of the usual hangouts for New York reporters and photojournalists. It was understood that the event would be casual: a handful of therapists and a group of wearied journalists taking an evening to put the trauma of the past two weeks on pause, to decompress, and just share a drink. My fellow therapists and I would mingle, and where desired and appropriate, could provide information to the group about dealing with traumatic events and experiencing stress reactions. When we arrived, it was clear that the journalists were enjoying the congregation, needing a respite from the barrage of 9/11 itself and the seemingly endless stream of funerals that followed. The majority had not stopped reporting since the attack, and the weight of death and dying pervasive in every story was taking its toll.

David, who was on crutches after being injured by falling debris while trying to report at Ground Zero, made an introductory speech, which was followed by a few comments from my colleagues and myself about traumatic stress and ways of taking care of oneself. The next few hours were spent conversing with the journalists, photographers, and the handful of editorial managers who had come to learn more about what they could do to support their staff. I was struck by how many of them were eager to talk and share their experiences with us, their emotional vulnerability perhaps being mediated by the comforts of compassion and a cold beer. I talked to people like Todd Maisel, a photographer for the *Daily News* who said:

> It was a horrific day, when many people saw their friends lose their lives. Body parts were on the ground, along with pieces of airplane and luggage ... lungs filled with an unforgettable taste and smell. A firefighter was fatally hit by something that turned out to be a body.... But he saved all of those around him, because we realized we needed to move back from the towers.

Another journalist told me she had been covering two or three funerals a day, and each time relived the pain of her own 9/11 experience, in addition to witnessing the grief of yet another family.

These journalists expressed feeling like they had little time to deal with what had happened. The demands of their profession kept them constantly moving, witnesses to other people's experiences, and they had no quiet moments in which to reflect on what had happened to them. I was struck by the variable degree of sensitivity demonstrated by the journalists' organizations: some responded to their staff's emotional needs, while others seemed unaware of the need for these journalists to take a break. More than anything, this gathering of journalists, editors, photographers, and mental health professionals demonstrated a deep need for this kind of conversational space, and that such a space was lacking, with potentially dire consequences for the well-being of the exhausted reporters. This collaboration helped shed light on the fact that journalists needed to be able to communicate with other journalists and to talk collectively about their highly stressful experiences, so that they might find sustenance in understanding and sharing.

After this first informal meeting we organized two more. The next was aimed at giving people a safe space to comment on sources of support in their professional community, and to identify without possible repercussion what was and was not working. Bruce Shapiro, the head of the DART Center, gave an introduction followed by Carol Prendergast, our center's managing director, and then by therapist Liz Margolies and myself. Next, Adam Lisberg, a staff journalist at New Jersey's *The Record* who had helped David organize the events, stood up and addressed his peers:

> The response has been amazing.... Look around you. We've published this for barely ten days very haphazardly, and still dozens of people are here. We think it's proof of what we've long suspected, that the people who covered September 11 still think a lot about what they saw and what they went through ... that we have a lot on our minds and not enough chances to talk about it. That's why we're here.

Adam went on to define the meeting as "a safe space to talk openly." He explained to the group:

> We want to hear what's on people's minds, not just about that day, but about what support we got or didn't get from our bosses, how

it's changed what we do. We want this to be a place where you can admit that you don't like covering stories in Lower Manhattan anymore, or that you can't stand taking picture of people in pain anymore, or that you sometimes think you're the only person who still thinks about it every day.

Therapists were present as a resource, but they did not run the event. "We have some therapists here who have studied how people react to traumatic events," Adam explained. "They're here to listen and learn, and if you want, they can offer some thoughts on how other people have reacted to other traumas in different situations. Nothing was normal about September 11, so no reaction is wrong."

Most importantly, Adam emphasized that the gathering was private and protected:

We want to be very clear on this point: this gathering is off the record. Maybe it's a little ironic to tell that to a room full of journalists, but we want people to participate and talk honestly, without worrying how it might sound to the world at large.

He then gave the floor to David, who framed his colleagues' psychological responses in the context of their profession. The culture of journalism "forbid[s] us from talking openly about how we are affected by the stories we cover," he said. "We are entitled to have emotions, we are entitled to grieve and recover, and we need to know that our newsroom culture, our managers and employers, will support us as we wrestle with all types of new challenges." The goal of the evening was to get a sense of what journalists needed.

David put forward several questions that were later compiled and distributed as a survey, and opened the floor to the journalists. The questions asked them to reflect on their experiences, on what they might have done differently, and what advice they might give to other journalists going into a crisis situation. He asked them if they felt they had received support from their editors and directors, and what they felt they still needed. After the open discussion, the journalists broke into small groups, with a mental health professional and note taker in each. The questions here were more focused on the future, on what could be done to improve support for journalists going forward. In these groups they generated ideas about what could be done as a community, and about what format new interventions might take. After 15 minutes the large group reassembled to share their thoughts, and, significantly, the discussion centered largely on how the journalists could define and harness their strength as a community. After that, the organized event ended, but many people lingered to have another drink and continue the conversation. On their way out, there were handouts available for the DART Center and other mental health services.

Our second large meeting (and third meeting altogether) was held on September 4, 2003. We hoped this might help journalists process any feelings that might surface in response to the two-year anniversary, and also to see how the sense of solidarity and community among them had developed. Familiar faces were present: David, Adam, my colleagues and myself, but the crowd had grown significantly. One of the most impassioned speakers at this meeting was Gabe Pressman, the president of the New York Press Club Foundation and the chairman of the Freedom of the Press Committee. He spoke candidly and critically about the restrictions placed on journalists after 9/11, emphasizing the importance of the fraternity among journalists in the face of institutional restraint. In the wake of 9/11, they faced a new obstacle: Mayor Giuliani's suppressive administration and the restriction of the site below Canal Street. Journalists were being denied access, and government officials were providing only minimal coverage, most of which focused on interviews with the mayor. For Pressman it had become an issue of democracy, and he called on his colleagues to defend the freedom of the press, and together to do the job they needed to do for the citizens of New York City.

This meeting contained many echoes of the previous one, and the survey data collected two years earlier showed that many reporters, especially the independent freelance writers, really had no formal support system, but only a few colleagues they could talk to. Yet they all expressed that simply having someone to talk to—to talk about the experience of being covered in pulverized glass that grated like sandpaper and would not wipe off; to talk about conflicting feelings when asked to write yet another story on a victim's family—that just having someone to talk to was what got them through the day. In pursuit of their profession, journalists give themselves over to the narratives of others. They write stories, express voices, and become the conduit for human experience so the public can keep abreast of the wraiths that threaten it, stay informed about the actions of its government, and exercise its legal right to knowledge and transparency. The journalist connects the individual narrative to society at large, and, in doing so, surfaces a civil narrative to which we all can and must relate.

To do this, they put themselves in harm's way more frequently than is effectively acknowledged. The cultural romance of the journalistic endeavor persists undaunted, but the experience of physical and emotional danger, of trauma when all that is taken for granted as social reality begins to collapse, is the moment in which journalists most need and often are lacking adequate support. The journalist seeks to capture moments of social upheaval to ensure that the public does not lose touch with the events. The journalist seeks to render readable the incomprehensible, and in doing so throws himself into the crucible of social dissolution. For thousands of people, the world fell apart on September 11, and journalists on the scene that day were in many ways first responders. They were not medics or firefighters or police officers, but they were among the first witnesses, ready to collect the shards of humanity being blown to pieces by an angry world.

One of the most important lessons of September 11 is that journalists need to be trained and treated as first responders. When disaster strikes, they are there. They come in to tell the story, to witness what is happening, and they come very close to the danger themselves. Those that covered September 11 realized they were not adequately equipped to be in a disaster situation. They did not know how to assess the real physical risk when they were running up to buildings as debris rained down. They need to be trained to administer first aid, to accurately gauge physical danger in the moment, and to read the traumatic potential of a crisis situation. Being prepared in this way will help journalists write better stories about their subjects, and take better care of themselves in the process.

It is often thought that the journalist needs to detach himself emotionally to be able to cover a story objectively and accurately, but sometimes the opposite is also true. Sometimes being in touch with one's own emotional reactions is an important element of conveying empathy, and providing the safety the interviewee might need. This tension between objective facts and subjective experience has always been a part of journalism, but there may be ways to get better, truer facts if a journalist has been trained to provide a safe space of understanding. Recognizing the need for safe communicative space within their profession makes this facet of empathetic reporting all the more relevant. It recalls the humanity that exists in both subjects and storytellers, and this is what gives journalism power as collective narrative. They weave stories for others, yet must not lose themselves in the process, for they are part of the same story. They are both participant and storyteller. To live that role holistically, they need to support each other through the liminal spaces, the spaces where they find themselves betwixt and between roles, speaking for someone else's pain but reckoning with pain themselves, conveying someone else's disbelief while they still have not overcome their own. While telling the stories of others, sometimes they need to tell their own stories, and creating a stronger and more unified community of journalists has the potential to create a meaningful social space where that can happen.

Artist Studio Tours: A Site for Reflection

After 18 months of dialogue and exploration, artists displayed their work in a collective show they called "Through Our Eyes" at the Lower Manhattan gallery, Art in General. At the opening, a panel discussion examined art, mourning, and community, and considered the impulse to create an understanding of 9/11 that was personal, local, and distinct from the omnipresent public narrative. The evening focused on the importance of constructing a historical perspective on 9/11 through art, exploring how the sublime might intersect the traumatic through artistic representation. The artists talked about "nudging the boundaries of perception," about weighing premonitions of disaster, about art as moving toward the site of painful experience versus art as moving away from it, and about the existential reckoning with temporality, ephemerality, shared memory, religion, the sacred, and the unspeakable. Their conversations were complex and emotional, but through a common language they began to untangle the thick web of personal and interpersonal experience that they were carrying with them, and that infused the world around them in the aftermath of 9/11.

In 2011 I sat down with artists Katy Martin and Jo Wood-Brown to learn more about the project they had started nearly a decade earlier. Jo explained that she had been driven by a desire to foster "deeper contemplation of the times," and so reached out to painters, sculptors, filmmakers, photographers, printmakers, performance artists, installation artists, and multidisciplinary artists from all across the city. She invited them to visit the spaces of artists in the neighborhood around Ground Zero, embarking on what became known as "Artist Studio Tours." According to Jo,

> After a major traumatic event, there's a tendency to attempt a fast getaway, to simplify and fall back on clichés. But artists have an impulse to question, to look deeply into the complexity of the event and all that surrounds it.

Following this impulse, Katy and Jo set out to foster a community dialogue among the city's artists who had experienced 9/11 as New Yorkers and had the capacity to question it as artists. They believed that the trauma was exacerbated by a narrative in the mainstream media that did not resonate with their own experiences. As artists, they had something important to say about what had happened, and an unconventional way of saying it. Artists share a unique language for making meaning out of broader historical events, and they wanted to reach out to people using that language in order to convey versions of the events that connected more powerfully with the complexity and variability of experiences.

The idea of organizing artist studio tours came to Jo during the summer before 9/11, but the tragedy spurred her to take action. She consciously selected experienced and diverse artists, which attracted a core group of about 15 members who regarded one another with warmth and respect. Once a month, an even larger group of up to 25 people would gather at an artist's studio and share something to eat. There was no agenda, and no expectations. It was just the creation of a close community that wanted to speak through a mutually understood visual language. With support from the Downtown Community Resource Center, they increased the number of meetings they held and the group expanded to a larger circle of over two hundred artists. The rapid growth of the project surprised even its creators.

Although never explicitly stated, there was a common impulse to find a non-linguistic, embodied way to reconcile with 9/11. Talking about artists, Katy explained, "We don't speak in words; material is our language. We don't speak in words, we speak in materials." It was important for the group to have a space to process the events in their own language, through another way of knowing and expressing themselves while maintaining the integrity of their experience. Traumatic experience can defy language; it often defies linear coherence and literally cannot be spoken about. Art allows for a rare freedom because it is non-verbal and open to interpretation. It is under no constraints to be linear and so can circumvent the restrictions imposed by social norms on how we feel and how we express those feelings. Art can hold multiple meanings simultaneously and allows for contradiction as part of the whole, and in this way can speak to people with different feelings, different experiences, different memories, and different meanings through a common prism.

Jo and Katy expressed feeling a strong sense of alienation following 9/11. They felt cut off from the neighborhood. They tried group therapy sessions, but found them too upsetting, too raw. People in the neighborhood were responding to the events in very physical ways: they were jumpy, on edge, always waiting for another attack. Jo and Katy did not want to lose their deep experiences and complex memories to the images propagated by television, so they turned to work to connect them to the present, and to begin an investigation that blurred the distinctions between "art" and "city." Discussing the artistic process, Katy explained that artists set parameters, and then turn things over and over until they become something else; something true to but distinct from what they were. Through this process they reconfigured the trauma of 9/11 until it became an organic articulation of the community, a true alternative to the narrative presented by the media. They felt like they were stitching together a new sense of neighborhood, and they slowed down to contemplate this process, recognizing it as an "awakening" of great significance.

The process of turning inward for support, of turning to a common group with a common language and a common need to reconnect, often produces a reciprocal need to turn outward once reconciliation has been found. The process results in a sense of empowerment and desire to connect to other communities, to share the experience of healing and rebuilding and to pass it on to others. The communal support and communal recovery that takes place on the local level releases an energy that wants to connect with others, to find more connections across broader boundaries, and to establish a kind of external validation for what has been suffered, learned, and overcome. The smaller community processes seek to become part of larger global processes and find something of a universal resonance.

Jo and Katy experienced this transition in their project. In the years following its original establishment, the Artist Studio Tours initiative evolved into an international program connecting New York artists to others in Belfast and Berlin to develop collaborative projects. They called themselves Artist Exchange International, and examined their experience as a part of cities with different histories and uncertain futures. They reflected on recent history in relation to vast breadths of history, looking at the unspeakable atrocities of the contemporary moment in relation to the continuum of the known and unknown past. Artists from Belfast had come together during the period of ethno-political conflict between Protestant unionists and Catholic loyalists known as "The Troubles" in Northern Ireland. They continued to work even after the ceasefire, and brought memory, ritual, and traditional emblems together to create insightful work about Northern Ireland's difficult transition.

The artists from Berlin worked with the artists from New York to contextualize events like 9/11 and the fall of the Berlin Wall on 11/9 within cycles of civilization. There was concern in the United States that 9/11 was being a-historicized as an exceptional event outside the timeline of history used to justify the War on Terror. It was critical to the artists that they challenge this decontextualization through their work. With the artists from Berlin, they co-created an exhibition called *9/11 11/9* in which both cities offered their perspectives on the dialogues that were built around the events of 1989 and 2001. The New York artists exhibited their work in Berlin, and the Berlin artists brought their work to New York. The project initiated an ongoing dialogue between the two groups, and gave rise to a new program, *Gap Junction in Urban Life*. *Gap Junction* refers to the relationship between the two cities, a physically divided space across which artists could engage in respectful and productive cultural exchange. As Jutta Goetzman, curator for the project in Berlin, put it, the exchange happens "without covering the tracks of cultural peculiarities. A gap junction enables the interchange of elements only of a certain size without changing the cytoplasm of the cell. Information can flow faster, joint projects can accelerate" (Goetzman, 2012). The collaborative presentation is set to take place in Berlin and New York in 2013.

This work is an example of how to communicate across boundaries. It examines what kind of information—literal, physical, emotional, interpretive—can be transferred through an artistic medium. It is an act of reaching out and overcoming isolation, of exposing groups that are similar across their differences to new stimuli, and engaging in a process of mutual witnessing. The international artistic resonance demonstrated between these cities raises questions about urban communities in a globalized world. The process of collective recovery, and within that the process of collective resilience, is very much defined by the community's cultural and situational context. Yet the potential for international collaboration suggests something unique about the urban recovery process, about how the urban community understands its internal and external relationships. By reaching out to artists in other cities in other countries, the New York organization engaged in collaborative creative activity on a social level that blurred boundaries and challenged geographical limitations. The meaning of the recovery process is constantly constructed on an ongoing basis, and for this particular group of artists the connection with other urban artists who had suffered similar traumatic circumstances was an important exercise in reciprocity and validation.

8

Collective Narration and Performance

While many of the projects discussed previously provide spaces for people to come together for shared activity and support, the projects in this chapter differ in that the safe environments and structure they provide enables people to reflect on their experiences and connect them with the larger context of community life and history as well as universal themes of suffering and transformation. After a disaster, people often wish to speak about their experiences, to tell their stories—and most prefer to do this outside a therapeutic or clinical context. Moreover, they often desire the opportunity to make their personal story public.

In the archive and theater projects that follow, mental health professionals, community members, and artists came together in teams and created an opportunity for people to reflect on their experience in a safe, controlled environment. In these projects, people were given permission to talk about not only the horrors of what they had experienced but also their continued anxieties and struggles to make sense of the events surrounding 9/11 through a creative endeavor. In these spaces they could discuss experiences that they would not normally talk about on the street to create something meaningful.

Drawing on inspiration from testimonial work that had been done with survivors of political violence, we at the Downtown Community Resource Center sought to implement similar projects in Lower Manhattan. We were particularly influenced by: the South African Khulumani Theater Group; the testimony therapy work of Chilean psychologists Cienfuegos and Monelli (1983); Inga Agger's and Soeren Buus Jensen's testimonial work with refugees in Denmark (1990); and the testimonial/expressive therapy work of Melinda Meyer de Mott (2007) in Norway. Our project, Theater Arts Against Political Violence, had done narrative theater work with former Chilean political prisoners now living in New York, and with the population in post-war Kosovo.

The driving idea behind this work was that public opportunities for collective reflection were important in a post-disaster/terrorism environment—that avoidance and silence may be counterproductive. I knew from my connections in Lower Manhattan that people still wanted opportunities to speak about what they and their families and friends had been through. Though counselors had been available in the first months following the attacks, in later months many still felt the need to recall their experiences on 9/11 and gain some perspective through reflection. Another idea that drove our work was the need to create public spaces where a diversity of experiences about 9/11 could be voiced and heard. At the time, the predominant voices were those of the heroes (first responders) and victims (families of who experienced loss). It sometimes seemed that only these victims had the right to speak publicly, and that only they had the moral authority to speak about how the country should respond (Stern, 2010). Many people had witnessed horrors, suffered severe distress, and had their lives altered, but their stories had not found a place as yet in the emerging collective narrative.

Stories From the Ground: Creating a Video Narrative Archive

Not long after the first anniversary of the attack, I started to meet with parents who had been active in the family and community support networks around the New York public school known as PS 234. These parents worked together to maintain their children's school in the aftermath of 9/11, as well as to build a downtown Manhattan community resource center. A small group of us met each week at Bazzini's, a local nut store and factory that had been transformed into a gourmet market and café, to discuss the possibility of creating a video narrative archive. We felt that such an archive would not only document the stories of residents and others who had lived and worked in Lower Manhattan, but also provide a space for people to reflect on their experiences and thus invite others to engage in mutual reflection. We were interested in their personal experiences, their experiences as members of the community, and their views about how the community was affected and had responded to the events.

The parents I worked with came directly from the community and brought an array of perspectives and resources to the project: Hally Breindel, a social worker, photographer, and long-time Tribeca resident; Liz Margolies, a therapist; and Linnae Hamilton and Nisi Jacobs, documentary filmmakers. We included the project as part of the grant proposal for the Downtown

Manhattan Community Resource Center. The archive project was seen as a useful community-based intervention, and therefore we secured funding through various complementary avenues. At our weekly meetings we brainstormed how to conduct the interviews. We were particularly concerned with the technical aspects of filming because we wanted to create a professional-level production. That made Linnae and Nisi valuable resources. Linnae had already completed a film titled *Our School*, about the evacuation of PS 234 and the teachers' responses to 9/11.

Several other documentary projects were already under way, but we hoped to do something different through the use of oral history and video documentation. In the spirit of our community-oriented project, we wanted to engage with fellow residents about not only their personal experiences on 9/11, but also their histories of living in Lower Manhattan with their families and neighbors before the attack. As a first step, we invited oral historians through the International Trauma Studies Program Disaster Response Workshop Series to speak to our group on oral history theory and methodology. Then we developed our own methodology to suit our community-based narrative project. We decided early on that we would videotape the interviews, with the long-term goal of editing them and making them publicly available to the wider community. We also felt that by having community members conduct the interviews, we would avoid an imposed insider–outsider dynamic. We hoped for a more conversational dialogue, and through this to create a space for interviews that demonstrated more of a shared history.

On March 7, 2003 the International Trauma Studies Program conducted a workshop titled "Supporting Traumatized Communities through Narrative and Remembrance," which was attended by roughly 60 academic and health professionals who were working on 9/11-oriented projects. Mary Marshall Clark, director of the Columbia University Oral History Office, and Silvia Salvatici, professor in the Department of Media Studies at the University of Teramo, Italy led the presentation. Silvia began the workshop by explaining an earlier project, "Archive of Memory," which was the oral history component of a larger psychosocial program implemented by the International Organization for Migration (IOM) immediately after the war in Kosovo in 1999 and 2000. The project aimed to provide a space for expressions of suffering through both narrative and body language, and to contextualize the experiences of suffering within Kosovars' history and culture.

The Archive of Memory project looked at narrative in multiple forms, including oral histories, diaries, lectures, drawings, and photographs (Salvatici,

2001). The researchers were sensitive to the fact that the interviews were being conducted through interpreters, and consequently across cultural and national boundaries. They understood that the presence of international actors shaped both the context and the content of the narratives being recorded. While the tensions created by an insider–outsider dichotomy could not be denied or completely avoided, the researchers worked to establish an environment of non-hierarchical discourse by using terms like "conversation" rather than "interview" to emphasize the equality of status between interviewers and interviewees.

In conducting our own interviews, we had the opportunity to employ locals in the act of researching their communities. We were conscious of how the shared histories and experiences of the downtown Manhattan community before 9/11 might facilitate a uniquely collaborative context for the construction of their narratives of life before and after the attack. We wanted to allow people to tell their stories and to speak about their experiences, but we also wanted to add the extra dimension of their histories within the community, their experiences as community members, and how they perceived the community's response to 9/11. We structured the interviews to encompass this broad, multifaceted perspective, and because we placed it within the context of our identities as community members, the discourse shaped in the interview process was inherently one of "our experience" rather than "my experience." In many interviews, the participants began with a history of their place in the community, their roles, and their responsibilities and identities in relation to their families, friends, and neighbors. They were talking about a collective history, a critical part in the construction of the collective narrative (Saul, Breindel, Margolies, Hamilton, & Jacobs, 2004).

Susan Sonz—a local artist, mother of two, and Tribeca resident since 1976—recognized the need in her community for a gradual process of healing. While the broader New York City and federal government were encouraging residents to return to normal, Susan explained that "normal" was not necessarily a reachable state, either in the immediate wake of the tragedy or perhaps ever, because the lives of Lower Manhattan residents had been permanently changed:

> The whole neighborhood had trouble recuperating quickly, as it should have. I don't think we should have pulled together any quicker than we did. We went through a natural grieving process, and should have. I think the city wanted us to snap out of it very quickly, and probably the federal government; I'm not sure, I'm not

one of them so I wouldn't know. I got the feeling when they were making the Stuyvesant students go back so quickly, and pushing our kids to go back into PS 234 and 89 that they wanted us to, as they kept saying, "get back to normal." We all knew that normal was a long way away, if ever, because you're changed forever by an experience like that. And I know the whole world had a strong reaction, but of course Tribeca had a very personal, individually personal, reaction to the tragedy, and we were changed forever.

Susan was able to take on a healing role within her community, treating the adults and children she saw struggling to orient themselves within the incomprehensibility of what had happened. Describing the weight of witnessing death and destruction on such a vast scale, and trying to find some means of reclaiming normalcy, she said:

I treated a lot of people, if they wanted it, just by having seen them and seeing the different stages they were in. Some people couldn't stop crying, some people were shaking all the time, they were so scared.... Around Halloween, we felt compelled as a neighborhood to celebrate it that year, [but] it was such a strange feeling, the smoke was hanging in the air, we were afraid to even be out those few hours ... and then the smoke started getting thicker so no one went around trick-or-treating. We all ran to people's homes. It was a strange time. But that was when I noticed that people ... didn't seem so shocked anymore. They were going into the depression, you know? It was too heavy, it was too sad. The feeling of spirits in the neighborhood was very, very strong, and all of that, I think that being overwhelmed by the number of people who had lost their lives here, the grief just became so huge for most people that they stopped being afraid so much. I noticed that a lot of us went into this reaction of actually being fearless, which is a common post-traumatic reaction as well.

Despite these feelings of depression, and perhaps denial, Susan said that, in time, the community rebounded. She conveyed with deep emotion the fact that the children in the community seemed to have recovered, and contextualized this as both critical to the shared recovery of the neighborhood, and as indicative of a traumatic burden that will be transferred and carried by future generations. She explained:

I do think for the most part that the children recovered beautifully. I know that they'll tell their children and their grandchildren about this thing that happened, but I think deep in their souls and their beings they recovered. I think the school did a beautiful job, I think the neighborhood did a beautiful job, and that's where this all started. I thought the neighborhood needed to grieve properly, and I think we did.... In spite of the fact that we were being asked to act normal and be normal, I think the neighborhood took its time and grieved; unfortunately when that year came, as it does, everyone looks at you like, "Now everything's OK, right?" And it isn't, you're changed forever, and people have trouble—Americans have trouble—recognizing or accepting that about someone else. So a lot of us in this neighborhood had to keep going in the grief, and finish it up, and I do think, now, most of us have gone through that place.

With a smile, Susan recalled the moment two years after 9/11 that she first felt like herself again, and she recognized that while the community and its individuals may have been forever changed, they are still, in a significant if subtle way, the community of individuals they were before. Rediscovering that is a way to reclaim the possibility of an optimistic future:

And it was a wonderful thing to know, both things. Yes, I'll be changed forever, but also yes, I'm still there, you know? It's two years, I knew I was there somewhere, because I feel much better than I did a year ago ... everything was light. It was a real, as they say, lightness of being, that I recognized, you know, old optimism, I started fantasizing, I had a fantasy, I have a small piece of land and I started drawing plans for a house! I'd never—I haven't had a fantasy in over two years, you know, it's been ... daydreaming, that's something that went away, that kind of foolish optimism. It's hard to have that again. Those are the things that I think change, those deep, deep ways of looking at life.

Saul, Breindel, Margolies, Hamilton, & Jacobs, 2004

Liz Berger and Fred Kaufman are Lower Manhattan parents who have lived in that community since the early 1980s. The archivists interviewed them in their home, where they have a large living room window that looks directly onto the site of the collapsed towers. For months they watched as firefighters and rescue workers sifted through massive piles of debris, and they found themselves constantly aware of the death and devastation just outside their home. Describing the emotional weight of that presence, Liz and Fred said:

FRED: So two months after, about eight weeks after, our view, you know, we're looking right over the site here. The building is still about 14 floors high on Liberty, just the wreckage, and the cranes are working–

LIZ: The picture of the façade of "One World Trade" was taken from our corner.

FRED: You know, everybody knows that they couldn't just take the garbage away, they had to go through it first to find remains. And I think that's ultimately what changed my consciousness the most, was having for so many days and weeks and months in a row, having outside my window seeing the off-duty firefighters raking through every last thing.

LIZ: And you knew when they found someone because there was an ambulance, that's how you knew, you'd hear the siren and you would know…

FRED: You'd see the ambulance and everyone would stop working, and you just see it again and again and again and again and again, and it, you know, you go through stages, you won't look out the window, you stare out the window, you won't look out the window, you can't help looking out the window, and so by—

LIZ: You cover your window.

FRED: Right, so you cover your window.

Liz and Fred have children who were in PS 234 at the time of the attack. Like Susan Sonz, they recognized the significance that being parents in this particular community at this particular time had for the creation of a collective network. The role and identity of "parent" seems to have created a necessary support network for the adult community, as well as a shared focus of responsibility and purpose in the protection and continued care of their children. Fred explained:

After September 11 down here, you would literally hear parents and your friends vowing, "I'm going to keep this together, I'm going to make this happen," insisting on opening their houses and keeping it going and keeping the kids on track and everything.… And that was interesting too, and nobody of course knows what's going on, nobody know what's happening or what's coming next, and that's something which had a tremendous effect on me in terms of the community and my feelings and my place in it.... The entire community is suffering in their own way from post-traumatic stress syndrome, it becomes their way of life. That's part of what makes us a community also, is that nobody else really understands that very basic, psychological way in which we're dealing. For example the first time we went to California—my folks are in California—we went out to LA, I felt like I was on another planet! And finally you go back and it's like, here's a 234 parent! They understand! They understand what we've been through.

His wife Liz expressed a similar sentiment when she explained how 9/11 actually created a space in which parents *could* focus on their families and their children, and that by focusing the energy of the community in this way, they were able to keep the children socially active, academically successful, and emotionally supported. She said:

I think it's a very important value, and one that's missing from our culture generally, and I think people are reluctant to acknowledge the positive impact of September 11 on their life. Certainly on their school, on their families.... People are so surprised that after all that the kids went through, the kids at 234 went through, they scored number one on the citywide test. Well hello! You had six hundred kids and twelve hundred parents, all they did for four months was hang out! What did you think was going to happen? It's the parents, stupid! And that seemed to be such a *new* concept, people seemed so delighted to lose temporarily their worldly conceits and focus on each other.

Echoing Susan's story about the first Halloween after September 11, Fred said the first birthday party was intensely emotional because this traditionally "normal" event took place within a deeply altered social space:

It was a very interesting fulcrum that you go through, when you go through such a terrible thing, and you add into this what had previously occurred, such as the marriages, and purchases, and the children.... And then you get these very intense experiences, for instance you have the first birthday party after September 11 for the children. Not my children, but the first birthday party of the group of children, and having all the parents back together again, and seeing all those children that hadn't seen each other for a month or so, and seeing this party happen, and all of us are walking around dazed but also just kind of crying and talking to each other and so happy.

Liz reflects on this relationship between the community's parents and their children, drawing out a significant existential tension between the desire to reclaim the optimistic future described by Susan Sonz and the weight of having lost faith in the promise of another day. Describing the process she went through in deciding whether to remodel a portion of their home, Liz articulates the fear of uncertainty that she discovered to be at the root of her apprehension:

I realized that to build in a homework desk, we needed to reverse the sliding doors. It was a huge issue, it couldn't be accomplished, technically. We did a lot of research and I found the company that could tell me, so I called them up, could they come switch the door? Well, it's a hundred-dollar consultation fee that you can apply to services or purchases. I couldn't schedule the appointment. I just couldn't schedule the appointment. And after six or seven weeks I realized that the reason that—this is in the spring of 2002—I realized the reason that I couldn't schedule the appointment was that I just didn't feel confident enough that we would be here in the fall to make the hundred bucks worthwhile. Not that we would leave, but that something would happen. So not that we would leave voluntarily. And when I realized this, I just thought, well that's ridiculous! How can I live that way? I can't live that way. I mean that's like dying a little death every day, I cannot live that way. And I called American Door and they came, and the jury's still out, they'll get back to me. But it was one hundred dollars to learn that I could live with the uncertainty of not knowing how long we'll live. And, I don't know. Maybe this is kind of a romantic notion; I mean, I think that that is a fear that parents experience on behalf of their children. I know that I still look at my children and I see death, and that, that is truly horrible, to have to live with that and keep on living. To have to encourage your children to think about their future while not knowing, or not necessarily

believing one hundred percent that they have a future, that's hard.
I think that's a new thing.

Saul, Breindel, Margolies, Hamilton, & Jacobs, 2004

The collective narrative emerges in two ways: first in the content of the interview itself, but secondly in the interview as a social and cultural object. What is the collective narrative? Who puts it together? The community's story should create a space for everyone, yet at the same time it will never be everyone's story. One of our goals with this project was to create space for alternative narratives, for the stories that are too often silenced or put in the margins by the dominant narratives—be it for social, political, or economic reasons. We took initial inspiration from the Archive of Memory project in Kosovo, but our framework was quite different; we were not so much listening to narratives of suffering as we were allowing people to speak about their individual experience as a community member. Our interviews were not structured around a dialogue or rhetoric of suffering, but rather served as an open space, a more flexible and interpretive setting, in which individuals could validate their experiences and engage in collective meaning-making. This was something people needed; they were very interested in having this space to talk about their experiences, and we felt that this opened up a site unavailable in the larger public conversation.

The project in Kosovo focused on understanding experiences of suffering in a way that created an alternative to the normal pathologizing of responses to traumatic events. In the 9/11 video narrative archive, we tried to take this a step further. We were deliberately looking at what kind of positive social processes can be supported by providing a space for people to engage in conversations about their experiences. The project was not a neutrally-minded initiative in which people were simply speaking, as we hoped to demonstrate that there is a positive individual and collective benefit from creating spaces for people to talk about their experiences. We saw that many people in the community genuinely desired such an opportunity. The dominant social narratives at the time were of "heroes" and "victims," and the primary national narrative developed around the War on Terror, but people in Lower Manhattan were living with a very different kind of narrative, and the community had gone through a very different kind of experience. Sharing individual stories within the community validates the experiences of marginalized groups in the wake of traumatic events. This brings a diversity of experience into the community's story, giving it a richer texture and making it easier for the individual to find resonance with his or her own story.

Our purpose in pursuing this project was to prevent alienation. One factor that can be very traumatizing for people after an event like 9/11 is the feeling that their personal stories do not matter, or that their experiences do not exist. It is as if their experiences of trauma have been invalidated, and what they have experienced is not important to the formation of the collective narrative. On one hand, this can be related to the "conspiracies of silence" that often emerge in the wake of major traumatic experience. People can choose to be silent, but if there is some manner of imposed silence, a collusion of silence, it toxifies both the opportunity and the nature of communication. People can expend an extraordinary amount of energy by avoiding speaking about certain events. Consequently, it is not just that the processes of collective narration may motivate people to talk, as in itself talking is not necessarily helpful. Rather, it is that people need to feel that they *can* speak about their experiences, if and when they want to. They need to know and understand that there is no prohibition on speaking.

On the other hand, meaning-making is necessarily a collective process, particularly when the shared experience is a historic event. This suggests that after a traumatic experience people *want* to get together and try to make sense of what they have gone through. They want to speak about what happened and to try to understand why it happened, and what the implications for future action are. Lower Manhattan has very few public spaces where such community dialogue could occur. This physical reality, the lack of space for public gathering and collective discussion, interferes with the meaning-making process.

We saw the narrative video archive as a way of promoting public discussion and the struggle to find meaning. Opening the conversation to be simultaneously within and about the community has a significant impact on people, and may sensitize them to their connection with the community. This project provided opportunities for certain people to become storytellers, an important role in many traditional societies. The storyteller is in many ways a performer, and that social role is critical to the collective narrative because it shifts the individual experience from a written textual transmission into an embodied transfer of knowledge (Taylor, 2003).

Theater of Witness: Constructing Meaning After Tragedy

A group of actors sat in a circle to listen to the story of John Scott and Diane Lapson, two leaders of the Independence Plaza North Tenants Association. Abby Gampel, the Downtown Theater Project's director, explained: "We try to hear you with all of ourselves, and then, from that, find parts of ourselves that resonate and then tell it, tell the story, tell your story."

Stephen Reisner, a psychologist and actor, added:

> Even though you may have had the opportunity to tell the story over and over again, in this context it's an opportunity to tell the story to artists who will then take your stories with others in the community to create a theatrical performance. Our theater group has been working for the past five years, meeting with communities who have endured some form of political violence and creating theater out of the experience.

The Lower Manhattan theater project stemmed from earlier work among traumatized and refugee communities, to harness the potential of theatrical performance to elicit and facilitate public discourse. The use of social theater to express, explore, and represent traumatic experience, as well as to provide a public space for groups to reflect on that experience, shifts the focus from an individualized clinical encounter between patient and therapist, to a collaborative artistic endeavor in which survivors, artists, and mental health professionals meet in a more dynamic and phenomenological environment of memory and discourse. In the case of the Lower Manhattan community, we wanted to explore the local experience of 9/11 that represented the multifaceted "truths" of our interlocutors and also rendered those individual narratives comprehensible, relatable, and legitimate in a way that resonated with the larger community.

To begin the theater project, the directors and producers held auditions and were able to assemble a group of actors that brought together artists from Lower Manhattan and the rest of the city. The versatile group could give voice to diverse narratives, and the combination of local affiliations with more geographically distant orientations supplied varied perspectives that facilitated a more richly textured artistic collaboration.

With a group of actors established, we began to conduct interviews with community members to record their memories, stories, and experiences of 9/11, and began working them into characters and narratives in a script. Throughout this process, we were sensitive to the tension between the artistic goals of the performance as theater and the responsibility to the members of the community and the authenticity of their stories. While we wanted the project to meet certain standards of artistic and aesthetic quality, we also wanted to stay close to the original sentiments of the material entrusted to us by the community.

One such story was that of Ernesto Castillo, a Chilean who had been living in exile in New York following his imprisonment and brutal treatment under the Pinochet regime after the overthrow of President Salvador Allende in 1973. Ernesto had participated in a theater project with the Chilean community we had run years earlier (see Chapter 2). When interviewing Ernesto, the group of actors was struck by the parallel traumas he had faced in his Chilean homeland and later as a New Yorker. Prompted by the group to speak about his experience in any way that he wanted, Ernesto began: "Let me tell the story this way." He recounted how on the morning of September 11, as he rode the Staten Island ferry to Manhattan, he happened to have been reflecting on the memory of planes bombing the presidential palace in Santiago, nearly 30 years earlier. While caught in his memories, someone on the ferry exclaimed that the World Trade Center was on fire. Ernesto looked up just in time to watch the second plane fly into the second tower. "For a long time I avoided the connection, tried not to think about it. Eventually I went to therapy.... It brought a lot of memories—everything I'd been trying to push back." In Ernesto's story, the trauma of September 11 in New York resonated with and recalled his previous trauma in Chile, and illustrates the myriad ways traumas may be carried with us, to be recalled in unexpected places and unanticipated moments.

In reflecting on these two experiences, Ernesto lapsed into a more existential dialogue and told the group about his grandfather and his inherited conceptions of truth and human nature:

> My grandfather was like my father. He used to tell me a story about the gods who were sitting around celebrating after they had created everything and one of them said, "Let's create The Truth." And The Truth was beautiful and strong and everyone loved The Truth. And then they created The Lie. And The Lie was really, really ugly. People would chase it away and throw rocks. And one day they had a meeting and said it wasn't fair, that The Lie should at least be able to defend herself, so they gave her a sword. And one day they met, The Truth and The Lie, and The Lie said, "It's your fault for everything that happened to me." So she took the sword and killed her, took her head, and put it on top of her own. From then on, The Lie has walked around with the face of The Truth, fooling people.... It's a reminder of what human beings are capable of doing to others.

This story demonstrates an intergenerational contextualization of trauma in which Ernesto actively connects his experience of 9/11 to his experience of Santiago, to his experience of being Chilean, and to his understanding of human nature in its darkest, deepest moments—which he learned from the most intimate and influential members of his paternal line. It is a weaving of self that suggests the past is never divorced from the present, and that the weight of trauma as experienced by an individual is rarely held in isolation. Rather it is communicated via narrative, myth, history, and even silence, in a way that leaves an indelible imprint on a network of persons, tied by kinship, by friendship, but most importantly by the struggle to come to terms with a determinedly incomprehensible experience of human suffering.

One of our goals was to include a wide range of community voices in the production. This created an account of the traumatic experience that resonated broadly with a diverse audience and gave the greatest number of people a connection to the action on the stage. We wanted them to find an emotional truth in which to recognize themselves or a piece of their own experience. It was also important to represent the diversity of experience within the Lower Manhattan community, so that the project remained grounded as being *for* the community. Because the project was developed in partnership with the community and based on community input, we had to make sure that it was going to serve them and devote appropriate attention to their concerns. We did not want to offend, alienate, or minimize the individuals willing to share their stories. We wanted this to be an inclusive collaborative process that respectfully and conscientiously incorporated their input.

The interviews done over the next few months were interpreted by the actors and creatively explored using improvisation techniques. This created a shared language within the group, such that the process of interpretation and integration created cohesion among the actors just as it created cohesion in the theatrical representation of the community's experience. The group of actors formed deep bonds with each other through the processes of interviewing, of recollecting their own 9/11 memories and experiences as triggered by the interviews, and in navigating the tensions of melding their own recollections with those of the characters they were creating for the stage. Among the voices portrayed by the group were: a great-grandfather who lost a grandson in the towers; a chaplain who worked among the cranes and wreckage to bless any recovered remains and who found herself struck by the gentle grace with which the huge machines sifted through the massacred acreage; and a man who watched the smoke rise over the towers from Harlem, knowing that his son had gone downtown to school by himself for the very first time that day. There was a Chinese woman living in Chinatown who came to feel more patriotic and more American than ever before, and there was a construction worker who haltingly recollected digging for 12 to 13 hours a day, desperately hoping to find someone alive. The group wanted to present a diversity of voices to the people who were seeing this play, hoping that it could convey experiences not portrayed in the media. By working together to uncover important themes, and their individual orientations in relation to those themes, the actors became a collective body with the capacity to process many different experiences and shape them into a coherent theatrical performance. The theater group is, in and of itself, a collective process engaging in collective meaning-making, and thus the nature of this endeavor lends itself to the productive discovery of an alternative kind of emotional truth and conception of the collective narrative.

In reflecting on the process of creating social theater with the Lower Manhattan community, the theater project's director Abby spoke about the significance of finding this kind of experiential truth and the potential of the theater to facilitate its communication. She explained:

> When you're doing theater of this kind, you approach it with very deep care, and what you find is that the people who have experienced it really want to see what happened, but that doesn't mean they want to see a replay of what happened. They want to see a representation of the truth of what happened, something that has truth to it.... The story is two planes going into the World Trade Center and millions of lives being decimated. That's the first story. But then you have all these infinite secondary stories, and it's like a prism. Each story is a reflection of how the light hits a different part of the prism. There's not one person who's going to interpret it the way you mean it, it's about finding something that has the same violence of intention, that's how you create the storytelling. That's what I call truth in theater.

By rendering individual experiences as part of a collective narrative within a performance space, the theater group creates a safe opportunity to recreate, recollect, relive, and reincorporate the memories of traumatic experience as understood by both the group itself and the audience. The literal and figurative bounds of the performance space create a lived moment in time and place in which painful memories of loss, devastation, and confusion can be revisited while reducing the risk of being retraumatized. The composite nature of the characters on stage and the collaborative product of the script itself create a record of experience that is at once singularly unique and recognizably human. Through the prism of the production, individual narratives of trauma merge, and refracture, such that community members, actors, directors, producers, and audience members access simultaneously the legitimate singularity of their own experience and the shared moment of emotional truth that resonates across the boundaries of the individual and brings them, if only temporarily, into being with the collective.

How does this kind of work have the potential to affect the collective narrative? When the collective narrative is taken as something *felt*, something experienced in the body and through the senses, it becomes a social object different from the dominant narrative as constructed by the media, by history, and by the individual in isolation. By reconstructing the traumatic experience within an artistic context, particularly the theater with its physical and sensory authenticity, it becomes a story not just cognitively perceived, but phenomenologically experienced. Trauma is given a space as embodied memory in both the individual consciousness and the collective realm, to be accessed through nonlinear processes not constrained by our usual mode of thinking with language.

An important example of this is the story of a Greek woman whose experience of 9/11 resonated with her mother's experience of the Axis invasion of Greece in 1941. This scene is portrayed during one of the climactic moments of the play, when the emotional resonance of the stories and the confusion and disorientation of the traumatized characters is almost palpable. As in earlier examples, this story also highlights the weight of intergenerational trauma. The scene begins with two women seated on stage, representing the mother and grandmother of the woman who tells the story. They share a basket on their laps. The youngest woman narrates the scene, explaining how on 9/11 all she could think of was the story her mother had always told her as they would break the ends off of string beans, of the day she and *her* mother had been sifting through lentils on their porch in Greece. On that day, the grandmother had prompted her to dust the furniture once more, because "this is how we care for things," and the mother got up and walked inside the house. As she did, a plane flew low across the Mediterranean sky, and "the lentils began to fall from her hands, and then she fell on her knees, and then slowly to the ground." Empathizing with her mother's memory, the youngest woman said:

There was her mother lying on the ground covered in blood. Nothing made any sense.... My mother used to tell me this story as we sat breaking the ends off string beans, and as my mother wept, bean end clicked off and clicked off, I listened to her repeat and repeat, "This is how we care for things ... this is how we care for things ... this is how we care for things ..." trying to make history make sense.

On September 11, she called her mother immediately, even before her husband or other relatives, to assure her that she was fine, and to try to protect her from the traumatic associations.

This scene is a critical moment, demonstrating how trauma is shared physically and emotionally and may lie deep within habitual bodily experience. The basket on the laps of the two women represents simultaneously lentils and green beans; it is the physical focal point for intergenerational transfer of unforeseen trauma raining from the sky. Like Ernesto, the Greek women associate the planes on the morning of September 11 with planes from earlier traumas, which, in the case of the youngest woman, are known only through repeated narrative, yet hold deep psychological significance.

The full-length theater piece, *Everything's Back to Normal in New York City: Below Canal, a Work in Progress*, was publicly performed over three weeks around the second anniversary of the attacks (Saul & ITSP Performance Group, 2010; Saul, 2006). Each performance was followed by talk-back sessions with the theater group, in which audience members, including Lower Manhattan residents, other New Yorkers, and visitors from elsewhere in the United States and abroad recalled their experiences on 9/11 and its aftermath. People shared stories, spoke about the artistic process of performing trauma, and speculated about the intense political competition surrounding the development of the historical narrative of September 11, 2001.

PART

3

WAR AND MIGRATION—LITTLE LIBERIA, STATEN ISLAND, NY

9

Little Liberia

Fostering Community Resilience

I was in the closet the night I got attacked and shot. I had bled so much that night. On that night of October 20, 1994. I was there watching the men in the house, and I'm just sitting there trying to give up my ghost. Just let it go. Let it happen. I close my eyes.

I was feeling another world, just feelings you know, in another world. And I saw my late father. And we had a brief chat. My father, telling me, "I know you can make it. You can make it. You can make it. You can make it." I just keep hearing the voice. "You can make it. You can make it. You can make it."

From that time, about 20 minutes later, the peacekeeping force came, and the men escaped. So I always remember that moment. That's a magical moment. That moment of joy. So I always remember that moment, when I almost threw out my ghost. I know I should've died that night. That's why I am here. Why am I here? Why am I here?"

Jacob Massaquoi, *Checkpoints* **(Theater Arts Against Political Violence)**

Engaging the Community

In the spring of 2002, a young man named Jacob Massaquoi joined a small group with two women to share stories at an experiential disaster-response workshop in a New York University classroom. He spoke of his recent arrival in the United States from the war-torn African country of Liberia, where he had been shot repeatedly in his leg, leaving him limping and handicapped. Mr. Massaquoi recounted one of his most painful experiences during the war, witnessing his brother's murder by soldiers. In order to save his own life, Jacob was forced to deny knowing his brother.

This workshop, on the topic of transforming traumatic experiences into theatrical expression, was led by John Burt, an expressive arts therapist, and Arn Chorn, a community activist and survivor of the Cambodian "killing fields." John and Arn had worked together for years to promote healing through the arts. They established an important organization in Cambodia, named Cambodian Living Arts, to link the few surviving elder Khmer artists with youth who had an interest in preserving their cultural and artistic traditions.

I had met Mr. Massaquoi on a visit to the Liberian refugee community in Staten Island, New York. In the fall of 2002, I began to explore providing psychosocial support to community members who had suffered torture and other forms of traumatic human rights abuses. Mr. Massaquoi was seeking political asylum, having been tortured by both government and rebel forces. He had worked for years as a human rights advocate in Liberia to develop psychosocial programs for youth, many of whom had been compelled to fight at a very early age.

I was the director of Refuge, a family and community resilience program sponsored by the International Trauma Studies Program at New York University. Refuge was a member of the Metro Area Support for Survivors of Torture Consortium (MASST) in New York, training mental health professionals and community workers in the city. We were now interested in developing a community resilience program with a refugee community. The program aimed to engage community members and support them in their efforts to promote psychosocial well-being for youth and families.

Service provision in Staten Island's Liberian community began on the soccer field. In 1994, Rufus Arkoi, founder and executive director of ROZA Promotions Inc., organized pick-up soccer games with adolescent Liberian refugees. A former soccer player himself, Mr. Arkoi saw the potential of working through sports to organize and communicate with Liberian youth. The Liberian boys' soccer team progressed from pick-up games in Staten Island to inter-borough competition and eventually a state trophy. In 1999 ROZA Promotions formalized this after-school program. The company was the first Liberian-run social service agency established in the community. Mr. Arkoi established ROZA to address challenges faced by resettled refugees on Staten Island. He hoped to provide recreational activities and educational support for refugee youth.

Soon, ROZA began to work with mainstream providers like Lutheran Social Services, which resettled the majority of Liberians in Staten Island,

and the Safe Horizon/Solace Program for Survivors of Torture and Refugee Trauma. One afternoon in 1998, Mr. Arkoi met Ernie Duff of Solace on a playground—Mr. Arkoi's informal office. They discussed the Liberian community's needs and Mr. Arkoi's dream to establish a not-for-profit agency to work with African immigrants and refugees. In 2000, the Queens-based Solace program, assisted by intensive case manager Sowore Omeley, opened an office on Staten Island where he and staff later worked with torture survivors from Liberia's civil war. Soon after, Solace's senior intensive case manager, Ayalnesh Mekonnen, connected Liberian women with a micro-lending program. One graduate from that program went on to own and operate Kortu's Place—a popular Liberian restaurant in Staten Island.

One of the first events I attended at ROZA was a forum for Liberian political leaders to discuss their home country's political concerns. About 100 people attended the event, held in a space normally reserved for an afterschool program. With children's art on the walls, representatives gathered from every Liberian political party, as well as soldiers and warlords from Liberians United for Reconciliation and Democracy (LURD). "Some of the worst human rights violators were right there," Mr. Massaquoi recalled.

Mr. Massaquoi organized the meeting to discuss Liberia's future and the possibility of an election in 2005. His group was discouraging the election and pushing for the prosecution of war crimes as a means of forming a unified party against President Charles Taylor. Mr. Massaquoi remembered the meeting as being simultaneously "reflective, retrospective, and accusative."

"It was a very bitter meeting. Everyone was against each other. The conversation turned out to be very brutal," he said.

It was my introduction to Liberian discussion, and I was not prepared for debates that ran from 6:00 p.m. to after midnight, though I remember fondly the late Liberian dinner of sweet potato leaves, rice, kala (fried corn bread), and fish stew.

Background

My first experience with Little Liberia, as it turns out, was not unrepresentative of Liberia as a whole. The small, West African country had been enmeshed in ethnic and class conflict since it was colonized in 1847 by freed American slaves who called themselves Americo-Liberians. When Samuel Doe, of the marginalized Krahn people, led a coup d'état that ended 135 years of Americo-Liberian domination, he continued the tradition of ruthless political repression, state terror, and personal greed. A failed counter-coup led Doe to tighten his reins even more, creating an environment of extreme desperation. Charles Taylor, an Americo-Liberian and former official in the Doe government, took this opportunity to mobilize an army (The Advocates for Human Rights, 2009).

From December 1989 to September 1990, Taylor's National Patriotic Front of Liberia (NPFL) campaigned around the country's capital, Monrovia, recruiting thousands of Liberians, including prepubescent children. Doe was executed. Conflict within the NPFL led the organization to splinter, and eventually, to an eight-year civil war, referred to in Liberia as the First World War. When Taylor became president in 1997, the fighting briefly cooled. He established a pariah state of militocracy and diamond-smuggling. In 1999, LURD rebels followed by the Movement for Democracy in Liberia mounted another attack on Taylor, which plunged Liberia into its Second World War. Liberia didn't know peace again until 2003, when Taylor was indicted for war crimes, exiled to Nigeria, captured and sent to The Hague in the Netherlands to be tried by an international court. Two years later, Liberia had a presidential election recognized by the international community as among the most democratic in African history. In 2005, Ellen Johnson Sirleaf was elected the first female president in Africa.

By the end of the wars, about 250,000 people had died, 20,000 children had become soldiers, countless others had been tortured and raped, and some had even resorted to cannibalism—an entire generation had been uprooted (The Advocates for Human Rights, 2009). Figures on the amount of Liberians living in the United States after the war vary widely, ranging from tens to hundreds of thousands (Frontline World, 2005; The Advocates for Human Rights, 2009). The number of Liberians living in Staten Island is debated as well, but most sources estimate the number as ranging between 8,000 and 10,000, more than half of which live in Park Hill (Clerici, 2012).

Park Hill, the site of a notorious federally subsidized low-income housing project nicknamed "Crack Hill" for its drug-pushing, had little institutional capacity to support this massive wave of immigration. The neighborhood had already seen years' worth of violent crime—for an example, just listen to 36 Chambers by the Wu-Tang Clan, long-time residents. It was not the best place of refuge for a war-ravaged people. Conflicts between the African-American, Hispanic, and immigrant African communities quickly emerged, as the first two fought to protect their territory and the third returned to the state of conflict that had defined its generation.

Liberian youth—many of them former combatants—ended up on the streets, perhaps feeling more at home there than in the schools, where they were often years older than their classmates, who outpaced them in literacy and math skills. With few employment opportunities, some turned to drugs and looting, and found themselves in squat houses.

Of every 10,000 people in this section of Staten Island, 100 were hospitalized because of drugs and 1.2 died because of drug use (New York City Department of Health and Mental Hygiene, 2006). Furthermore, many struggled to acclimate to live in the United States in the aftermath of their war experiences, and in an unsafe neighborhood at that. Many had not been able to see doctors in Liberia during the war and as a result there were about twice as many admissions for mental health in the area as the city average. The HIV rate was twice the national average, and 22% of pregnant women received late prenatal care, if at all (New York City Department of Health and Mental Hygiene, 2006).

Mapping Out Crucial Needs of the Community

One-on-one work with the Liberian refugee community transitioned to community-level work in 2001. The Safe Horizon/Solace program began collaborating with ROZA and the International Institute of New Jersey (IINJ) to initiate a community needs assessment. Based on the Australian Transcultural Mental Health Network's model, *Assessing Needs for Mental Health and Culturally and Linguistically Diverse Communities: A Qualitative Approach* (Larson, 1998), the Staten Island and New Jersey-based needs assessment hoped to engage survivors, families and communities to address concrete needs and de-stigmatize the violence and stress they had endured. Solace and IINJ hired individuals from the community to interview other survivors about issues they had suffered during the war. The report resulting from these interviews recommended that Solace improve access to mental health services while IINJ would do the same for physical health. A mental health promoter training program was the first follow-up step to the needs assessment. Community members in both New Jersey and Staten Island enrolled in a ten-week training program to learn skills to help them support and negotiate the emotional needs of their neighbors.

In the fall of 2003, Safe Horizon/Solace continued its macro-level approach by facilitating focus groups around domestic violence. Serena Chaudhry, Solace's director of health and community services, organized four focus groups—male, female, youth, and mixed. Confusion and frustration were the pervasive feelings felt within all four groups. Parents voiced frustration about raising children in the United States, while their children now labeled their traditional approaches, such as spanking, as child abuse. Youth argued that they were constantly challenged by the difficulty of integrating into U.S. culture—how to dress, how to talk, and how to assert themselves without a gun. Women spoke of their gender's positive power shift and the extent to which this humiliated African men. Before the war, women were given a space in the political domain but, in the end, men still had control.

Following these dialogues, it was evident that these families could benefit from additional support. Chaudhry organized a community meeting and invited New York Police Department (NYPD) officers to field questions and discuss child abuse laws. This initial dialogue with mainstream providers transitioned into a series of workshops hosted by the Staten Island Liberian Community Association's (SILCA) Adult Literacy Program on issues ranging from parenting to HIV/AIDS. These community needs assessments, dialogues, and workshops proved the power of a macro-level approach and set the stage for future multisystemic interventions.

In the winter of 2003, Refuge joined Safe Horizon/Solace in exploring how to better address psychosocial issues in the community. Refuge was particularly interested in identifying community members who could act as "community links" (Landau-Stanton, 1986). Community links become effective change agents from within a community, who can mobilize a broad base of support to address what the community members themselves define as priorities. Together with Dr. Judith Landau, a community psychiatrist who developed the LINC model, we invited community leaders from the Staten Island community to a class at the International Trauma Studies Program.

Following Landau's LINC model, we approached the Liberian community guided by the following 14 principles:

1. Ensure that we have an invitation, authority, permission, and commitment from the community.
2. Engage the entire system of the community, including representation of individuals and subsystems from each cultural and ethnic group, and all economic, cultural, and status strata.
3. Identify scripts, themes, and patterns across generations and community history.
4. Maintain sensitivity to issues of culture, gender, and spirituality.

5. Encourage access to all natural and ancillary resources (bio-psychosocial, cultural, and ecological).
6. Build an effective prevention/management context by collaborating across all systems.
7. Foster a balance of agency and communion across the community.
8. Build on existing resources.
9. Relate program needs to goals, future directions, and best interests of the community.
10. Utilize resources, turn goals into realistic tasks, and turn those into practical projects.
11. We provide the process; the community takes responsibility for the content and goals.
12. Encourage community links (natural change agents) to become leaders in their communities.
13. The more peripheral we are, the more successful are the program and the community.
14. Success of the project belongs to the community (Landau-Stanton, 1986; Landau & Saul 2004).

Landau and I also identified four factors that come into play during disaster recovery. These factors can be categorized into: disruption (family and community systems: process, function, structure, and organization); stressors (transition, catastrophic event, unresolved grief, and loss); multisystemic impact levels (loss of ability to contextualize, family dynamics, bonding patterns and communication patterns, social and community levels); and transitions (emergence of resilience and transitional pathways) (Landau & Saul, 2004).

The first part of the class at the ITSP involved discussing resources, themes, and scripts that most characterized Liberia in general. Scripts are a set of prescribed present and future actions, based on beliefs people have about their families, communities, and cultures. From our discussion that day, it became apparent that Liberians had a tremendous sense of pride in their heritage—they referred to Liberia using its old moniker, "the light of Africa." Their love of country was only matched by their love of soccer, a unifying force. People took pride in Liberia's historical role in international affairs, for example its involvement in the Organization of African Unity (OAU) in 1963, membership in the League of Nations and later the United Nations, and status as the home of the first African female president of the United Nations—Angie

Brooks. The challenging history of the country played an important role for the Liberian community in Staten Island. Three percent of Liberians, the Americo-Liberians, were descendants of former slaves who had immigrated from the United States. They ruled over the rest of the Liberian population. The Americo-Liberians and the indigenous people at times worked toward positive change, but at other times engaged in brutal conflict, with atrocities committed by both sides.

The second part of the presentation simulated a meeting in which community members articulated goals in response to country needs. In this role-playing exercise, Liberian community leaders assigned roles to class participants and guided the improvised conversations. The exercise was then repeated to discuss the community goals of Staten Island Liberians. The participants voiced the opinions of key players and demographics within Liberia.

A university professor spoke about the need for both sides from the former conflict to work toward reconciliation and build a new Liberia. A U.N. representative sought to promote peace and educate the people about the upcoming 2005 election. A business leader spoke about creating a caucus to put more businesses in the hands of the indigenous population.

In the Staten Island role-play, a minister recommended bringing together church leaders to promote educational and social programs. A single father of two teenage boys, who worked two jobs, spoke of his desire for his children to know and value the Liberian part of their identities. The director of a local Liberian association spoke about the need to convene various groups and to find places for the entire community to engage in conversation and resolve conflict. As ideas came together and the group prioritized community goals, it became clear that they uniformly desired a geographically accessible multi-purpose drop-in center.

In my capacity as director of Refuge, I visited the West African community with a visiting student of ITSP NYU from Liberia, Famata Gibson. We made weekly trips to Staten Island to interview community leaders and providers on current needs, problems, and obstacles to community development. The community leaders expressed a wide array of perspectives.

Rufus Arkoi, the first to be interviewed about mental health concerns, set the tone with these words of caution:

> When it comes to mental health, we are currently getting enough services here from Solace. But there has been a problem with outside organizations coming to our community, especially those

seeking [to] assist people with problems related to 9/11. They came ready to work, without asking you what you need, like if the plumber comes to your house and says, "Okay, I'm going to replace all of your bathroom fixtures."

He went on to say:

What the community needs now is mental stability; this is a community of people coming from terrible, tough war experiences, and they need mental support. I am no mental health expert, but at the end of the day, I even just keep people company, people who can't be alone, can't sleep because of the experiences they've had. We need for organizations to leave something behind here. It would be helpful to have someone who could act as a link between the community and the organizations who are providing services.

Many leaders pointed to the need to help the youth. There were about 40 adolescent boys at Park Hill who were hanging out on the streets, occasionally getting into trouble with the police. Most of the boys were high school drop-outs; "hungry for family and public support," said Arkoi. As in other Liberian communities in the New York/New Jersey area, some of the boys had fought in the war and were potentially violent. "A kid who has been carrying an AK-47 is not going to take much from other kids," one provider said. "Fortunately, these kids are not usually getting into trouble because they have strong families and strong values about education, social obedience, and order."

Providers described families as having many hardships. One provider noted that he worked with many men in the community whose wives had left them because they had not been able to financially provide for their families. Many parents had to work long hours and did not feel they had enough time to spend with their children. Often adults worked as home health aids and in other careers with a high time commitment and low advancement opportunities because of their education levels.

"They are constantly worried about their families back in Africa, which feeds their depression. Everyone has a story about a family member who has disappeared and they have no way of contacting them. The uncertainty is unbearable," one provider said. "There were many obstacles to building support for services in the community." Another provider said:

The West Africans have had a great deal of difficulty organizing themselves effectively—they talk a lot about what they want to do but don't act. They make appointments but don't follow through. Many have a "mañana" attitude. They have difficulty following through on projects. They need to be accompanied to carry out tasks.

Another provider said, "They need social support, but at the same time they need to help themselves. One of the most important things that outsiders can provide them is information." He went on to say:

While there needs to be support for grassroots organizations, many people do not trust community organizations. There has been a real problem in this community with abuse of power by some people who are providing services. People may have a hard time trusting community organizations and often they will choose to go outside the community for services.

One provider said that attempts had been made to create a neighborhood association that could apply for grants collectively. But some organizations received money while others did not, and this led to fighting among the small organizations. "While the churches are trying to address needs, the problem is that there is a lot of fragmentation in the community, and the Africans I know who can help are too busy," Mr. Arkoi said.

Establishing a Drop-In Center

We soon found that a number of community members were already undertaking volunteer work with youth and were looking for a site to establish their own community-based psychosocial program. At the time, ROZA was very busy with its recreational activities and did not have the capacity to take on psychosocial programs for youth and their families. Instead, Mr. Massaquoi joined with Reverend Annie, a pastor from Mali, and four men and women from the Liberian community to create a pilot project for youth to meet for ten weeks on Saturday mornings and afternoons during the summer of 2003.

The project tapped into the creative talents of the community. One man, a drummer and musician, put together a rap music group of eight boys, which performed songs portraying the plight of African immigrant kids in their schools. Another program, called "Memories of Liberia," gave teens who had recently arrived in the United States an opportunity to videotape stories of their lives in Liberia. David Kpomakpor, an elderly man in the community who had been one of the interim presidents of Liberia, was a special guest in the program. Referred to as the "Professor," he was a former attorney who was appointed head of the first Liberian National Transitional Government in 1994. When he sought refugee status in the United States in 1999, he became a community leader and took an active role in spreading the story of Liberia's history to the youth. On Saturdays, "Prof" told groups of about 40 curious Liberian children about his short time as president, and the day when two Liberian warlords took him to the national bank to withdraw most of what remained in the national treasury to be split between them.

The Saturday morning pilot project gave us a good sense of what youth in the community were facing. It also gave us an idea of what challenges a program of this scope would face, including the need to base a community program within the housing project where most of the refugee families lived. We found that the closer a program was to the community, the greater access members had to available resources. The program was an initial step to build trust with members of the community.

The pilot project also identified two organizers who had the qualifications needed to work as change agents or "links" in the community: Mr. Massaquoi and Mr. Sam Emmanuel. The two men received support to establish an organization called African Community Resource to assess the successes and failures of the previous project and to plan the next phase of capacity building in the community. It seemed clear that the next step should be securing an easily accessible space for community members. It did not take long for Mr. Massaquoi and Mr. Emmanuel to get a housing complex to donate a space for African Community Resource to operate as a drop-in center at Park Hill. This space became the basis for the development of this new non-profit organization, initially called African Community Resource (ACR) and then changed to African Refuge. Mr. Massaquoi and Mr. Emmanuel invited a third partner, Mr. Ernest Cassel, an accountant and financial advisor to join them, and they quickly became incorporated.

The drop-in center opened in October 2003. After it was furnished with donated tables, chairs, and desks, the one-bedroom basement apartment became the gathering place for a number of community youth to stop in to watch television or use the office computer. The three men running the drop-in center started to get the word out that the community had a space where people could come for information, referral, and possible assistance. A few community members volunteered to work shifts at the center to help connect people with the appropriate services. Edwin Chuku, for example, was a graduate student in disaster studies, and he used the computer room in the center to do his work. He gave back to the center by assessing the community's job development needs, and helped to find them employment.

Around this time, we also had a volunteer who helped find employment for refugees in Canada. Together, Danielle Filion and Mr. Chuku created a comprehensive job development program complete with assessment and counseling services. This collaborative pairing of a local community member with an outside volunteer was a crucial component of our work in Park Hill. It allowed us to take stock of sources of resilience in the community, and also to support and enhance them. The employment development program was one of the first projects to employ the collaborative and improvisational approach that helped the drop-in center grow.

People from the community started to drop in for assistance on a number of different issues. Immigration concerns were some of the most common, including applications for asylum, temporary status, and work permits, as well as financial issues such as tax forms and financial planning. Mr. Massaquoi turned his attention to developing programs for children in the community. In the spring, a community volunteer and a student from ITSP NYU created a Saturday afternoon arts program that focused on Liberian history, storytelling, and cultural values. Each week an elder person or other community member with artistic talents would come to the center and meet with the groups of pre-teens, give a presentation, and engage them in conversation. An art activity followed, inspired by the presentation that day. The pre-teens had an intense interest in learning about the country of their parents.

A Solace case-worker began coming on Friday afternoons to meet with families referred to her. By the end of the drop-in center's first year, there had been more than 1,500 visits, and 430 children and adults had received services. Amid the hustle and bustle of people coming in and out of the drop-in center, the small volunteer staff was able to develop a simple system to track the needs presented and addressed each day. It became apparent that to best address the community's psychosocial needs, the center needed a more formalized method of needs and resource assessment. The center partnered with university-based public health researchers to apply for funding for such an assessment. Their efforts, unfortunately, were unsuccessful. We had to rely on our organic assessment based on information culled from daily logs at the center. Volunteer student researchers entered information into a database and did basic statistical analyses.

Staff at the center recorded information on services received for each visit to the center. They found that 26% of visits were for computer education and assistance (including contacting family in Africa), 20% for social services (counseling, group discussion, family support, and advocacy), 15% for employment or vocational assistance, 12% for educational assistance (including help with homework, school projects, and college applications), 8% for general assistance (accompaniment, information, or help with documents), 8% for youth arts or recreation, 5% for immigration assistance (status, citizenship tutorial, green card, travel documents) 5% for referrals to health or mental health services, and 2% for assistance with finances and taxes, or with health insurance forms.

A sample of the those seeking services were asked to participate in a survey to get some sense of whether the center was addressing the needs of those who had experienced trauma prior to arriving in the United States. Fifty-eight different community members were surveyed, 26 male and 32 female. In that group, 68% reported the murder of at least one family member, 60% had directly experienced Liberia's recent wars, 58% had experienced property loss, 53% had experienced forced migration, 51% were missing family members, 47% reported having been tortured, 28% reported being victims of sexual violence, and 42% reported that they had experienced other crimes.

Unsupervised Youth Come to the Center

In an article in *Mother Jones*, journalist Alissa Quart wrote about ex-combatant children living in Staten Island (Quart, 2007). She cited a study that estimated that one in five youth who had emigrated to the United States from Liberia had participated in the war. Furthermore, the study said that government and rebel forces had "recruited" one out of every ten children— roughly 20,000 in all. Quart cites Amnesty International's figure that up to 40% of all fighters in the Liberian civil war were under 18. Conscripted into groups such as Taylor's infamous Small Boys Units when they were as young as ten, they were handed Kalashnikovs, sent to fight on the front lines, and forced to commit atrocities, even killing friends and relatives. After the war, many children were raised by foster parents or tertiary family members, such as aunts, uncles, or grandparents. Many joined gangs. When they grew up, these former combatants often would not speak about their past, for fear of becoming ostracized or put in danger if neighbors learned of their involvement.

There was a tendency, Ms. Quart noted, for the American public to fixate on media stories of African child soldiers without ever engaging the issue head-on.

> This sudden fascination with photogenic survivors such as [Ishmael] Beah [author of *A Long Way Gone: Memoirs of a Boy Soldier*] seemingly reassures us that Africa's young fighters can be redeemed if only they step forward to share their stories or win the heart of a kindly Westerner. But most former child soldiers remain in the shadows, whether they're in West Africa or Staten Island, home to as many as 8,000 Liberian immigrants, and consequently what might be the largest concentration of child soldiers in the United States.... Not only is telling soldier from victim often impossible, but both groups suffer many of the same problems—growing up amid bloodshed, leaving their families behind at a young age, trading Third World poverty for First World alienation.

Quart, 2007

Not only were children in the community haunted by the traumas of war and the destruction of their families, they also often found Liberian ethnic conflicts replaying themselves in this so-called Little Liberia. Clashes with other African immigrants from countries such as Nigeria and the Ivory Coast were common, as were quarrels with local African-Americans. Just like in the war, the youth lost faith in institutions around them, often falling into cycles of drug abuse and gun battles. With so many desperate youths, African Refuge was to have been the long-hoped-for solution.

Fifteen to twenty boys came to the drop-in center almost daily, hungry and looking for snacks, often having slept in hallways or on the roofs of buildings in the projects or in abandoned buildings. Many of these youth had been soldiers in the wars in Liberia, though they were not willing to speak about it. Many of the kids had difficulties at home, and when tensions became too great, they were sent to stay temporarily with another family, as was the practice in Liberia. For most of these kids, their problems had not abated with a temporary stay in another household, and they passed from one house to another until they found themselves on the streets. Many had been attending middle or high schools and very much wanted to continue, but without a stable home, or even a bathroom and shower, they eventually dropped out.

Others were interested in job training. But when opportunities came up for them to join a residential program in the city where they could get this training, they often failed to show up for the van that would take them to Manhattan. They could not leave their group of peers and did not want to move too far from their community on Park Hill.

As the youth became comfortable spending time at the center, more of them came by. We learned that close to 100 youths, ages 14 to early 20s, were living unsupervised and on the streets. The Liberian community had known about this for quite some time and were concerned about their welfare and safety.

We held a number of meetings during those months to determine how best to approach this problem. The community wanted to care for the youth despite knowing that many had been former combatants. They did not want them to be further victimized here in the United States. It soon became clear that many of these kids were most likely not the biological children of the families who brought them from Liberia. It was not uncommon for a family to send their child with another family out of the country to save their lives. Many found themselves in families that did not have the same level of commitment to care for them as their own, especially when they began to exhibit behavioral problems at home and in school. Members of the community thought that a desirable long-term solution would be to rent a house and have volunteers care for the youth, but a more immediate solution was needed to accommodate these at-risk youth.

I found that we were in a familiar situation. Community members cared for other more vulnerable community members and had gained their trust, but were in need of greater resources in order to offer effective assistance. The youth posed more of a problem than untrained part-time volunteers could tackle on their own. Once more we found ourselves able to act as mediators between a community in a position to respond to a crisis and possible resources outside the community. But with the Staten Island Liberian community, this situation proved much more difficult and complex than we had imagined.

The drop-in center had come at an ideal time for those children, who flocked to the place in search of food, education, and general support. This provided an excellent opportunity to work with the children together with their families. The goodwill of community members, and their capacity to connect with and support these youth, outpaced the resources needed to provide effective assistance.

In the fall of 2003 I reached out to the U.S. Office of Refugee Resettlement about the number of unsupervised Liberian youth in Park Hill. The Office directed us to the New York State Bureau of Refugee and Immigrant Affairs (BRIA). Upon hearing our concerns BRIA reacted quickly. We were urged to provide the names of the youth so that the resettlement agency that had primary responsibility for them could respond. Unfortunately, we heard reports that the agency's response was to seek out each child's guardians and raise fears of deportation if they did not take the kids back into their home. In the process, our organization was demonized in the community for having brought attention to the plight of these youth, and the youth in turn felt betrayed by our program for "turning them in." They stayed away from the drop-in center.

As a consequence of the state's action, community attention shifted away from the youth and toward the goal of establishing a consortium through which leaders and stakeholders could come together to best address the needs of the community. In such a situation of tremendous community need, there were not enough resources available to promote community development while simultaneously addressing the needs of at-risk youth. An experienced case-worker with volunteer support might have been able to provide some effective assistance to the youth and their families. Instead, after the state decision, these at-risk children were less accessible to community intervention.

People wanted to do something for their community. We, on the outside, were ready to provide support with African Refuge as a centerpoint, giving out small stipends from a grant we had received through MASST. Our limited resources only allowed us to provide for those people who actively sought help at the drop-in center. We built relationships with these people, and trained outside service professionals, essentially serving as a bridge between the two. As our focus changed to address these needs, the state provided funding for a social worker who could formalize and strengthen the existing consortium of community providers and community organizations.

Consortium Building

The Consortium of African Community Service Providers on Staten Island (CACSP) began in the spring of 2004 to help find answers to the growing needs of West African immigrants, refugees, and asylees on Staten Island. Recognizing the needs of other immigrant, refugee, and asylee populations, the consortium redirected its focus to provide services to the greater African immigrant community on Staten Island. The mission of this consortium was to build a cohesive, seamless system of service delivery to help immigrant, refugee, and asylee communities acculturate into mainstream society.

As the CACSP continued to develop, these goals coalesced:

- To facilitate communication between service providers, schools, and communities, by providing a forum where providers can come together and discuss issues affecting the community.
- To strengthen and support the capability of families to care for their children.
- To build community opportunities for positive youth development through neighborhoods, schools, parks, and religious facilities, and expand opportunities for youth leadership and opportunities for youth to serve as problem-solvers.
- To mobilize resources (public and private; state and local) through collaborations and partnerships with businesses, media, and civic organizations.
- To encourage collaboration between educators and human services providers to strengthen connections between the home, school, and community.
- To establish common outcome measures for programs, common goals, objectives, and core measures to enhance accountability and gaps in services.

The consortium became the mechanism that strengthened the mesosystem of organizations and provider groups for the African immigrant community on Park Hill. One of the greatest benefits of the consortium's collaborative work was to facilitate a number of linkages between established social services and health organizations and the drop-in center. But this positive momentum was disrupted by a period of intense community tensions and conflict.

Community Crisis

During the African Refuge weekly staff meetings, tensions seemed to develop among the three leaders of the program, but their underlying causes were not discussed. One day, a community volunteer brought a woman from the community to meet me. The woman's son had been arrested for his participation in a crime, and the woman had sought help at the drop-in center for legal assistance. A program director at the drop-in center referred her to a lawyer, and the woman sent all of her savings to the lawyer to defend her son. The lawyer was not able to intervene and returned a check made out to her through the program director. I learned that the program director had deposited the check in his own account; I contacted him and requested that he return her money. When I met with the other staff members of African Refuge, I soon found that this director had been making money off the drop-in center for some time, repeatedly jeopardizing the program. On top of this, he allegedly had a long history of involvement in illegal activities, including theft of Social Security numbers, and possible tax return fraud.

I only realized the full scale of the corruption when community members started to call me, asking me not to fire this director. Instead, they simply wanted him to return the money and go on as if nothing had happened. Community members not involved in the corrupt activity, such as Mr. Massaquoi, had been aware of these dirty dealings, but had been too intimidated to denounce them. By the following week, the program director had returned the money to the woman, sparing me from involving the police, but I refused to accept his continued employment and dismissed him from the center.

At a meeting of the Staten Island Liberian Community Association the following week, I realized this was only the tip of the iceberg. Many corruption cases began to surface. Cases of embezzled funds and exploited community members were even more extreme and disturbing than the one I had reported. The community was clearly in crisis but community leaders' capacity to collectively address needs was severely limited by pre-existing factions and conflicts. From this, we learned that despite the displays of constructive energy we had seen and tried to cultivate in the community, an unspoken vacuum still drained community members' efficacy and optimism.

The community members working and running the drop-in center chose to move in the direction of polarization rather than collaboration. During this time Mr. Massaquoi and others in the community felt a renewed impetus to challenge the status quo. They started to engage in local politics, making inflammatory accusations in public and on the Internet, demanding investigations, and threatening those they held accountable with lawsuits. When African Refuge affiliates created a political party with a platform to challenge and weed out corruption in the community, a heated campaign and collective debate ensued. Members of the community became angry with the African

Refuge staff for getting so involved. Operating as the financial conduit and supporter of the drop-in center, Africa Refuge faced a dilemma. Did we have the authority to prevent the center's staff from participating in community political activity? Others from the community who were members of the opposing political party certainly felt that our organization should rein in the staff. We had conversations with Mr. Massaquoi and the staff at the center about their political activities, and they clearly felt strongly that the system of corruption and the prior power dynamic had to end and that they would do what they could to promote change. The new political party was now headed by Jennifer Brumskine, a project coordinator at the center, and she was nominated to run for president of the Staten Island Liberian Community Organization. Unsurprisingly, this tacit support of the political conflict put the center in an adversarial position with other community organizations.

While a peace agreement had gone into effect in Liberia in 2003, a war was now taking place in the Staten Island community, resembling the tensions back home. Now that the wars had ended, people were concerned that the country would revert to the prior socio-economic and political structures, the very same systems of corruption and exploitation that led to the civil wars in the first place. Mr. Massaquoi and others on Staten Island saw a similar need for structural change in their own community, which fueled their determination. These adversarial political tensions affected the community's functioning and sense of collective efficacy. The divisiveness undermined the capacity of local community organizations and unfortunately affected perceptions by local foundations that could have provided them financial support. As a result, the Staten Island foundations refrained from providing funding to the African community organizations on Park Hill for many months.

Further Developments at African Refuge

Despite the communal tensions, the staff at the center continued to work hard to provide services to needy community members. By 2006, the drop-in center had become a landmark service-provider in the community, operating under the name African Refuge. Programs organized by other providers regularly operated onsite, including legal and employment services, and a food pantry. African Refuge continued to be a place where the community's particular needs could be expressed, and where volunteers could focus on helping other community members. During this phase, projects expanded and became formalized. The center staff learned about the needs of the community and addressed them collaboratively. The space served as a bridge between community members, who started working together to create their own programs. Among the many groups run by community members, the center provided space for a women's project run by Esther Sharpe. She was one of the Staten Island Liberian community members given a scholarship to attend the International Trauma Studies Program for training in psychosocial and mental health response and received ongoing support from the program. A social worker and pastor by training, Ms. Sharpe was the founder and executive director of Living Hope Outreach Ministries Inc., a non-profit organization with a "mission," she said, "to empower African women and children to improve their self-esteem and maximize their potential that they too may find fulfillment in life." This facilitated peer support group met weekly, providing a place where women could speak about traumatic events they had endured during the war.

As the director of African Refuge, Mr. Massaquoi had started sitting on official community boards and task forces in Staten Island to work on social and economic issues, and established a network of political contacts with stakeholders and decision-making organizations. With this strong leadership, he expanded services through local partners, such as the Wagner School of Nursing, which established a nursing training program based at African Refuge. His main partner in this effort was Cheryl Nadeau, a faculty member at Wagner, who mobilized much-needed resources. Each week, ten nursing students came to the center, which had its own dedicated room for what was to be named the Partners in Community Health program (PICH)—a program that was still running in late 2012. The center saw tremendous activity on Tuesdays and Thursdays, when the program was running. Many people seeking health services were elders coming in for blood pressure monitoring or treatment for diabetes, as well as basic health services and assistance with medication.

One of the more innovative projects developed at this time was *Coming Home: Connecting Liberian Elders in the Diaspora with the Family and Friends at Home* (www.itspnyc.org/african_refuge/cominghome.html). Started by Serena Chaudhry, this photovoice project brought together a group of elders in Staten Island to take photos and create video messages to carry to their friends and family in Liberia. Chaudhry then delivered these messages on a trip to Liberia, filmed the family members' responses, and returned the films to the Staten Island community. The project culminated in a multimedia exhibit, featuring stories, photographs, and films by these elders and their

Liberian friends and families in late 2006 at the Snug Harbor Cultural Center in Staten Island (Chaudhry, 2008).

With the increased number of youth seeking after-school help at the center, Mr. Massaquoi was able to get additional space donated by the housing management. Through volunteer help, donations, and a Herculean effort, staff and volunteers completely rehabilitated a long-abandoned work-room into a Youth and Family Center. The center ran an after-school program with homework assistance, art projects, and Liberian cultural heritage programs.

In September 2007, we launched the new Youth and Family Center with a huge party that involved youths and parents from the community, as well as leaders and political speakers. One of the most touching moments of the evening was when James Davis spoke up from the back of the room and said he wanted to offer a few words to the crowd. Mr. Davis, an outspoken elder of the community, said that, on his way to the event, other community members had approached him and urged him not to attend. They said he shouldn't support African Refuge, but he had turned them away. Not only did he want to come, he said, but he brought with him a donation to support the new Youth and Family Center. He handed the director a $500 check, said it was time people stood up to corruption in the community, and congratulated African Refuge for taking such a stand and providing valuable services for Liberian youth.

The endurance of African Refuge was made possible by a number of Staten Island supporters, particularly by Gene Prisco, a retired educator and public school advocate who headed the advisory board and later became the chair of the board of directors of African Refuge when it became an independent nonprofit organization in 2008. Soon after the opening of the new Youth and Family Center, Mr. Prisco played a key role in organizing the Family Advocacy and Support Project, regular discussions to address the challenges faced by African youth struggling to succeed in the local public schools. These discussions, which included schoolteachers, principals, youth organizations, the NYPD, and parents, led to the development of specific advocacy projects to support families, parents, and children in the community. These projects grew out of an early research study focused on school and family outreach, involving five schools where the majority of African refugee youth were enrolled. The research focused on how to create a closer collaboration between school staff and parents. Essentially, the Family Advocacy and Support Project was geared to empower community members to become advocates on issues such as education, housing, and benefit entitlements. The project group met every other Sunday at the center to create sustainable support for effective parenting skills, parent–school collaboration, and recognition of children's difficulties in adjusting to their environment.

Summary

The work promoting community resilience with Liberian immigrants and refugees in Staten Island took a different shape from such work with other communities. First, the population lacked a coherent sense of community, since most had immigrated from different villages and towns in Liberia during the recent civil wars. It was a community with many factions, based on tribal and political affiliations. Consequently, legacies of victimization and betrayal from the wars were often replicated on the streets of Park Hill. The majority of adults and youth in the community were deeply affected by their war experiences, most had suffered the loss of family, friends and property, and yet they remained very attached to their homeland. Most reported that they wanted to return to live there one day, but since the economy was so poor, they saw it as their duty to work in the United States and send money back home to support family and friends. Most of the community members' immigration status was temporary, and they lived under the chronic stress of possibly being sent back to Liberia.

As we began our work, we realized that people drew on many resources in the community for emotional, social, and spiritual support—most importantly, the church and the family. The majority of the population belonged to one of the 11 Liberian churches and mosques in the neighborhood. In these churches, community and family life was most active and visible. Community organizations provided alternative spaces for activities that did not fall under the churches' mission.

Our project was initially funded through a U.S. Department of Health and Human Services grant through the Torture Victims Rehabilitation Act (TVRA). Rather than screening for survivors of torture, assessing for mental health difficulties, then offering targeted clinical services, we took a community resilience approach aimed at strengthening the community's capacity to support families and individuals in recovery. Since we suspected and then later confirmed that significant numbers of community members had suffered from torture and political violence during the wars, our goal was to take a multisystemic community approach that would: (1) work in partnership with the community through local "links" or change agents to facilitate community capacities to promote psychosocial well-being; (2) build community capacity through training and ongoing supervision and support; (3) strengthen the mesosystem of community organizations and provider groups in order to share resources and work collaboratively to address community challenges; (4) respond to needs and sources of distress as defined by community members; (5) provide opportunities for recovery through non-stigmatizing activities, gatherings, educational meetings, discussion groups and cultural activities designed by community members; (6) provide extra support to vulnerable populations, i.e. isolated elderly, at-risk youth affected by war, overburdened families; (7) provide accompaniment and referral for community members who needed health and mental health services not provided on site; (8) create links between community members and affiliations and resources outside the community; (9) raise public awareness and support about the community through media and the arts; and (10) support linkages to processes of recovery and reconciliation that were taking place in the Liberian diaspora and in Liberia itself.

Due to the project's minimal funding through small grants, with not more than three part-time staff, when the TVRA funding ran out the project was able to sustain itself, buttressed by almost 20 volunteers and a tremendous amount of in-kind support, until it found alternative funding a few months later.

What we had not initially anticipated was the degree of fragmentation and the absence of non-polarizing leadership in the community. Some people did not trust outside organizations and refused to participate in cooperative activities. Unlike in some other communities, these community members were very overstretched, often working more than one job, and had very little time to be with their children, let alone devote time to working on a community task force. Students from local colleges and universities who had an interest in refugee or African studies helped supplement volunteer work at the center. However, community members' limited time and involvement seriously constrained the center's ability to be directly run by community initiative and interests rather than by outsiders, despite its intent to do so. We were always seeking to keep a balance between insider/outsider collaboration and prevent the organization from being overly controlled by outsiders.

The crisis in the community reached its height when corruption surfaced and brought intense conflict to the forefront. However, this appeared to be an unavoidable stage for the community to enter in order to continue the process of collective recovery. From a systemic perspective, with the many changes taking place initiated by different community organizations and provider groups, the status quo had been challenged, and the community was going through a stressful transition toward a new steady state. As will be presented in the next chapter, collective recovery encompassed processes active both at a diaspora community level in Staten Island and at a national level in Liberia.

10

Seeking Truth and Justice

Unfold my story gently.
There are secrets.
I was 18 when the war started.
One morning you wake up and there's a war
And you don't know where to begin,
You don't know where to start.
Trauma is different from what you remember.
People die because of fear.
Checkpoints, checkpoints.
My life, it's been all about going back and forward.
Which war is this?
Octopus.
Three months of hell.
You see people die every day.
Our family's made up of women.
We are all women.
Crossing over death.
Crying river.
Women crossing with babies.
I dream for her to get out.
My belly is empty,
Cooking life,
Stewing generations.
My heart cries tears into the ground
To grow a new Liberia.
Fly away Africa.
Keep returning to the heart, to the home.
Keep a part of yourself hidden.

**Poem from Mary's testimony, *Checkpoints* (Theater Arts Against
Political Violence)**

The TRC Comes to Staten Island

Excitement filled the Christ Assembly Lutheran Church in Staten Island in September 2007. The Liberian Truth and Reconciliation Commission (TRC) Diaspora Statement-Taking Program was about to come into being. Reverend Philip Saywrayne welcomed the crowd to his church, the largest Liberian church in New York City, a few blocks from the refugee community at Park Hill. He prayed for the success of the project initiated that day.

Liberian government representatives were in the audience, as well as those of several human rights organizations, and members of the Staten Island Liberian community, the media, graduate students, and Massa Washington, commissioner for the TRC's diaspora arm. Having worked as a prominent journalist in Liberia for years, including during the civil war, Ms. Washington had come to the United States in 1999, and by 2004 had enrolled at Temple University in Philadelphia for a Masters in social work. She had finished her first year in clinical training, which focused on systemic family therapy, before being appointed by the TRC to serve in Liberia in 2006.

Commissioner Washington introduced the TRC and explained that this would be the first TRC to include the testimony of a diaspora community. Liberians the world over, in Ghanaian refugee camps and in communities in the United States and Europe, would have the opportunity to testify on the events of the war. The purpose of the program, she explained, was to give the Liberian diaspora the opportunity to voice their experiences during the civil wars, to hopefully prevent their country from engaging in such violence again. The Minnesota Advocates for Human Rights acted as the primary facilitators in the U.S. diaspora statement-taking program.

Despite the excitement that morning, there was also palpable tension in the meeting hall, following recent and heated community organization officer elections. Jacob Massaquoi, a founder of the African Refuge drop-in center, had vocally opposed some members of the Staten Island Liberian Community Association (SILCA) who had been running in the elections. His passionate opinions had provoked a backlash against African Refuge, which often implicated me through guilt by association. I frequently found myself walking a thin line between supporting Mr. Massaquoi's good work and trying to stay out of local politics. But my efforts to remain neutral were interpreted otherwise—as tacit approval of the political activities and aspirations of some members of African Refuge. The community became so incensed that accusations were even made during the ceremony, suggesting that Mr. Massaquoi and I were terrorizing the community. Fortunately, however, this presented an important opportunity for us to publicly acknowledge the need to engage in a local process of reconciliation. After the ceremony, the rival organizations got together for a photo-taking session, and agreed to address the sources of this tension and work toward their resolution.

A few weeks after the inaugural meeting, the statement-taking began. Minnesota Advocates for Human Rights organized a statement-taker training program in the boardroom of the Fried Frank law firm in downtown Manhattan. The primary statement-takers were lawyers and paralegal workers affiliated with major New York law firms. I asked Agnes Fallah Kamara-Umunna, a Liberian journalist who had been active in the TRC statement-taking in her home country, to co-lead a training session with me. Ms. Kamara also ran a counseling center and a radio program in Monrovia where she spread awareness about the TRC and addressed lingering legacies of the civil war. She even brought victims of war crimes and their perpetrators together on her radio program to discuss the possibility of reconciliation.

Ms. Kamara had come to the United States on a scholarship through the International Trauma Studies Program, and later enrolled for her Masters degree at Columbia University's School of Journalism. For our training session, we discussed psychological effects of trauma and how they might manifest themselves in interviews with survivors. At one point, Ms. Kamara and Commissioner Washington spoke about Liberian spiritual beliefs and practices, which would be important to consider for effective interviewing. It had been my impression from working with Liberians that these sorts of beliefs were not usually shared with outsiders. But once asked, Liberians were often more than willing to speak about their experiences growing up with spirits and witches that intervene in the daily affairs of humans. These beliefs, it turned out, played an important role in how Liberians remembered and interpreted many of their wartime experiences.

Truth and Reconciliation Commissions

The world has seen more than 30 truth commissions since Uganda released its first report in 1974 (The Advocates for Human Rights, 2009; Avruch & Vejarano, 2001). Each commission differed from the last in title, context, mission, and source of support, but they all found common ground in seeking justice following human rights crises. Results have also varied greatly, ranging from the prosecution and conviction of war criminals to their full-fledged impunity. Most of these commissions, however, are instigated by the very same national governments that committed the atrocities. That has sparked ongoing debate over the resulting value of "truth" in their reports.

Liberia's commission was mandated in 2005 to "promote national peace, security, unity and reconciliation" by following a six-point framework. The commission would: (1) investigate human rights violations, violent abuses, and economic crimes, searching for evidence of systematic planning in their execution, and identifying perpetrators; (2) provide a space for public discussion between victims and perpetrators, which would create a shared narrative of the war and guard against impunity, thereby cultivating a system of healing and reconciliation; (3) identify the historical antecedents of the conflicts in Liberia; (4) correct misinformation about Liberia's socio-economic and political past; (5) develop procedures for addressing gender-based violations, and rehabilitating affected women and children, as well as disabled individuals and former child soldiers; and (6) publish a report about the processes of the commission for the purpose of transparency (The Advocates for Human Rights, 2009).

Compared to many other truth commissions, the Liberian effort had a particular focus on reconciliation and healing, much like the oft-praised South African TRC model. Additionally, the inclusion of diaspora communities as well as nationals in the dialogue represented a unique approach to the Liberian effort. Diaspora Liberians provided advisory input on the operation of the project, participated in outreach, gave statements, and testified in public hearings held in the diaspora. This groundbreaking effort gave the diaspora a crucial voice in the truth-seeking, accountability, and reconciliation processes in Liberia.

Local Reconciliation on Park Hill

Commissioner Washington met with a cross-section of members and leaders of the Staten Island community. Like many of the Liberian communities in the United States, she soon found that different groups were engaged in various conflicts with one another, each vying for their own exclusive partnership with the TRC. She told them that the TRC would not work with any individual group, but with the entire community.

"The TRC is for all Liberians," she said. "People will be watching you here in Staten Island."

By the end of the first workshop on the TRC, competing community groups were working together.

African Refuge's drop-in center was an obvious site for conducting TRC interviews. Later, it also became a key organizer to motivate community members to give testimony. The Staten Island community, however, was doubly occupied with supporting families back in Liberia and adjusting to life in the United States. They were reluctant to give up their minimal spare time to the TRC, and some individuals also felt that the details of past suffering were now quite beside the point.

To rally the community to give testimony, Mr. Massaquoi directed an outreach campaign through African Refuge to distribute flyers, and held informational meetings. Seasoned Liberian interviewers, like Ms. Kamara, started tailoring the statement-taking approach to the refugees in Staten Island.

Ms. Kamara-Umunna's innovative, often aggressive, approach to interviewing victims and possible perpetrators sometimes conflicted with the more neutral, politic approach of the diaspora TRC. In her book *And Still Peace Did Not Come*, Ms. Kamara described the diaspora TRC as well organized, but she thought it was problematic that almost all the statement-takers were non-Liberian lawyers, unversed in the cultural and historical complexities of Liberia (Kamara-Umunna & Hollander, 2011). According to her, they didn't seem to realize that the process of getting statements, getting at the "truth" of the war, was not as straightforward as asking direct questions and writing down responses.

Many people were afraid to speak for fear of retaliation from potentially dangerous neighbors. Some were traumatized and said they couldn't remember their stories. Others said that their memories were too painful to recount, and that revisiting the loss of loved ones was not a burden they wished to bear. Moreover, many Liberians saw no practical reason to recall the past: nothing could be done to change it. There was a sense of disconnection from Liberia too. Most members of the community had not returned to Liberia since the war. Many felt estranged from the daily activities in the country since they had left. Their main focus was getting ahead in Staten Island—securing income, assuring their residency, ameliorating their life styles. Because of the diaspora's distance from Liberia, there was no greater challenge for the TRC than explaining the connection between revisiting the past and healing for the future.

Like many Liberian communities in the United States, issues from the war were often "spilling over" into community life. There were tensions between ethnic groups, between the haves and the have-nots, between those who had supported and those who had opposed the rebels. Now, there were also tensions over leadership, and, as is typical in a diaspora community when they begin to organize, tensions over funding intensified (M. Washington, personal communication, September 24, 2012). In Staten Island, intense competition for limited resources led groups to sabotage one another's funding by making accusations and undermining fellow community organizations' reputations. Seeing organizations with limited accountability and transparency, potential funders were discouraged from providing direct funding to African-run organizations in Park Hill.

Following the rise of the collaborative spirit galvanized by the presence of the TRC, Reverend Saywrayne decided it was time for a community-wide reconciliation process. For years, Liberians in Park Hill had lacked a leader free from community conflict. Reverend Saywrayne had spent much of the preceding decade in Liberia ministering to congregants during the wars and their aftermath. In 2007, he returned to his base church in Staten Island. As the elected leader of the Staten Island Liberian Ministerial Association, composed of more than 11 congregations, including one or two Liberian mosques, he was in a position to address the ongoing tensions that were having a destructive impact.

One afternoon in the fall of 2007, not long after the TRC meeting, Reverend Saywrayne came to African Refuge to meet with Mr. Massaquoi and myself. With some sadness and concern, he said that African Refuge was under fire. Although the drop-in center had contributed much to Liberians and others living in Park Hill, its true potential to serve the entire community was hindered by damaging rumors spread by certain members of the community. Furthermore, other community organization leaders urged people not to attend the drop-in center and the recently opened Youth and Family Center.

In response, Reverend Saywrayne organized a series of public encounters aimed at reconciliation, hoping to wipe the slate clean in the best interests of the neighborhood. He invited us to a meeting with other leaders of non-profit service organizations to air grievances and renew our common purpose. He held similar meetings among Liberian business owners and faith-based organizations, to culminate in a community feast held later in the year.

We met at the Liberian Association offices one evening. The non-profit organization leaders attended, as did members of other provider groups that had been in the consortium of African community services. After praying for a successful meeting, the Reverend asked Mr. Massaquoi and Rufus

Arkoi of ROZA to recount the story of their conflict, the misunderstandings and accusations hurled at each other for years. Eventually, each man had a better understanding of the resentments that had accumulated and of his own responsibility for exacerbating the conflict. The reverend asked them to apologize and move on.

In Liberia, each village traditionally has a "palaver hut," a round thatched-roof hut for meetings with elders to resolve conflict and to discuss local challenges. As a result of this Staten Island-style palaver hut, mutual respect and collaboration between previously warring parties recognizably increased for many months.

The Fate of the TRC

When the TRC officially launched in 2005 President Ellen Johnson Sirleaf supported its formation (The Advocates for Human Rights, 2009). At the time, tales of extreme brutality during the war were surfacing, including stories about widespread physical and sexual violence toward women, even reports of raped children and infants. Popular sentiment favored establishing a system of accountability for these atrocities. President Sirleaf promised that perpetrators of these horrors would be punished.

The TRC began its investigations and traveled throughout Liberia to document the testimonies of victims and witnesses of atrocities during the civil wars. But when the mandated public hearings started and those testifying began naming perpetrators, government support of the TRC process waned. According to Commissioner Washington, President Sirleaf asked that any large-scale hearings be staged, if they were held at all, and otherwise, statement-taking should be done in private. The TRC commissioners felt that private statement-taking was only appropriate for interviewees whose safety would have been at risk in public.

Jerome Verdier, chief commissioner of the TRC, responded that they would not let the truth and reconciliation process be stage-managed. President Sirleaf was reportedly concerned about testimonies regarding the crimes of former warlords who had joined the government, and particularly about her own involvement with Charles Taylor's rebel group.

According to Commissioner Washington, the Liberian government then initiated a public relations campaign attacking the credibility of the TRC commissioners, and even of witnesses. Due to this campaign, international support for the TRC process diminished. By the time the TRC released its final report in 2008, the Liberian government had cut funding for the TRC by half, including salaries for commissioners and staff; even the rent for their office space was neglected. Despite little pay and eviction notices from landlords of the TRC offices, the commissioners persisted. Even though the United Nations Development Program (UNDP) printed 2,000 copies of the report, it was distributed mainly to Liberian government offices and the international community; it did not reach the general public in Liberia (M. Washington, personal communication, September 24, 2012).

To distribute its findings to the public, the TRC would have needed to organize its own public forums. One of the commission's more innovative recommendations was to set up a network of palaver huts across the country as sites where villages could discuss the TRC findings. Palaver huts would be natural sites for public discourse and for addressing survivors' needs. But the continued suppression of the TRC hindered this important process. Many felt that a public discussion about the prevention of future violence would never take place. A majority of Liberians still have not read or heard the TRC's findings and recommendations. In Staten Island's Little Liberia, interest dwindled over time, and attention returned to the struggles of everyday life. However, many in the community still wanted to resist the "efforts to scratch away our history," as Mr. Massaquoi described it.

"In order for someone to heal, you have to rock the boat. You have to discuss what's happened in the past. You have to rattle it. Loosen it up. You have to cry. And then you can move on," he said.

The community was tangibly divided between those who supported the Liberian government's efforts to rebuild the country and those who were concerned that the process of addressing the past had been aborted. Many found it intolerable that egregious perpetrators of war crimes were members of the new government, rewarded rather than punished for their crimes; their impunity suggested that similar violence could happen again in the future. Furthermore, the needs of those most victimized during the war were not being addressed; there was no further validation of their experience and no course of redress. The TRC had recommended resources be directed to the rehabilitation of the tens of thousands who had been harmed both physically and psychologically during the war. There was concern that this was no longer a priority with the current government.

A variety of perspectives circulated in Staten Island's Little Liberia. African Refuge took the position that it was important to provide public spaces where the past could be addressed. With future visions of peaceful Liberia in question, former tensions reawakened in the community.

Checkpoints

Imagine someone going through a checkpoint guarded by rebels, dressed with leaves or all sorts of horrible things, and you go in through the checkpoint. Imagine what happened in all of those massacres ... I'm thinking that bringing them on stage ... would be of interest to people in our community ... People come to the center and talk about it, but for someone to bring those stories on stage ... I think that would be the most profound way of promoting healing in the community.

Checkpoints: A play by Theater Arts Against Political Violence

In 2009, the International Trauma Studies Program decided to run a theater workshop in partnership with a refugee community to create a collaborative theater arts project with its advanced training course. We accepted Mr. Massaquoi's invitation to come to the Staten Island community and to put the story of his fellow countrymen on a public stage.

The theater workshop faculty included actors and trauma specialists, who developed a theater ensemble in collaboration with community members. The trauma-training students in turn served as both witnesses and participants. Following our collaborative model, we invited community members to work with our theater group, to discuss the kind of story they wanted to tell about the wars in Liberia.

One woman who took part in our project was named Mary. When she arrived at the theater workshop, she was very shy and taciturn. We talked with her before the class, and she seemed anxious about the process but also motivated to be involved. Megan Auster-Rosen, one of the actors leading the workshop that day, began the class with a physical warm-up as an empowerment exercise. The class divided into groups and each group was instructed to make a tableau with their bodies to represent the experience of oppression. While in the scene, Mary's body shook as though overcome with fear. Then the class was asked to physically represent the feeling of liberation. Mary stopped shaking and a huge grin spread across her face. She described feeling empowered by enacting the transition.

Mary had lived through the Liberian wars and had endured multiple violent experiences. In our conversations prior to the group meeting, she let me know that some of her experiences would be too painful to share with the group. I assured her that she should feel free to tell us what she wanted and not feel compelled to describe experiences that were too difficult. Part of our process was to film the interviews and improvisations, and, with Mary's permission, she decided to tell her story with her back to the camera as she faced the class.

She spoke about how war destroyed any sense of normalcy; life was unpredictable with few normal routines. Children did not attend school; no one celebrated birthdays or holidays. Before the war, she explained, there were frightening rumors of the massacres and destruction to come. Worse still, no one knew whom to trust or what to do, but they overwhelmingly felt that they needed to leave.

One day, a troop of soldiers rounded up her community; they were accused of harboring rebels. The soldiers said if they failed to produce a hidden rebel by the next day, they would all be slaughtered. That night, 18-year-old Mary fled with her grandmother, daughter, and a few neighbors. They crossed the river at night by boat, carrying their children on their shoulders. Scared, tired, and disoriented, Mary accidentally dropped all of her food provisions overboard.

That night, they docked by an expansive field and were silently led across— by whom it's not clear—until they encountered a "mess of corpses strewn left and right." Thus began a decade Mary would remember as full of bitter violence and disarray; her only recurrent hope was that somehow her daughter would escape. For many Liberians, this period of war, with the sense that you were never safe, that an amorphous darkness lay ahead and could snatch you out at any moment, became known as the "octopus."

"As soon as you started picking up the pieces," Mary said, "another war would come—this was the octopus."

By giving this testimony and going through the Theater of the Oppressed exercise, Mary felt reaffirmed about how far she had come from the war to a new life with her daughter in New York City.

We then performed an expressive therapy activity in which everyone in the class made interpretive crayon drawings of Mary's story. Some pulled select words from her story; others drew figurative images, like an octopus whose tentacles each led to another of Mary's memories. When everyone finished, we organized the 18 drawings in a circle, and each person wrote a response to every other piece of art. By the end, each person had 17 other comments about his or her piece. From this, each participant wrote poems about Mary's story, drawing only from words used in the comments about their piece of art. Each person read his or her poem to Mary, and with each demonstration of empathic witnessing she was visibly moved.

One actor, Lucy McLellan, wove together the responses into one, collective poem that eventually translated into a scene in the theatrical performance. Using the poem and the recorded testimonies of community members, the theater ensemble worked improvisationally for weeks to develop a play they performed for the Staten Island Liberian community. This trial performance of the play, entitled *Checkpoints*, was intended to gauge how appropriate and representative it was of community members.

By this time, Garrison Sherman, a talented Liberian performer without formal theatrical training, had been invited to join the ensemble. At the African Refuge Youth and Family Center, an audience with quite a few young Liberians had come to see the play performed, and especially to see Mr. Sherman act. When the ensemble presented a piece about rebel soldiers stopping civilians at a checkpoint, Mr. Sherman played a soldier. He acted with an intensity based on his experience that caught the attention of the audience, resonating with their own war experiences. Feedback from the audience was important and helped grow the collaborative efforts of community members, organizers, and actors.

The completed theatrical piece included scenes reflecting testimonies of war experiences given by community members. Mr. Massaquoi interpreted his survival against all odds as a call to advocate for survivors and bring the perpetrators to justice (see introduction to Chapter 9). Mr. Sherman's story told how he wanted to join the rebels at the age of 17 as a means to gain control over his life. There was a video segment of Mary's testimony, followed by a theatrical re-enactment of the poem created from her story.

The play ended with Mr. Sherman singing the Liberian gospel song, "I Know Not What Tomorrow," the song his mother sang to comfort him and his siblings during the war, a song familiar to all Liberians. The audience joined in as Mr. Sherman sang:

> I know not what tomorrow has for me.
> It may have great mansions or palaces,
> Hardship or poverty.
> No matter what it has, I'm gonna trust you,

For you know what's best for me.
You didn't say...
My tomorrow, will all be bright
You didn't say
There'd be rivers of tears to cross
You only say
That I shall trust you, for I never know
What tomorrow has for me.

By asking people to tell their stories and then playing them back to the community, our theater pieces gave them an opportunity to illustrate their experiences, but in a way that provided them with some distance. That is the power of theater—it creates a communal space in which people can relive experiences in the safety of the present context. In this theatrical space, survivors may exert some choice over what they choose to experience. When done well, we believe these theater pieces could take people through a number of emotional experiences, dynamically shifting the expressions of pain, sadness, humor, absurdity, love, and anger to allow for a sense of transformation and catharsis.

Checkpoints became a medium with which Liberians could collectively remember the war, but also a means to convey the extreme experiences of the war to an outside community. It was a story that needed to be expressed, and, in being heard by outsiders, publicly validated. The play provided a space where meanings could be revised and negotiated and ultimately shared. *Checkpoints* was performed in its entirety later in the fall, at a symposium on the Liberian Truth and Reconciliation Commission.

The TRC Conference

On October 29, 2010, the "Symposium on the Liberian TRC Process: Reform, Redress and Recovery" was held at the New School for Social Research in New York City. Sponsored by African Refuge, the International Trauma Studies Program, the New School University Graduate Program in International Affairs, and the Institute for the Study of Human Rights at Columbia University, the two-day conference hosted experts to converse about the TRC process, its accomplishments, and how individuals and organizations could contribute to the future of the process.

Members of the Liberian community attended the meeting, as well as speakers from around the country, Europe, and Africa, including three commissioners from the Liberian TRC: the TRC Chair Jerome Verdier, and Commissioners Massa Washington and John Stewart. Half the audience consisted of students and members of the international humanitarian community interested in the future of Liberia.

Before the conference, Mr. Massaquoi, director of African Refuge, was highly involved in the planning process. But as the event drew near, his participation diminished. As it turned out, he and some of his fellow organizers were using the conference to spark a political discussion about justice and accountability, and to create the foundation of a political opposition to the current Liberian government. Mr. Massaquoi had been meeting with members of the U.S. State Department, encouraging them to honor the TRC's recommendations, to hold accountable some of the most well-known perpetrators of war crimes, and to exert influence to attempt a postponement of the Liberian elections.

With politics looming large, my colleague Michael Keating and I had to make it clear that the purpose of this conference was constructive dialogue. Nonetheless, rumors flew that the conference had been hijacked by opponents of the government. This was clearly false, according to Keating, as members of the current government were invited well ahead of time (unfortunately, none chose to attend), and the panel was carefully arranged to represent an array of diverse voices.

At the end of the first day of the conference, *Checkpoints* was performed for the mixed audience of Liberians and non-Liberians. After the show, many audience members said that a performance of this sort was important not only in diaspora communities, but in Liberia itself, to keep the memory of the war alive. A number of Liberians who had experienced the war—including commissioners of the TRC—came up to the members of the theater group to privately disclose their own checkpoint stories after the performance. The play had clearly hit upon a common point of experience for the large majority of Liberians. Furthermore, it became clear that many Liberians wanted a creative and communal context in which to express their stories.

The conference also provided a fitting opportunity to discuss reform. Questions at hand included the status of the TRC process and the government's response to it, as well as the need to establish a human rights agenda in Liberian society. But it also sparked discussions on redress, the likelihood of holding war crimes tribunals in Liberia, and the social effects of impunity. It asked, "What kind of reparations could be considered—for whom and when?" Additionally, the conference examined the role that the international community might play to help Liberia seek justice and reparations. Some Liberian speakers asked whether a different set of expectations for justice held for an African country versus a European one, and hinted that racism might be at the root of such a difference.

On the second day of the conference, we held a panel to discuss the impacts of the war, especially regarding gender-based violence and former child combatants. Commissioner Washington, David Backer, Louis Bickford, Joseph Gbaba, and Jennie Annan presented on these topics, and we discussed implications for promoting mental health and psychosocial well-being. We talked about the importance of redress and reparations in the recovery process, and the role Liberian diaspora communities could play in the healing process. Mr. Bickford had been working on themes related to memory, memorialization, and transitional justice. As a founding member of the International Center for Transitional Justice, he had worked with a number of countries, including Liberia, to devise strategies of confronting the past through the construction of memory. He presented on Liberian "sites of memory," which included a photo presentation on the emergence of memorials at some of the more well-known sites of the checkpoints during the wars.

In a powerful reminder about the trajectories of many Truth and Reconciliation Commissions, Mr. Backer, a researcher in transitional justice, reminded us that it had taken Chile and Argentina decades to actively pursue prosecutions of crimes against humanity. Justice is more often a long-term process. As Michael Keating summarized,

> In the end, the question that was left hanging at the end of the conference was whether there can be reconciliation—in Liberia or anywhere—without justice? This is a question that should be asked at a neutral forum in Monrovia with representatives of the victims given full voice to express their opinion.

Keating, 2010

After the conference, a coalition of community and political leaders came together to aggressively challenge the policies of the Liberian government, calling for war criminals to be prosecuted. The following week, President Sirleaf visited the Staten Island Liberian community and was warmly welcomed and applauded for the work she had done to bring stability and economic progress to her country. Mr. Massaquoi dedicated himself to a new political organization he co-founded and decided to resume his doctoral studies in organizational psychology. He also stepped down as director of African Refuge. A celebration was held in his honor at the Christ Assembly Lutheran Church in January 2011, officiated by Reverend Saywrayne. Gene Prisco, the chairman of the board, introduced the new executive director, Reverend Judy Brown, to the community and supporters.

The Liberians in Staten Island taught me that, for many, collective recovery must embrace the pursuit of truth and justice in the aftermath of horrendous civil wars. For others, the most important road to recovery lay in helping those victimized during the wars. And still many more focused on reconstructing their own lives in the United States while supporting the rebuilding process in Liberia. Collective recovery for Liberians, it seems, comprises a number of forces yet to be integrated into a coherent narrative with a positive vision of the future.

Summary

Collective trauma threatens to undermine people's basic sense of communality. It can severely disrupt the networks of relationships in families and communities, organizations, and societies at large. People and their communities often harbor remarkable capacities to rejuvenate, to revive, and even to thrive in the aftermath of tragedy. In this book I have presented a response to massive trauma and adversity that focuses on recognizing and enhancing the collective capacities of communities to recover from catastrophe. To best promote an effective and sustainable recovery process, communities must utilize their own resources to address the challenges they see as their greatest priorities, often with the help of outsiders. Community initiative and participation are crucial at every stage of the recovery process.

Taking a multisystemic approach to collective recovery means affirming both community and individual strategies in a way that utilizes creativity and improvisation. This approach may incorporate more structured and manualized methods of mental health and psychosocial work as well as more flexible methods, which can respond organically to changes as they emerge in the aftermath of disaster. Such a creative/improvisational approach harnesses a community's unique resources and capabilities and takes advantage of exceptional circumstances and opportunities. As opposed to methods that assume similarity across contexts, this approach recognizes and works with the dynamic differences taking shape in disaster situations.

As such, this approach to promoting community resilience and recovery needs to be adjusted to fit different situational, communal, and cultural contexts. And we must go about this work with particular tools, skills, and guiding principles, recognizing that no single solution will apply consistently across different communities. The particular shape that recovery will take is culturally based and socially constructed over time and will thus vary tremendously by circumstance.

Improvisational work requires being clear on basic principles that can guide us in times of uncertainty and ambiguity; this enables us to embrace the creative potential of chaos rather than retreating into familiar and ineffective solutions. In each of the communities we served, our artistic engagement in theater as a communal intervention helped steer the larger creative process of collective recovery, and became a metaphor for the performance of recovery itself. As we saw in many projects, such work often produced unintended outcomes that opened up new connections and understandings in communities, and led to new directions in their development.

It is critical to remember that collective trauma requires collective responses. As we observed, there is a constant interplay between individual and collective healing. This collective dimension was both necessary for and desired by many of the people with whom we worked. For them, this dimension was an important first step on the road to individual healing, whether it involved public memorialization, acknowledgment, or accountability. Similarly, the process of collective narration is crucial to give the shared experience of trauma both meaning and purpose. Above all, recovery is a relational process; its success depends on competent leadership and the restoration of trusting caring relationships.

References

Advocates for Human Rights, The. (2009). *A house with two rooms: Final report of the Truth and Reconciliation Commission of Liberia Diaspora Project.* Saint Paul, MN: DRI Press.

Agani, F. (2005). Building community based mental health services in a post war Kosova. KFPEC consultative meeting. New York. October, 10.

Agani, F., Cardozo, L. B., Vergara, A., & Gotway, C. (2000). Mental health, social functioning, and attitudes of Kosovar Albanians following the war in Kosovo. *Journal of the American Medical Association, 284,* 569–577.

Ager, A. (1997). Tensions in the psychosocial discourse: Implications for the planning of interventions with war-affected populations. *Development in Practice, 7,* 402–407.

Ager, A., Strang, A., & Abebe, B. (2005). Conceptualizing community development in war-affected populations: Illustrations from Tigray. *Community Development Journal, 40*(2), 158–168.

Agger, I., & Jensen, S. (1990). Testimony as ritual and evidence in psychotherapy for political refugees, *Journal of Traumatic Stress, 3*(1), 115–130.

Agger, I., & Jensen, S. B. (1996). *Trauma and healing under state terrorism.* New Jersey: Zed Books.

Anthony, J. A., & Benedek, M. D. (1975) *Depression and human existence.* Boston: Little, Brown.

Antonovsky, A. (1979). *Health, stress, and coping: New perspective on mental and physical well-being.* San Francisco: Jossey-Bass.

Avruch, K., & Vejarano, B. (2001). Truth and reconciliation commissions: A review essay and annotated bibliography. *Social Justice: Anthropology, Peace, and Human Rights, 2*(1–2), 47–108.

Baron, N., Jensen, S. B., & de Jong, J. T. V. M. (2002). Mental health of refugees and internally displaced people. In J. Fairbanks, M. Friedman, J. de Jong, B. Green, & S. Solomon. (Eds.), *Guidelines for psychosocial policy and practice in social and humanitarian crises* (pp. 243–270) New York: Report to the United Nations.

Barrera, M. (1986). Distinctions between social support concepts, measures, and models. *American Journal of Community Psychology, 14*, 413–445.

Bava, S. & Saul, J. (2013). Implementing collective approaches to massive trauma/loss in western contexts. In K. M. Gow & M. J. Celinski (Eds.), *Mass Trauma: Impact and Recovery Issues*. New York: Nova Science Publishers.

Bell, C. C. (2001). Cultivating resiliency in youth. *Journal of Adolescent Health, 29*(5), 375–381.

Berg, I. K., & Miller, S. D. (1992). *Working with the problem drinker: A solution-focused approach*. New York: WW Norton.

Bloom, S. L., & Farragher, B. (2013) *Restoring sanctuary: A new operating system for trauma-informed systems of care*. New York: Oxford University Press.

Bonanno, G. A. (2005). Resilience in the face of potential trauma. *Current Directions in Psychological Science, 14*(3), 135–138.

Boss, P. (1999). *Ambiguous loss*. Cambridge, MA: Harvard University Press.

Boss P. (2004). Ambiguous loss research, theory, and practice: Reflections after 9/11. *Journal of Marriage and Family, 66*, 551–566.

Boss, P. (2006). *Loss, trauma, and resilience: Therapeutic work with ambiguous loss*. New York: Norton.

Bourdieu, P. (1986). The forms of capital. In J. G. Richardson (Ed.), *Handbook of Theory and Research for the Sociology of Education* (pp. 241–258). New York: Greenwood.

Chaudhry, S. (2008). Coming home: Connecting older Liberians in the Diaspora with the family and friends at home. *Refuge: Canada's Periodical on Refugees*. Spring 2008.

Cienfuegos, A. J., & Monelli, C. (1983). The testimony of political repression as a therapeutic instrument. *American Journal of Orthopsychiatry, 53*(1), 43–51.

Clerici, C. (2012). Life in Little Liberia. *Capital*. Retrieved March 25, 2013, from www.capitalnewyork.com/article/culture/2012/06/6069279/life-little-liberia-staten-island.

Cottrell, L., Jr. (1976). The competent community. In B. Kaplan, R. Wilson, & A. Leighton (Eds.), *Further explorations in social psychiatry* (pp. 195–209). New York: Basic Books, Inc.

Danieli, Y. (1982). Families of survivors of the Nazi Holocaust: Some short- and long-term effects. In C. D. Spielberger, I. G. Sarason, & N. Milgram (Eds.), *Stress and anxiety* (vol. 8) (pp. 405–421). New York: McGraw-Hill/Hemisphere.

Danieli, Y. (1985). The treatment and prevention of long-term effects and intergenerational transmission of victimization: A lesson from Holocaust survivors and their children. In C. R. Figley (Ed.), *Trauma and its wake* (pp. 295–313). New York: Brunner/Mazel.

Danieli, Y. (1998). *International handbook of multigenerational legacies of trauma.* New York: Springer.

De Shazer, S. (1985). *Keys to solution in brief therapy.* New York: W.W. Norton.

Dixon, L., McFarlane, W. R., Lefley, H., Lucksted, A., Cohen, M., Falloon, I., Mueser, K., Miklowitz, D., Solomon, P., & Sondheimer, D. (2001). Evidence-based practices for services to families of people with psychiatric disabilities. *Psychiatric Services, 52*(7), 903–910.

Epstein, H. (1979). *Children of the Holocaust: Conversations with sons and daughters of survivors.* New York: Putnam.

Erikson, K. (1976). *Everything in its path: Destruction of community in the Buffalo Creek flood.* New York: Simon and Schuster.

Figley C. R. (Ed.). (1985) *Trauma and its wake.* New York: Brunner/Mazel.

Figley, C., & McCubbin, H. (Eds.). (1983). *Stress and the family: Coping with catastrophe.* New York: Brunner/Mazel.

Fraenkel, P. (2001). The new normal: living with a transformed reality. *Psychotherapy Networker, 25*(6), 20–22.

Fraenkel, P., Hameline, T., & Shannon, M. (2009). Narrative and collaborative practices in work with families that are homeless. *Journal of Marital and Family Therapy, 35*(3), 325–342.

Frontline World. (2005). Liberia: No More War, Facts & Stats. *Public Broadcast Service,* New York City, NY. Retrieved March 23, 2013, from www.pbs.org/frontlineworld/stories/liberia.

Fullilove, M. (2002, April). Together we heal: Community mobilization for trauma recovery. Paper presented at a meeting of Columbia University School of Public Health. New York.

Fullilove, M. (2004). *Root shock: How tearing up city neighborhoods hurts America and what we can do about it.* New York: Ballantine Books/One World.

Fullilove, M. (2013). *Urban alchemy: Restoring joy in America's sorted-out cities.* New York: New Village Press.

Fullilove, M., & Hernandez-Cordero, L. (2006). What is collective recovery? In Y. Neria, R. Gross, R. Marshall & E. Susser (Eds.), *9/11: Mental health in the wake of terrorist attacks* (pp. 157–163). Cambridge: Cambridge University Press.

Fullilove, M., & Saul, J. (2006). Rebuilding communities post-disaster: Lessons from 9/11. In Y. Neria, R. Gross, R. Marshall, & E. Susser. (Eds.). *9/11: Mental health in the wake of terrorist attacks* (pp. 164–177). Cambridge: Cambridge University Press.

Furman, B., & Aloha, T. (1992). *Solution talk: Hosting therapeutic conversations.* New York: Norton.

Garbarino, J. (1992). *Children and families in the social environment* (2nd ed.). New York: Aldine de Gruyter.

Garbarino, J., & Kostelny, K. (1996). What do we need to know to understand children in war and community violence? In R. J. Apfel & B. Simon (Eds.). *Minefields in their hearts: The mental health of children in war and communal violence* (pp. 33–51). New Haven: Yale University Press.

Goetzman, J. (2012). Gap junction: 9/11, 11/9 in urban life. Project proposal. New York: Artist Exchange International.

Gonzalez, J. (2002) *Fallout: The environmental consequences of the World Trade Center collapse*. New York: New Press.

Hamber, B. and Gallagher, E. (Eds.) (forthcoming). *Social transformation, peacebuilding and psychosocial practice*. New York: Springer.

Hardy, K. & Fraenkel, P. (2002). Trauma-based family therapy. Mental Health Association of New York City in collaboration with the Ackerman Institute for the Family. Post 9/11 Training Program.

Hobfoll, S. E. (1998). *Stress, culture, and community: the psychology and philosophy of stress*. New York: Plenum.

Hobfoll, S. E., Watson, P., Bell, C. C., Bryant, R. A., Brymer, M. J., Friedman, M. J., Friedman, M., Gersons, B. P. R., de Jong, J. T. V. M., Layne, C. M., Maguen, S., Neria, Y., Norwood, A. E., Pynoos, R. S., Reissman, D., Ruzek, J. I., Shalev, A. Y., Solomon, Z., Steinberg, A. M., & Ursano, R. J. (2007). Five essential elements of immediate and mid-term mass trauma intervention: Empirical evidence. *Psychiatry: Biological and Interpersonal Issues, 70*, 283–315.

Independence Plaza North Tenants' Association. (2003) Neighbor to neighbor – the downtown solution: IPNTA's guide to community healing. Retrieved March 25, 2013, from http://ipnta.org/book/index.html.

Inter Agency Standing Committee (IASC). (2007). *IASC guidelines on mental health and psychosocial support in emergency settings*. Inter-Agency Standing Committee.

Jensen, S. B. (2001) In the aftermath of 9–11–01: A European perspective? *International Trauma Studies Program*. Retrieved March 23, 2013, from www.itspnyc.org/perspective_911.html.

Kamara-Umunna, A., & Hollander, E. (2011). *And still peace did not come*. New York: Hyperion.

Kaniasty, K., & Norris, F. (2004). Social support in the aftermath of disasters, catastrophes, acts of terrorism: Altruistic, over-whelmed, uncertain, antagonistic, and patriotic communities. In R. Ursano, A. Norwood, & C. Fullerton (Eds.), *Bioterrorism: Psychological and public health interventions* (pp. 200–229). New York: Cambridge University Press.

Keating, M. (2010). "Dubious value" in some recommendations at TRC symposium in America. *Operation We Care for Liberia*. Retrieved March 23, 2013, from http://owcl.wordpress.com/2010/11/01/dubious-value-in-some-recommendations-at-trc-symposium-in-america/.

Kirmayer, L. J., Sehdev, M., Whitley, R., Dandeneau, F. S., & Isaac, C. (2009). Community resilience: Models, metaphors and measures. *Journal of Aboriginal Health, 5*(1), 62–117.

Klein, H. (1982). Children of the Holocaust: Mourning and bereavement. In: Anthony, E. James, & Koupernik, Cyrille (Eds.), *The child in his family*. New York: Taylor & Francis.

Klein, H. (2012). *Survival and trials of revival: Psychodynamic studies of Holocaust survivors and their families in Israel and the diaspora*. Brighton, MA: Academic Studies Press.

Klingman, A., & Cohen, E. (2004). *School-based multisystemic interventions for mass trauma*. New York: Kluwer.

Landau, J. (1982). Therapy with families in cultural transition. In M. McGoldrick, J. K. Pearce & J. Giordano (Eds.), *Ethnicity and family therapy* (pp. 552–572). New York: Guilford Press.

Landau, J. (2007). Enhancing resilience: families and communities as agents for change. *Family Process, 46*(3), 351–365.

Landau, J. (2010). Communities that care for families: The LINC model for enhancing individual, family, and community resilience. *American Journal of Orthopsychiatry, 80*(4), 516–524.

Landau, J., & Garrett, J. (2003). *Motivating Change: A Counselor's Guide for Harnessing Family Motivation to Change™ to Engage Resistant Substance Abusers in Treatment*. Submitted for publication.

Landau, J., & Saul, J. (2004) Facilitating family and community resilience in response to major disaster. In F. Walsh and M. McGoldrick (Eds.), *Living beyond loss*. New York: Norton.

Landau-Stanton, J. (1986). Competence, impermanence, and transitional mapping: A model for systems consultation. In L. C. Wynne, S. McDaniel, & T. Weber (Eds.), *Systems consultations: A new perspective for family therapy* (pp. 253–269). New York: Guilford Press.

Landau-Stanton, J. (1990). Issues and methods of treatment for families in cultural transition. In M. P. Mirkin (Ed.). *The social and political contexts of family therapy*. Boston: Allyn and Bacon.

Larson, A. (1998). *Assessing needs for mental health in culturally and linguistically diverse communities: a qualitative approach*. Australian Transcultural Mental Health

Network, Department of Psychiatry, The University of Melbourne.

Lifton, R. J. (1968). *Death in life: Survivors of Hiroshima*, New York: Random House.

Lifton, R. J. (1979). *The broken connection: On death and the continuity of life.* New York: Simon and Schuster.

McCann, I. L., & Pearlman, L. A. (1990). *Psychological trauma and the adult survivor: Theory, therapy, and transformation.* New York: Brunner/Mazel.

McCubbin, H. I., & Figley, C. R. (1983). *Stress and the family: Coping with normative transitions* (Vol. 1). New York: Brunner/Mazel.

Meyer de Mott, M., (2007). Repatriation and testimony: Expressive arts therapy. Oslo: Norwegian Centre for Violence and Traumatic Stress Studies.

Miller, K., & Rasco, L. (2004). An ecological framework for addressing the mental health needs of refugee communities. In K. Miller & L. Rasco (Eds.), *The mental health of refugees: Ecological approaches to healing and adaptation.* Mahwah, NJ: Lawrence Erlbaum.

National Institute of Mental Health (n.d.). Helping children and adolescents cope with violence and disasters. Retrieved April 12, 2013, from www.nimh.nih.gov/health/publications/helping-children-and-adolescents-cope-with-violence-and-disasters-parents/introduction.shtml.

New York City Department of Health and Mental Hygiene. (2006). *NYC community health profiles* (2nd edition). New York City, NY.

Norris, F. H., Friedman, M. J., Watson, P. J., Byrne, C. M., Diaz, E., & Kaniasty, K. (2002). 60,000 disaster victims speak: Part I. an empirical review of the empirical literature, 1981–2001. *Psychiatry: Interpersonal and Biological Processes, 65*(3), 207–239.

Norris, F., Stevens, S., Pfefferbaum, B., Wyche, K., & Pfefferbaum, R. (2008). Community resilience as a metaphor, theory, set of capacities, and strategy for disaster readiness. *American Journal of Community Psychology 41*, 127–150.

O'Hanlon, B., & Bertolino, B. (1998). *Even from a broken web: Brief, respectful solution-oriented therapy for sexual abuse and trauma.* New York: John Wiley & Sons, Inc.

Omer, H., & Alon, N. (1994). The continuity principle: A unified approach to disaster and trauma. *American Journal of Community Psychology, 22*(2), 273–287.

Padgett, D. (2002). Social work research on disasters in the aftermath of the September 11 tragedy: Reflections from New York City. *Social Work Research, 23*, 42–53.

Parsons, T. (1951). *The social system.* New York: The Free Press.

Perel, E., & Saul, J. (1989). A family therapy approach to Holocaust survivor families. In P. Marcus & A. Rosenberg, (Eds.) *Healing their wounds: Psychotherapy with*

Holocaust survivors and their families. New York: Praeger.

Peskin, H. (1981). Observations on the first international conference on children of Holocaust survivors. *Family Process, 20*(4), 391–394.

Pfefferbaum, B. J., Reissman, D. B., Pfefferbaum, R. L., Klomp, R. W., & Gurwitch, R. H. (2007). Building resilience to mass trauma events. *Handbook of Injury and Violence Prevention* (pp. 347–358). New York: Springer.

Porter, M., & Haslam, N. (2005). Determinants of refugee mental health: A global meta-analysis. Unpublished, Columbia University.

Pulleyblank-Coffey, E., Griffith, J., & Ulaj, J. (2006). The first community mental health center in Kosovo. In A. Lightburn & P. Sessions. (Eds.), *Handbook of community-based clinical practice* (pp. 514–528). New York: Oxford University Press.

Putnam, R. (1993). *Making democracy work: civic traditions in modern Italy.* Princeton, NJ: Princeton University Press.

Quart, A. (2007). The child soldiers of Staten Island. *Mother Jones.* Retrieved March 23, 2013, from www.motherjones.com/politics/2007/06/child-soldiers-staten-island.

Reisner, S. (2003). Private trauma/public drama: Theater as a response to international political violence. *The Scholar and Feminist Online, 2.1.* Retrieved April 12, 2013, from http://sfonline.barnard.edu/ps/reisner.htm.

Rolland, J., & Weine, S. (2000). Kosovar family professional educational collaborative. *American Family Therapy Academy Newsletter, 79*, 34–36.

Salvatici, S. (2001) Memory telling. Individual and collective identities in post-war Kosovo: The archives of memory. In N. Losi, L. Passerini., & S. Salvatici. (Eds.), *Psychosocial Notebook: Archives of memory: Supporting traumatized communities through narration and remembrance.* Geneva: International Organization for Migration.

Saul, J. (2000). Mapping trauma: A multi-systemic approach. *Psychosocial Notebook.* Geneva: International Organization for Migration.

Saul, J. (2003). *Spring and slaughter: Kishinev pogrom 1903 –2003. A multimedia web installation commemorating the 100th anniversary of the Kishinev Pogrom.* Retrieved March 25, 2013 from www.kishinevpogrom.com.

Saul, J. (2004) *Stories from the ground: The Lower Manhattan video narrative archive project.* Retrieved March 25, 2013 from http://itspnyc.org/archive.

Saul, J. (2006). Trauma and performance: constructing meaning after tragedy, theater of witness in lower Manhattan post 9/11. Presented at Trauma and Research Net, Hamburg Institute for Social Research, St. Mortiz.

Saul, J. (2007). Promoting community resilience in lower Manhattan after September 11, 2001 [monograph]. *American Family Therapy Academy: Systemic Responses to*

Disaster; Stories of the Aftermath of Hurricane Katrina, Winter 2007, 69–75.

Saul, J., & Bava, S. (2008). Implementing collective approaches to massive trauma/loss in Western contexts: Implications for recovery, peacebuilding and development. *Sponsored by INCORE*. Retrieved June, 5, 2009 from www.incore.ulst.ac.uk/pdfs/IDRCsaul.pdf.

Saul, J., Breindel, H., Margolies, L., Hamilton, L., & Jacobs, N. (2004). *Stories from the ground: The Lower Manhattan video project archive project*. Retrieved June 20, 2012 from itspnyc.org/archive/archive_history.html.

Saul, J. (Producer), & ITSP Performance Group. (2010) *Checkpoints*. Collaborative Theater Project with Staten Island Liberian Refugee Community. International Trauma Studies Program, New York.

Saul, J. (Producer), and Ray, J (Director). (2002) *A partnership for kids: post 9/11 coping strategies for the school community.* [Video] New York: International Trauma Studies.

Saul, J., Ukshini, S., Blyta, A., & Statovci, S. (2003). Strength-based treatment of trauma in the aging: An Albanian Kosovar case study. In J. Ronch & J. Goldfield (Eds.), *Mental wellness in aging: Strength based approaches* (pp. 299–314). London: Health Professions Press.

Scheinberg, M., & Fraenkel, P. (2001). *The relational trauma of incest: A family based approach to treatment*. New York: Guilford.

Scott, J. (1998). *Seeing like a state*. New Haven: Yale University Press.

Seaburn, D., Landau-Stanton, J., & Horwitz, S. (1995). Core intervention techniques in family therapy process. In R. H. Mikesell, D. D. Lusterman, & S. H. McDaniel (Eds.), *Integrating family therapy: Handbook of family psychology and systems theory* (pp. 5–26). Washington, DC: American Psychological Association.

Silove, D. S. (2004). Challenges facing mental health programs for post-conflict and refugee communities. *Prehospital and Disaster Medicine, 19*(1), 90–96.

Somasundaram, D. (2007). Collective trauma in northern Sri Lanka: a qualitative psychosocial-ecological study. *International Journal of Mental Health Systems, 1*(5).

Stern, N. (2010). *Because I say so: The dangerous appeal of moral authority*. Minneapolis: Bascom Hill Books

Stinnett, N., & DeFrain, J. (1985) *Secrets of strong families*. Boston: Little, Brown.

Taylor, D. (2003). *The archive and the repertoire: Performing cultural memory in the Americas*. Durham: Duke University Press.

Tedeschi, R. G., & Calhoun, L. G. (2004). Posttraumatic growth: Conceptual foundations and empirical evidence. *Psychological Inquiry, 15*(1), 1–18.

Ungar, M. (2008). Putting resilience theory into action: Five principles for intervention. In L. Liebenberg and M. Ungar (Eds.), *Resilience in action.* Toronto: University of Toronto Press.

Ungar, M. (2011). Community resilience for youth and families: Facilitative physical and social capital in contexts of adversity. *Children and Youth Services Review, 33*(9), 1742–1748.

Walsh, F. (1998). *Strengthening family resilience.* New York: Guilford Press.

Walsh, F. (2003). Family resilience: A framework for clinical practice. *Family Process, 42*(1), 1–18.

Walsh, F. (2007). Traumatic loss and major disasters: Strengthening family and community resilience. *Family Process, 46*(2), 207–227.

Weine, S. M., Danieli, Y., Silove, D., van Ommeren, M., Fairbank, J., & Saul, J. (2002). Guidelines for international training in mental health and psychosocial interventions for trauma exposed populations in clinical and community settings. *Psychiatry, 65*(2), 156–164.

Weine, S. M., Raijna. D., Kulauzovic, Y., Zhubi, M., Huseni, D., Delisi, M., Feetham, S., Mermelstein, R., & Pavkovic I. (2006). Development and implementation of CAFES and TAFES: Family interventions for refugee families from Bosnia and Kosova. In G. Reyes (Ed.) *International Disaster Psychology.* New York: Praeger.

Weine, S. M., Ukshini, S., Griffith, J., Agani, F., Pulleyblank-Coffey, E., Ulaj, J., Becker, C., Ajeti, L., Elliott, M., Alidemaj-Seregi, V., Landau, J., Asllani, M., Mango, M., Pavkovic, I., Bunjaku, A., Rolland, J., Cala, G., Sargent, J., Saul, J., Makolli, S., Sluzki, C., Statovci, S., & Weingarten, K. (2005). A family approach to severe mental illness in post-war Kosovo. *Psychiatry, 68*(1), 17–27. doi:10.1521/psyc.68.1.17.64187.

Winnicott, D. W. (1971). *Playing and reality.* London: Burns & Oates.

Wirth, L. (1938). Urbanism as a way of life. *American Journal of Sociology, 44*(1), 1–24.

World Health Organization, War Trauma Foundation and World Vision International (2011). *Psychological first aid: Guide for field workers.* Geneva: WHO.

Index

Page numbers in *italics* denote tables.